KINSHIP ACROSS BORDERS

KINSHIP
ACROSS
BORDERS

A Christian Ethic of Immigration

KRISTIN E. HEYER

GEORGETOWN UNIVERSITY PRESS
Washington, DC

LIBRARY OF CONGRESS CATALOGING-IN-PUBLICATION DATA

Heyer, Kristin E., 1974–
Kinship across borders : a Christian ethic of immigration / Kristin E. Heyer.
    p. cm.
  Includes bibliographical references (p.) and index.
  ISBN 978-1-58901-930-0 (pbk. : alk. paper)
  1. United States—Emigration and immigration—Government policy—Moral and ethical aspects. 2. Emigration and immigration—Religious aspects—Christianity.
I. Title.
JV6483.H47   2012
261.8'36—dc23
2012001502

♾ This book is printed on acid-free paper meeting the requirements of the American National Standard for Permanence in Paper for Printed Library Materials.

15   14   13   12   9 8 7 6 5 4 3 2   First printing

For my partner,
MARK W. POTTER,
whose accompaniment of migrants
inspired this book
and accompaniment of our children
enabled its completion.

CONTENTS

ACKNOWLEDGMENTS

A T THE OUTSET I wish to recognize reluctant immigrants and their loved ones, as it is their griefs, anxieties, and hopes that inspire this book. For the opportunity to publish the resulting reflections in this series, I am grateful to Richard Brown and Jim Keenan at Georgetown University Press. A valued colleague over the years, Richard's courageous and significant contributions to the theological academy are rivaled, in my estimation, only by the joy he takes in parenting. Jim has been a stalwart advocate whose work continues to model the integration of rigorous analysis with humane reflection. His pivotal role in fostering a global community among Catholic theological ethicists bestows an enduring gift to the church and world.

I am also grateful for the support of my colleagues at Santa Clara University and Loyola Marymount University. Several friends read chapters and offered helpful feedback: Maureen O'Connell, Laura Nichols, David DeCosse, Soccoro Castañeda-Liles, Karen Peterson-Iyer, and Mark Potter. I likewise benefited from the suggestions from Georgetown University Press's anonymous reviewers. I am indebted to the valuable and committed research assistance Brittany Adams provided at Santa Clara University. Earlier assistance from the following alumnae/i of Loyola Marymount University also contributed to this volume: Isabel Arrastia, Charles Bergman, Karla Alvarado, and Jessica Osorio. During the book's final stages John Sealy and Michael Zampelli provided key assistance.

I received several grants to complete portions of this book: from Santa Clara University, two faculty-student research assistant awards; from Santa Clara's Markkula Center for Applied Ethics, a Hackworth faculty grant ("Gendered Vulnerability: Exploitation of Women on the Move"); from Loyola Marymount University, the Bellarmine research award ("Just Hospitality: Immigration and Catholic Social Ethics"); and a Jesuit Conference social and pastoral ministry research grant. A version of chapter 2 appeared as "Social Sin and Immigration: Good Fences Make Bad Neighbors," in *Theological Studies* 71, 2 (June 2010), pp. 410–36.

My own students' passion and questions regarding issues of immigration have fed my work here, as have the sincere concerns and needs of those I have encountered in other university, parish, and social outreach settings. I have also benefited from conversation partners at the Catholic Theological Society of America, the Society of Christian Ethics, and the Catholic Theological Ethics in the World Church conferences, where I presented portions of this project in recent years. I am thankful for the friendship and indefatigable leadership of Sean Carroll at the Kino Border Initiative in Ambos Nogales. I have also learned much from the work and witness of the community at Dolores Mission parish in East Los Angeles, Bill O'Neill, and Tom Greene. Support from my cherished long-distance and local friends, including the women of my Sacred Circle in San Jose, nourished and sustained me throughout this lengthy journey.

I dedicate this book to my partner, Mark Potter, whose insights on solidarity as spiritual praxis and ministry to immigrants continue to motivate and convert me. This book owes its birth to Mark's unfailingly generous support throughout its gestation. My parents, Bob Heyer and Jean Marie Hiesberger, offered faithful encouragement and assistance across the miles, sending along many relevant articles and previewing drafts. My in-laws, the Potter clan, offered vital support in the final week prior to the manuscript's submission, freeing me up to meet the major deadline. Owen and Luke, my amazing sons, proved flexible and understanding as this project's demands sapped their mother's time and attention. I remain deeply grateful for the perspective their love and nonacademic pursuits provide, and for the invaluable gift of a family undivided due to distance or documentation. May we labor so that every family enjoys as much.

Introduction

In this season of my life, I am an undergraduate student at a university in California. Like the typical undergraduate, I live in a dorm room and often stay up ungodly hours of the night typing away term papers like the rest of them. At my university, I am just your average nineteen-year-old fulfilling her educational requirements. But the truth is, nothing about me is average. I am eight hundred miles away from my Arizona home, a place where the racial prejudice burns my brown skin worse than the desert sun, especially for an undocumented student like me.

The immigration hardships and racial tensions heightened in Arizona with the passing of the infamous SB 1070 the spring of my senior year of high school. After such detrimental news, the only thing that was keeping my family thinking positively was the hope of a once-in-a-lifetime scholarship, which was awarded to me by a school in California. Unfortunately, SB 1070 was only the beginning; Arizona had more plans for us. A month after my high school graduation, ICE [Immigration and Customs Enforcement] agents with loaded guns, bullet-proof vests, and steel-toed boots surrounded my house and nearly pounded down my front door, demanding to see my dad and me. I came out to the front yard where the head agent asked my name while pulling out his handcuffs as if he was standing in front of some criminal. No GPA or letter of recommendation could save me then. I fell to my knees in front of the agent and began pleading with him to let me stay, telling him I was starting college in a month on a special scholarship. He said to me then, "Fine, I will let you go, but only if you tell me where your dad is." I stood there shocked and dumbfounded, completely unable to answer the question. Was this what normal students had to sacrifice for their education? I shot a look over at my hunched and mortified mother, who nodded yes to go ahead and tell them. My heart ripped in two as I revealed the precious information. The ICE vans sped off to my dad's work, where he was arrested in front of his boss and coworkers. Within a few minutes they had him back in my driveway for a quick goodbye, where he leaned in, handcuffed, to kiss each of us. When he came to me, he looked me in the eye and said, "Sigue adelante. Te quiero." "Keep moving forward. I love you." Seconds after, the van sped off. I stood in complete disbelief; I had sold my own dad for an education. I realized then that leaving for college now meant leaving my mom alone with two kids and a house she could no longer pay for. My heart was breaking. How could this have been my dream only one month ago?

I began my freshman year with a criminal record that required me to do immigration check-ins in Arizona with the agent who had separated my family. In those days, to everyone around me, I was just another college student, but when my dorm room door closed, instead of working on homework, often I was on the phone with my lawyer strategizing ways to keep myself in the country.

I am now a sophomore in college still fighting for my education while fulfilling my immigration requirements in Arizona, knowing that every time I fly back for a check-in I am at risk of getting deported back to Mexico, a country I haven't lived in since age two. Unfortunately, my only real legal salvation, the DREAM Act, didn't pass the Senate in December of 2010, which leaves me uncertain of what the future holds. However, I am still here today and I haven't forgotten my dad's last words, "to keep moving forward." Until my last day in this country (whenever that may be) I will continue to become educated and contribute as much as I can of myself to a school and community that has given me so much. Until my last day, I will learn, and do, and fight, and most importantly, I will be grateful for what I do have. Until my last day in college I will be grateful for the scholarship that saved me.[1]

T HIS TESTIMONY of an undocumented college student illuminates the impossible choices the contemporary immigration impasse foists upon residents in the United States, even those lucky enough to pursue higher education. In this brief account, questions of earned citizenship and violent enforcement tactics take on flesh and blood. I will not soon forget the stories of women I sat with in 2009 at Casa Nazaret in Nogales, Sonora (Mexico), who had been likewise separated from their families in the other direction: One had agreed to send her toddler daughter ahead "first class," while her smuggler assured her they would meet up with her after crossing the border on foot; the mother was caught and deported and unable to locate her young daughter whose driver successfully crossed. She had not eaten or slept in the week since. Another had raised her children in Los Angeles for two decades, and was deported abruptly after a domestic abuse complaint was filed nearby. Her teenagers were now caretakers for her US-citizen adolescent while she figured out her next move. The shelter for deported, unaccompanied minors we visited held children who had themselves attempted and failed the journey; most of the young boys looked dejected and reported they would try again so as not to let down their families back in Central America and across Mexico. One young girl rocked in her chair stretching her t-shirt over knees, her contracted posture suggesting trauma.

These experiences and others have prompted my reflections on what it means to take seriously the Christian narrative in light of contemporary immigration's urgent challenges. How are we to make sense of biblical injunctions of hospitality and neighbor love in a globalized context? World history and Christian history are histories of migrations, yet we live in an era witnessing intensified motilities. From 1970 to 2010 the number of international migrants worldwide more than doubled, such that by 2010 one in nine people lived in a country where international migrants comprised a tenth or more of the total population.[2] The United States is the world's leading destination for immigrants, and across new regions, US residents are increasingly confronted with newcomers.[3] In some quarters reactions reflect the nation's historic openness to immigrants, in others, its deep ambivalence about "outsiders."

As transnational migration increases, ongoing debates about cultural cohesion and national identity, the impact of neoliberal economic priorities, and tensions between protectionist and globalizing impulses take on increasing urgency. Whereas migration is a global phenomenon, the immigration debate in the US context focuses primarily on immigrants from Latin America, and that is my own focus in this book. From 1970 to 2010, the overall US immigrant population increased fourfold, whereas the Mexican and Central American population increased by a factor of twenty.[4] Due to a variety of factors explored in this book—including numerical limits on permanent migration from the Western Hemisphere, the termination of the guest worker programs of the mid-twentieth century, and demographic and economic shifts increasing the demand for low-wage labor—a substantial proportion of the immigrant population from these countries remain unauthorized.[5]

As the opening narratives suggest, the path of such migrants en route to the United States via Mexico is increasingly paved by suffering and death, as drug cartels overtake the profitable business of human smuggling, increased border fortification and surveillance reroute their paths, and record heat waves conspire with human hazards. At the same time, the intransigence of the electorate on matters of immigration reform has hardened. As presently framed, the immigration quandary pits the interests of different constituencies against one another: native and foreign-born workers, industry and organized labor, cultural conservatives and social justice advocates, even different generations of immigrants. The reality of undocumented immigration remains a complex matter. Legitimate concerns regarding disproportionate burdens on local social services and the need to set workable limits and procedures for border protocol understandably persist.

As has become increasingly apparent, immigration cannot be reduced to a security or legal issue alone; it also involves economics, trade policy, cultural tolerance, family values, and criminal justice. Grounded in its scriptural, anthropological, and social teachings, a Christian immigration ethic calls believers to promote structures and practices marked by kinship and justice. Mounting threats to human life and dignity indicate the deficiencies of an immigration paradigm centered on national interest, expediency, or economic efficiency. The person-centered approach proposed here demands basic changes to systems and rhetoric that abet and disguise immigrants' exploitation and death, such as enhanced human rights protections and an expansion of the reigning paradigm's scope. The practices that violate the human rights of the irregular immigrants not only threaten human life, bodily integrity, and family unity, but they also undermine the rule of law and its legitimacy.

My central goal is to offer a sustained analysis of immigration patterns in their wider socioeconomic contexts by developing four theses at the intersection of Christian theology and immigration: (1) the Christian vision of the person profoundly challenges patterns of commodification and exploitation at play in immigration matters; (2) the category of social sin elucidates the relationship between harmful ideologies and structural injustices related to immigration; (3) elements of Christian family ethics pointedly critique the impact immigration policies and practices have on women and families; and (4) a commitment to global solidarity contextualizes the relationship of migration to broader policy considerations. Attention to these Christian commitments can unmask the operative ideologies that frame and sustain exploitation of migrants.

As an endeavor in Christian social ethics, the project entails an interdisciplinary methodology with hermeneutical (or interpretive) and constructive dimensions, integrating the work of social scientists, historians, theologians, philosophers, legal scholars, and Chicano/a studies scholars. I critically appropriate insights from the traditional sources of Christian theology as they bear upon immigration, with special attention given to Catholic social ethics. My approach interprets and analyzes predominant contexts and experiences of undocumented immigration in light of fundamental Christian commitments, and articulates normative implications for individuals and institutions. I draw upon Protestant and Catholic sources with a hope of contributing to the field of Christian ethics and action in a broad sense, but in some cases I consider the Catholic ecclesial context in particular ways. Attending inductively to various dimensions of migrants' lives, I hope to offer what abstracted philosophical debates or typical political formulations on immigration may overlook.

Finally, my own social location is that of a white Roman Catholic whose immigrant forebears hail from Ireland, Germany, and Austria. At the ripe age of seven, my maternal grandfather traveled unaccompanied from Austria in the hold of a ship to Ellis Island, his sisters in his care. He went on to marry the granddaughter of an Irish immigrant housekeeper in Kansas City, his journey reflective of the countless personal stories of migration shaping the past, present, and future of the United States.

Overview of Chapters

Chapter 1 elaborates the ways in which a Christian anthropology (or vision of the person) challenges the widespread commodification and exploitation of immigrants. The articulation of an anthropology relevant to a Christian immigration ethic draws upon Catholic social encyclicals' principles of economic ethics, Reinhold Niebuhr's notion of collective egotism, and Margaret Farley's "obligating features of personhood." The resulting critique reorients the reigning immigration paradigm to one focused on transnational human rights. Attention to migrants' courage and resiliency amid such contexts challenges reductive perceptions and opens up new possibilities for their contributions to the national story. Chapter 2 builds upon the first chapter's discussion of collective egotism to probe how social sin elucidates structural injustice and ideological resistance. The chapter brings together articulations of social sin by the Catholic magisterium and liberation theologians to clarify the interconnection of structural injustices and the dominant ideologies that serve to legitimate them.

A Christian family ethic integrates a family's intimate communion with its charge to mutually engage the broader social good. Chapter 3 frames immigration as a family issue, indicating how gender-based assault, a backlash in family-based immigration policies, and traumatic enforcement mechanisms threaten families' well-being with social consequences. In addition to drawing upon Christian understandings of integral family humanism to interrogate practices that harm immigrant families, chapter 3 also uses migrant women's and families' experiences to critique idealized elements of Christian family ethics. Moving from familial spheres of kinship out to global networks, chapter 4 contextualizes immigration within broader political and economic arenas to reveal the international forces and actors at play even as state-centered responses and migrant-focused enforcement remain privileged. Given the reach and grip of exclusionary global dynamics, I analyze neoliberal globalization via the interconnected structures and internalized ideologies detailed in chapter 2. Chapter 4 forwards the virtue of solidarity (with institutional, incarnational, and conflictual dimensions) to help reframe migration as a shared international responsibility and cultivate conversion from pervasive idolatries.

In light of the basic Christian commitments I advance in order to reorient values in the immigration debate—relational agency, family flourishing, solidarity—chapter 5 concludes with an analysis of both how such resources shape an immigration ethic and how migrant experiences can, in turn, inform normative frameworks. The final chapter exposes operative ideologies and misleading frameworks at play in the debate, such as those evident in the immigration industrial complex and the function of arguments centering on the rule of law. Attentiveness to the experiences of migrants, the demands of justice, and a Christian summons to subversive hospitality yield the contours of immigration reform and integration proposals, as well as challenges to normative frameworks that privilege autonomy and overlook social contexts. Amid the pervasive misinformation and subterfuge that cloud the exploitation of immigrants, a Christian ethic of immigration can provide guideposts along the journey from exclusion to solidarity.

Notes

1. Testimony offered via proxy at "The Jesuit Family Welcomes the Stranger," liturgy convened by South Bay Area Jesuit Institutions, February 5, 2011. Text obtained from author and used with permission.

2. Aaron Terrazas, *Migration and Development*, 1–2. Today about 3 percent of the world's population lives outside of their country of birth; despite the higher estimates of those who would prefer to migrate given the opportunity (16 percent), such individuals' desires are frequently constricted by their capacity to do so. Most migration occurs from middle-income developing countries, and Sub-Saharan Africans emigration rates are among the lowest.

3. Terrazas, *Migration and Development*, 2. For example, Georgia, North Carolina, and Colorado count among new (nonborder) higher volume receiving states.

4. In 1970 Mexicans comprised 8 percent of the US foreign-born population and Latin American and Caribbean immigrants overall comprised 26 percent of all immigrants; by 2010 the Mexican and Central American populations reached 20.4 million, a twenty-fold increase over forty years (Latin American and Caribbean immigrants combined accounting for 53 percent of the US foreign-born population, with Mexicans comprising 30 percent and Central Americans, 7 percent). See Brick, Challinor, and Rosenblum, *Mexican and Central American*

Immigrants, 1–2; US Census Bureau, 2009 American Community Survey (ACS), available at www.census.gov/acs/www/data_documentation/2009_release/ (accessed July 11, 2011).

5. I use the terminology of "unauthorized," "irregular," and "undocumented" interchangeably throughout to refer to individuals who lack citizenship status whether due to unlawful entry or expired visa status. I also use "migrant" and "immigrant" fairly interchangeably, indicating the fluid status of many individuals who find themselves either reluctantly on the move or inadvertently remaining in the United States due, ironically, to enhanced enforcement measures. In 2009, 62 percent of Mexican immigrants to the United States were unauthorized, along with 42 percent of Salvadorans, 60 percent of Guatemalans, and 68 percent of Hondurans (representing the top four countries of origin of unauthorized immigrants residing in the United States that year). Brick, Challinor, and Rosenblum, *Mexican and Central American Immigrants*, 5.

CHAPTER ONE

Christian Anthropology and the De-humanization of Immigrants

This is the year that those
who swim the border's undertow
and shiver in boxcars
are greeted with trumpets and drums
at the first railroad crossing
on the other side;

—MARTÍN ESPADA, "Imagine the Angels of Bread"

SINCE FORTIFICATION escalated along the United States–Mexico border in the mid-1990s, deaths of border crossers have occurred at a rate of at least one every twenty-four hours, amounting to a humanitarian crisis that shows little sign of receding.[1] In spite of the economic downturn and drops in both migrant crossers and apprehensions toward the end of the first decade of the twenty-first century, deaths increased. In 2010 the Arizona desert claimed a record 252 lives; due to similar death rates across the southern Mexican border, Chiapas has been described as a "cemetery without a cross."[2] Since the early 1990s, an estimated 5,000 have perished crossing the US–Mexico border. It is increasingly palpable why the US–Mexican border has been described by Gloria Anzaldúa as *"una herida abierta* [an open wound] where the third world grates against the first and bleeds."[3] Amid concerns about the cultural and economic impact of the estimated 11 million undocumented immigrants residing in the United States, the centrality of human dignity and agency in Christian ethics challenges death-dealing policies and practices driven by a market logic, xenophobic fears, and indifference to vulnerable populations.[4]

The nearly 2,000-mile US–Mexico border, spanning six Mexican and four US states, bisects the sharpest divide in average income on the planet and constitutes its busiest frontier, with an estimated one million crossings daily.[5] As migrants traverse its yet unfortified stretches, their treacherous journeys frequently entail the following hazards: drowning, suffocation in overcrowded and perilous cargo transport, mutilations from accidental or coerced train injuries, fatal dehydration, high rates of physical violence, detention under inhuman conditions, and precious little recourse to protection or legal representation.[6] Almost half of total unauthorized migrants to the United States are female, and women are nearly three times more likely to die from exposure than men, with the vast majority falling victim to sexual assault.[7] For those who survive the passage north, life in the shadows dehumanizes in a host of ways, from precarious working conditions and wages to prolonged family separation to routine denigration.

Behind the brute facts of suffering and death lies a strategy that threatens lives, yet ultimately fails to deter crossings. The death risk "coincides with the unprecedented buildup of agents, fences, roads and technology along the US–Mexico border, casting doubt on a mantra often used by the Border Patrol that a 'secure border is a safe border.' "[8] In 2003 the Inter-American Court of Human Rights ruled that the deaths of nearly two thousand migrants from Mexico and Central America offer the strongest evidence that the United States "has violated and continues to violate human rights by maintaining Operation Gatekeeper." Other international human rights organizations, including the United Nations Human Rights Commission and Amnesty International, have reached the same conclusion in subsequent determinations.[9] As Gioachhino Campese puts it, despite Border Patrol search-and-rescue operations, "deaths continue to rise because it is the strategy itself—the rerouting of the immigrants toward the most dangerous terrains—that is causing the deaths. The US government refuses to take any responsibility for all of these casualties, which are considered one of the 'unintended' consequences of the nation's effort to protect its sovereignty."[10] Human rights abuses evident in a strategy that maximizes rather than minimizes death call into question the legitimacy of absolute claims to sovereignty and accompanying border control mechanisms.[11]

This litany of abuses and "unintended consequences" born of present US border policies makes apparent Gustavo Gutiérrez's assertion that "the central theological problem of our day is not the problem of the nonbeliever but the problem of those thought to be nonpersons by the reigning elites."[12] From the perspective of moral anthropology, respect for all persons as ends and as inherently relational poses considerable challenges to the ongoing dehumanization of migrant women and men. Examining matters of undocumented immigration through a lens of dehumanization does not resolve the complexities of law and policy, but it does bring patterns of objectification into relief and help reframe the debate. The title and subheadings hyphenate "de-humanization" to highlight the fact that whereas prevailing attitudes and prac-tices strike at the core of what it means to be human and obscure immigrants' humanity, their resilience and courage make clear that victimization is not the complete story nor the final word.

Chapter 1 elaborates the ways in which a Christian anthropology critiques patterns of dehumanization vis-à-vis undocumented immigration to the United States. Pervasive frameworks that reduce migrants to their economic function or cast them as threats to national security and cultural cohesion make it easier to lose sight of our common humanity. I draw upon Catholic social encyclicals' principles of economic ethics, Reinhold Niebuhr's notion of collective egotism, and Margaret Farley's obligating features of personhood to ground an anthropological critique of pervasive practices and inform a Chris-tian immigration ethic. These emphases indicate that deep Christian commit-ments regarding what it means to be human—not simply rights to migrate or duties of hospitality—radically critique pervasive exploitation and prevailing immigration paradigms. The chapter concludes by considering ways in which migrants' agency gets expressed amid such daunting constraints.

Economy and the De-humanization of Immigrants

The brutal border realities outlined above beg the question of why families and individuals risk crossing. The fact that the majority of those deported make plans to reattempt the journey suggests that beyond deep familial ties in the United States, it is dire economic need with no viable prospects that com-pels most irregular migrants crossing the US–Mexico border. Following the implementation of the North American Free Trade Agreement (NAFTA) in 1994, millions of Mexicans lost their jobs in agriculture and many have been forced to abandon their land and join irregular migrant streams to the United States, most without legal protection.[13] In the face of insurmountable com-petition from US-subsidized, imported agricultural goods, real income has dropped 25 percent in purchasing power and the poverty rate for female-headed households increased by 50 percent. Catholic Relief Service's (CRS) Mexico Country Manager Erica Dahl-Bredine laments that CRS efforts to improve family farmers' living conditions have been severely limited by the impact of such trade policies: "The price of corn in Mexico has been driven below the cost of production, leaving farmers with a crop literally not worth harvesting. The Mexican government's cuts to vital support and subsidy programs for farmers has [sic] only made matters worse. After generations of farming corn, families are giving up, abandoning their farms, and heading north."[14]

Free-trade policies like NAFTA facilitate the cross-border movement of capital, goods, and services, yet inhibit the movement of people. In the words of a 2004 document issued by the Pontifical Council for the Pastoral Care of Migrants and Itinerant People, globalization has "flung markets wide open but not frontiers, has demolished boundaries for the free circulation of information and capital, but not to the same extent for the free circulation of people."[15] In recent decades these priorities have become enshrined in neoliberal economic policies that have failed to improve the living conditions or prospects for a large percentage of the population living not only in Latin America but also in other developing regions.[16]

Hence, this tendency to prioritize capital to persons and reduce laborers to "factors of production" fosters dehumanizing conditions that generate economic refugees in the first place, and then exploit undocumented workers who remain precariously vulnerable once hired.[17] The Christian tradition's priority of the human person, by contrast, grounds an economic ethic that profoundly critiques these sources and conditions of undocumented labor. The tradition grounds its essential commitment to human life and dignity in a vision of the human person as created in God's image, social and political by nature, and endowed with inviolable dignity and human rights independent of citizenship status.[18] This vision undergirds its staunch subordination of capital to labor, a priority pointedly reversed in neoliberal trade polices and undocumented labor abuses.

Border deaths and policies that compel and then punish irregular migration are profoundly challenged by a Catholic defense of rights to emigrate and immigrate rooted in the tradition's understanding of human rights, the political community, and the universal destination of created goods.[19] In an interdependent context, human rights are not absolute claims made by radically autonomous individuals, but rather claims to goods necessary for each person to participate with dignity in society's communal life.[20] Catholic principles of economic ethics therefore protect not only civil and political rights, but also more robust social and economic rights and responsibilities.

From Pope Leo XIII's warnings that neither human nor divine laws permit employers to exploit another's need for profit in 1891, to Pope Benedict XVI's recent condemnations of global economic practices that hinder authentic development, the protection of human dignity remains the central criterion of economic justice. The encyclical tradition makes clear that "every economic decision and institution must be judged in light of whether it protects or undermines the dignity of the human person . . . realized in community with others."[21] In *Laborem exercens*, for example, John Paul II roots his condemnation of the social and financial exploitation of migrant workers in the principle that "the hierarchy of values and the profound meaning of work itself require that capital should be at the service of labor and not labor at the service of capital."[22]

Hence the Catholic social tradition explicitly protects the basic human rights of undocumented migrants in host countries in light of longstanding teachings on human and workers' rights, which do not depend on citizenship status.[23] The tradition promotes rights to just wages, benefits, safe working conditions, and health care assistance, especially in the case of on-the-job injuries, and rights to association.[24] Within the US labor market, the pervasive exploitation of undocumented immigrants in terms of substandard wages and protections, disproportionately unsafe conditions, wage theft, and a lack of mechanisms to enforce humane protections thus constitute basic violations.[25]

Catholic social encyclicals' defense of workers' rights also stems from a particular understanding of human work as necessarily "intelligent and free."[26] As Oscar Romero poetically elaborates:

How beautiful will be the day
when all the baptized understand
that their work, their job,
is a priestly work,
that just as I celebrate Mass at this altar,
so each carpenter celebrates Mass at his workbench,
and each metalworker,
each professional,
each doctor with the scalpel,
the market woman at her stand,
is performing a priestly office!
How many cabdrivers, I know, listen to this message
there in their cabs;
you are a priest at the wheel, my friend,
if you work with honesty,
consecrating that taxi of yours to God,
bearing a message of peace and love
to the passengers who ride in your cab.[27]

Not only are persons entitled to the right to the means of livelihood to sustain their basic needs, but the tradition recognizes that "when work is unavailable, or insufficiently satisfies the purposes of work, authentic development is jeopardized."[28] Pope Benedict's 2009 social encyclical evokes this deeper reach and meaning of work in light of the concurrent economic downturn: "Unemployment today provokes new forms of economic marginalization. . . . Being out of work or dependent on public or private assistance for a prolonged period undermines the freedom and creativity of the person and his family and social relationships, causing great psychological and spiritual suffering."[29] The tradition's understanding of work as a vocation reflects the core value of autonomy and suggests that the inability of many migrants to earn a living wage due in part to US trade policy strikes at the core of undocumented workers' humanity.

In contrast to the social and economic rights accorded all humans in the Catholic social tradition, within the framework of free trade, human services "become commodities to be traded for profit."[30] In the course of his analysis of outsourcing and deregulation in the global market, Benedict XVI similarly decries the "*downsizing of social security systems* as the price to be paid for seeking greater competitive advantage in the global market, with consequent grave danger for the rights of workers, for fundamental human rights and for the solidarity associated with the traditional forms of the social State."[31] His call for theological and moral reflection on the meaning of the economy, and its goals arises in part from his concerns about "the human consequences of current tendencies towards a short-term economy."[32]

Dehumanization persists by means of this operative value hierarchy in the objectification of workers as mere tools of production. The incongruence of the present system, given labor demands and practices, exhibits a civil societal deficit indicating an overextension of the market, as well: Undocumented laborers who are integrated chiefly through the market have no recourse to redress labor abuses, and local and state communities have proven ill-equipped to pay the social and humanitarian costs of enforcement raids.[33] Profits have significantly increased for private firms that contract with the government to detain immigrants in recent years, and the US immigrant detention system is expected to cost tax payers $2.75 billion in FY 2012. With a 200 percent increase in the number of beds in detention centers from 2000 to 2009, the Department of Homeland Security and its subcontractors now detain over 280,000 persons a year, more than triple the number of those detained just nine years ago.[34] In terms of daily averages, in 1994 officials held approximately 6,000 noncitizens on a given day and detained 33,000 daily by

2008.[35] Utilitarian analyses are operative for local governments in border towns who financially support the humanitarian organization Humane Borders, because they "find it cheaper to help provide water than to pay the costs associated with burying the migrant dead."[36] Drug cartels have increasingly taken over the profitable business of human smuggling, for undocumented migrants are preferable to cocaine bricks because they can be drug mules and their families extorted for ransom.[37] Hence a wide array of immigration practices reflects patterns of commodification that severely compromise immigrants' human rights and dignity.

Security and the De-humanization of Immigrants

The objectification of migrants may be more readily apparent in the economic sphere, but dehumanizing tendencies similarly pervade the security and cultural frameworks that also shape immigration debates. As the events of September 11 placed unlawful entry into the United States in a national security context, public figures have all but conflated southwestern border crossings with security breaches of large-scale, violent consequence. Conceptualizing unauthorized immigrants as willful lawbreakers who pose a national security threat evokes fears of anarchy and enables their mistreatment. Christian understandings of the human person as not only sacred and social but sinful shed light on entrenched tendencies to scapegoat immigrants as threatening economic and societal security.

Reinhold Niebuhr famously observed that original sin is the one empirically verifiable Christian doctrine. His insights on individual sin that becomes magnified in groups are particularly relevant for the inhumane trends impacting immigrants that seem to manifest in collective forms, whether government policies, nativist narratives, or media depictions. Niebuhr's understanding of sin as an attempt to overcome insecurity also bears on dehumanizing dimensions of undocumented immigrants' experiences and reception.

Niebuhr characterizes the paradox of human finitude and self-transcendence as a source of anxiety, which persons attempt to overcome through sensuality or pride. Resolving her anxiety in sin, a person grants ultimate meaning to a finite locus of value, rather than to God. In the course of this dynamic, the ego—"which falsely makes itself the centre of existence in its pride and will-to-power"—inevitably wreaks injustice, subordinating other life to its will.[38] Niebuhr characterizes even sins of ignorance in culpable terms, as ignorance entails efforts to overestimate our sight in order to obscure our blindness or stretch our power to obscure our insecurity.[39] As a result, the universal human experience entails the sin of "seeking security at the expense of another life."[40] From playground power struggles to uncompromising partisanship to golden parachutes, we encounter empirical evidence of this dynamic.

Beyond personal sinful tendencies, Niebuhr argues that the pretensions and claims of collectives far exceed that of the individual: "The group is more arrogant, hypocritical, self-centered and more ruthless in the pursuit of its ends than the individual."[41] He singles out the expression of group egotism in the nation-state, in particular, as the state gives the collective impulses of the nation instruments of power and imaginative symbols of identity such that "the national state is most able to make absolute claims for itself, to enforce those claims by power and to give them plausibility and credibility by the majesty and panoply of its apparatus."[42] Historical examples of state repression and national exceptionalism bear out this analysis. In his first volume of *The Nature and Destiny of Man*, Niebuhr concludes: "Collective pride is thus man's last, and in some respects most pathetic, effort to deny the determinate and contingent character of his existence. The very essence of human sin is in it. . . . This form of human sin is also the most fruitful of human guilt, that is of objective social and historical evil. In its whole range from pride of family to pride of nation, collective egotism and group pride are a more pregnant source of injustice and conflict than purely individual pride."[43]

Hence Niebuhr's cautionary tale for military and economic superpowers warns that where groups are endowed with power, prestige, intellectual eminence, or moral approval, "there an ego is allowed to expand. . . . Its vertical expansion, its pride, involves it in sin against God. Its horizontal expansion involves it in an unjust effort to gain security and prestige at the expense of its fellows."[44] Whereas varied motives and outcomes coexist in the contemporary global economy, and many legitimately question consequent patterns of migration without susceptibility to collective egotism, it is worth considering how Niebuhr's insights on sin in terms of insecurity and group dynamics elucidate patterns at play that generate reluctant migrants in the first place as well as inhibit their reception upon arrival. In particular, this section explores (1) how efforts to overcome insecurity contribute to undocumented migration and related abuses, and (2) the ways in which dehumanizing rhetoric and national ideologies that construe the immigrant as "other" manifest collective egotism.

Niebuhr's understanding of sin as anxiety illuminates US complicity in exacerbating push factors generating unwilling migrants. Causal factors for undocumented immigration are frequently cast in terms of the economic desperation and corrupt oversight characterizing sending countries, or demographic changes and labor market needs in host countries.[45] Yet as sociologist Yen Le Espiritu points out, this "disregards the aggressive role that US government and US corporations have played—through colonialism, imperialist wars and occupations, capital investment and material extraction in Third World countries and through active recruitment of racialized and gendered immigrant labor—in generating out-migration from key sending countries."[46] The temptations by those in power to attain and increase financial security directly contribute to undocumented flows and exploitation.

As noted, NAFTA's economic promise has proven illusory for the large majority of Mexicans. Hence for countries with intertwined histories like Mexico and the United States, it is critical to account for the host country's complicity in generating push factors.[47] Seeking economic security at the expense of neighbors' livelihoods occasions responsibility and guilt in Niebuhr's terms. His words about the practice of flooding the agricultural markets with subsidized grain ring eerily prophetic: "Man's sense of dependence upon nature and his reverent gratitude toward the miracle of nature's perennial abundance is destroyed by his arrogant sense of independence and his greedy effort to overcome the insecurity of nature's rhythms and seasons by garnering her stores with excessive zeal and beyond natural requirements."[48] Given the role the United States and other developed nations have played in shaping conditions that benefit their own interests and help drive migration—together with Christian convictions about the universal destination of created goods—we might consider comprehensive immigration reform that regularizes the status of most undocumented immigrants as a demand of distributive justice.[49]

Beyond the monopolization of financial security, matters of national security and societal security have become central to debates about the US–Mexico border. Interchanging certain undocumented immigration with national security concerns reflects the temptations of collective egotism rooted in what Niebuhr called the perennial anxiety inherent to the human condition. Whereas national security implicates the legitimate right to self-preservation, the Christian tradition rightly cautions against turning security into an absolute good.[50] Here Niebuhr sounds a relevant warning: "The pride of nations consists in the tendency to make unconditional claims for their conditioned values."[51] The tendency to seek security is not limited to those (in the United States) who fear terrorists, foreigners, or the loss of capital growth; Niebuhrian pride transgresses multiple borders, and we encounter oppressive temptations within migrant communities. For example, Chicano/a studies scholar Yvette

Flores-Ortiz recounts how "the many tensions generated by migration can exacerbate domestic violence in dysfunctional families through 'cultural freezing,' where 'tradition' and control are imposed as a means to cope with distressing disruptions."[52] Rising violence among Mexican crime syndicates likewise manifests the idolization of power and wealth in efforts to surpass finitude.[53] For example, in August of 2010, 72 undocumented migrants from Central and South America were discovered in the Mexican state of Tamaulipas, 58 men and 14 women slayed and then piled in a room as "discarded contraband."[54] Migrants from Central America traveling through Mexico report sexual violence, extortion by authorities, and collusion of government officials and train drivers with criminal kidnapping gangs during their journeys in Mexico.[55]

Culture and the Dehumanization of Immigrants

Beyond the basic propensity to pursue security, Niebuhrian group egotism is particularly evident in social construals of national identity over and against the outsider, together with strategies that obscure such endeavors. At a general level, the scale of recent migration to the United States has fostered a widespread conception of immigrants as threatening the rule of law, social cohesion, and the nation's economic health. As these concerns get amplified or distorted by ethnocultural nationalism or fear, anti-immigrant sentiment has led, in extreme cases, to the demonization of populations of color through increasingly mainstream outlets, as evidenced by the 40 percent increase in anti-Hispanic hate crimes between 2003 and 2007.[56]

Race and ethnicity continue to play a significant role in the pattern by which humans punish those whom we fear just as we fear those whom we punish, and, in so doing, produce the differences we fear.[57] Race and irregular immigration status have remained intertwined over the course of US history, and undocumented immigrants remain "at once welcome and unwelcome," economically integral qua disposable labor.[58] Campese decries this coexistence of anti-immigrant rhetoric about invasion by "foreign menaces" with the nation's "insatiable appetite for cheap immigrant labor" that invites immigrants across its borders.[59] Some situate this ambivalence within the historical subversion of Emma Lazarus's promise by persistent nativism and racism.[60]

Miguel De La Torre highlights the racial dimensions of the US fortification strategy, arguing that it rests on collective judgments about the value of certain persons: "Funneling migrants to the desert was based on a philosophy that the collateral damage of dead brown bodies would deter others from crossing. Even after recognizing that few were deterred, we continue to implement policies that lead to death. Not since the days of the Jane and Jim Crow South have governmental policies systematically and brutally targeted a group of non-white people."[61] Virgilio Elizondo characterizes racism as rooted in a fear of others as potential threats and the West's self-image as normative; his notion of racism's function as the justification and masking of economic exploitation likewise reflects enduring attitudes and practices toward certain immigrant communities.[62] Hence the "group pride" of socioeconomic, national, and ethnic elites eclipses immigrants' full humanity from considerations with violent and unjust consequences.

Outside the realm of policymaking, the reduction of undocumented immigrants to their legal status, actions, or parents' actions in wider culture has become so ubiquitous as not to shock. In some respects, reductive conceptualizations of immigrants are dehumanizing whether they cast persons as social burdens or economically beneficial. Lost in cost comparisons of federal revenues gained against local services strained is the primary humanity of such migrants. Media portrayals of an out-of-control border or immigrants as public charges and purveyors of disease help sustain dominant cultural ideologies and exacerbate immigrants' plight.[63] In his book *Brown Tide Rising*, Otto Santa Ana catalogs metaphors depicting Latinos in the media and public discourse. Images range from a "rising brown tide [that] will wash away Anglo-American cultural dominance" to immigrants as animals, as weeds that spring up and must be uprooted, to pathogens, enemies, criminals, and tax burdens.[64] Such characterizations shape a society's collective imagination, and "as the discursive practices are enacted, ideological practices are reproduced and reaffirmed . . . which define and confine both oppressor and oppressed."[65]

Collective egotism is evident not only in dehumanizing rhetoric and structural violence, but also in the ways we disguise sinful goals with lofty rhetoric about immigration aims. First-generation immigrant and comparative literature scholar Ali Behdad details the nation's repeated efforts to recuperate its national narrative of hospitality to the oppressed even as its actual pragmatic considerations have consistently held sway. He notes that since the nation's founding, legislative debates about immigration have centered around issues of national security, economic instrumentalism, and social costs rather than human rights. Yet the "celebratory narrative of immigrant America" relies instead on lofty ideas like hospitality, liberty, and democracy to justify the nation's desirability to outsiders.[66] In a similar manner, the trade policies of high-income countries that disproportionally benefited certain sectors within their nations while negatively impacting others have been masked by "stated commitments to promote development and poverty reduction."[67] As Niebuhr cautions in *The Irony of American History*, "despite the constant emphasis upon the 'dignity of man' in our own liberal culture . . . our culture does not really value the individual as much as it pretends."[68] Behdad argues that a "repetitive discourse of self-legitimation" generated to shore up patriotism "eclipses not only the economic dimensions of immigration, but also the disciplining of its aliens by . . . state apparatuses."[69] He contends that the contemporary US–Mexico border exemplifies the nation's treatment of its immigrants, marked as it is by militarization, surveillance, and discipline in the effort to produce a docile, cheap labor force.[70] He laments from personal experience that such "disciplinary practices of border control . . . play a critical role in normalizing an exclusionary form of citizenship and national identity."[71]

Nativist elements of US culture have thus historically served to manufacture an imagined sense of community.[72] Representations of the outsider as a social menace have been continually reinvented in moments of national crisis—for example, the Know-Nothing Movement in 1850s, the Chinese Exclusion Act of 1882, racist quota laws of 1920s, Proposition 187 in 1986, and post–September 11 laws.[73] While each presents a distinct and complex context, the general pattern evidences xenophobia's productive function in the national imagination. According to Behdad, in each anti-immigrant claim we encounter "a differential mode of national and cultural identification that posits a fundamental difference between the patriotic citizen and the menacing alien. The project of imagining a homogeneous nation is never complete. It requires the continual presence of the immigrant as other, through whom citizenship and cultural belonging are rearticulated."[74] These historical patterns have helped "transform xenophobia into an acceptable and powerful form of patriotism," manifesting and engendering nationalistic collective egotism.[75] Hence in the mythmaking that obscures self-interested considerations or social mechanisms that legitimate xenophobic practices, citizens may become co-opted by narratives that demean or obscure reality. Media and state apparatuses thus contribute to distorted consciousness that leads to collective destructive action.[76]

In recent years Samuel Huntington articulated his suspicion that the nation's ideals and Anglo-Saxon cultural identity were under threat from Spanish-speaking immigrants failing to assimilate.[77] His concomitant fears about declining patriotism among the nation's elites in threatening the nations' "historic sense of its own uniqueness" recall Niebuhr's warning that "the entrenched idea that America has a providential mission in the world and our nation's rendered uniquely virtuous and innocent by the blessings of that history" was even more perilous than the nations' tendency toward materialism.[78] Discourse regarding assimilation thus risks self-righteous exceptionalism along with ethnocultural nationalism. Both historical nativist concerns and ongoing efforts to subsume the immigrant are dehumanizing; put another way, both the fear of immigrants' inability to assimilate and the goal of their assimilation deny their particularity and agency. Different varieties of ethnocultural nationalism view nations as "distinct peoples connected most deeply by race, religion and other characteristics that they cannot change or should not have to change."[79] Nativists frequently charge that immigrants "balkanize receiving nations and undermine their core identities" or social cohesion.[80]

Whether we seek to expel or unilaterally assimilate newcomers, we are tempted by sinful motives and reductive perceptions. Cuban philosopher Raul Fornet-Betancourt has suggested that we must question whether the concepts that shape our way of thinking "from whose horizons we encounter the strangers are suitable instruments," or if they result from "prejudgments" we cultivate, since we are interested not in knowledge of the strangers, "but controlled and interested dealings with them."[81] The hegemonic manner wherein a subject appropriates an object does not lead to recognition but assimilation; hence, we need a "hermeneutics that is both liberated from the habits of colonial thinking and allows itself to be influenced by the strangers."[82] I return to the challenge of adopting more adequate forms of integration in chapter 5.

Christian Anthropology: Illuminating Immigrants' Constrained Agency and Relationality

The patterns of dehumanization witnessed across dominant perceptions, experiences, and functions of undocumented immigrants reflect sinful human tendencies that strike at the core of what it means to be human. As noted above, Christian critiques of such patterns are rooted in a vision of every person as not only sinful, but also sacred and inherently social. This notion is rooted in a philosophical anthropology that "regards human beings as naturally embodied, intelligent, free and social," grounded, in turn, in a "theological anthropology of human beings as created in God's image, wounded by sin, and redeemed by grace."[83] The basic elements of Christian anthropology illuminate the inner logic of an immigration ethic that contests dehumanizing economic, political, and social practices.

In her work in bioethics, sexual ethics, and feminist ethics, Margaret Farley has helpfully elaborated intrinsic features of personhood that claim our respect and "awaken our love." She probes whether there is "anything inherent in persons that forbids us to reduce them to what they can do for us, that prohibits us from invading their bodies or their lives, that requires us to pay attention to their needs and their beauty?"[84] Farley identifies autonomy and relationality as the two basic "obligating features of personhood" that ground the requirement to respect all persons in whatever manner we relate to them.[85] She notes that autonomy and relationality constitute the basis of our "obligation to respect persons as *ends in themselves* and forbid, therefore, the use of persons as mere means."[86] For Farley these elements are rooted both in Christian beliefs that humans are created and beloved by God, but also experientially in terms of humans' capacity for free choice, for self-determination as "embodied, inspirited beings," endowed with the "capacity to choose not only our own actions but our ends and our loves," the meaning of our lives and our destinies.[87]

On the first obligating feature of autonomy, Farley specifies that to "treat another human person as a mere means is to violate her insofar as she is autonomous"; hence individuals and groups may not achieve their purposes "at the expense of other persons' basic needs and purposes."[88] The second feature of relationality similarly grounds an obligation to respect persons as ends. Farley frames this capacity for relationship as intrinsic to personhood in the general acknowledgment that persons "do not just survive or thrive in relations to others; they cannot exist without some sort of fundamental relatedness to others." Hence our identity as persons is thus constituted by our self-transcendence through capacities for knowledge and love.[89] In her words, "the capacity to love one another and all things, and to love what is sacredly transcendent and immanent (that is, divine), makes persons worthy of respect."[90] Autonomy and relationality mark ways in which persons both transcend and possess themselves.

Farley's emphasis on autonomy and relationality (justice and love, respect and compassion) brings together a Kantian morality of respect for persons with a feminist ethic of care that attends to embodied particularities. She insists that "an obligation to respect persons requires that we honor their freedom and respond to their needs, that we value difference as well as sameness, that we attend to the concrete realities of our own and others' lives."[91] As suggested above, these concrete realities are often violated for marginalized groups when their members are reduced to a generalized other, as is evident in the construal of all Latinos as immigrants, of immigrants as the cause of domestic social problems, or of the need for "them" to become more like "us." Finally, freedom and relationality are also profoundly connected to one another, and together they provide the content for basic ethical norms.[92] Farley's vision of personhood unmasks the manipulation and exploitation of migrants as dehumanizing, for both the autonomy and relationality of the unwilling migrant are compromised at various stages.

Farley's Kantian insistence on humans' absolute value rather than contingent or conditional value excoriates the widespread exploitation and commodification of immigrants' bodies and their labor.[93] Personal agency is constrained for unwilling migrants or economic refugees and for members of mixed-status families; in significant senses they are unable to determine the direction their lives will take or ownership over their actions and lives.[94] To respect persons as ends, Farley insists, is to resist absorbing another into one's own agenda.[95] The sexual exploitation of migrants compromises the victim's autonomy for the perpetrator's physical self-gratification. More broadly, the mass absorption of small farmers and low-wage workers into certain transnational corporations' and employers' agenda of profit maximization likewise violates agency. The obligations Farley outlines emanating from respect for persons—honoring their freedom, responding to their concrete realities and needs—are disregarded for the migrant whose freedom to pursue a meaningful "agenda" in his home country is constrained, or whose freedom of movement and recourse are constrained once undocumented.[96] Certain detention and deportation practices that cause disproportionate distress and more indirect "deportation-by-attrition" strategies similarly dehumanize.[97]

Gutiérrez characterizes human dignity in a similar way in an essay on poverty and migration: "Dignity necessitates that the poor be subjects of their own history," he asserts, which "includes holding their own destiny in their hands."[98] Some may object that the ability to choose one's own agenda or destiny falls short as a useful norm for migrants—it is impossible to universally guarantee the substance of what a robust agenda for individuals (and family members) might entail. Certainly when it comes to obligations of host countries, limits may be set, yet in the case of much reluctant migration the basic opportunity to earn a living wage or reunite with family members seems to be constitutive of authentic subjectivity on Farley's account. Gutiérrez himself admits that "in the case of those who live their lives marginalized from our society this perspective may seem unrealistic, but such a situation must not be a reason to forget their personhood."[99]

The connection Farley highlights between freedom and relationality underscores the intrinsic nature of family relationships to personhood and the necessity of nurturing primary relationships for growth in freedom.[100] If family members constitute our most intimate relationships, protracted separation risks a fundamental denial of our humanity. For many undocumented migrants, immediate family members are their primary motive for crossing—to reunite with them or provide for them. Current US immigration practices undermine these primary relationships by disallowing "the legal immigration of otherwise eligible members from low-income families, and by forcing immigrants who have been approved for family-based visas to wait for years, occasionally decades, before they receive them."[101] Undermining family unity, such laws frustrate the core relationality Farley defends.

Apart from family separation, the mixed status of an intact family has significant consequences on children's education, future labor market experience, and integration into broader society. Forty percent of US-born children of Hispanic immigrants have at least one parent who is an undocumented immigrant (the large majority from Mexico or Central America), according to census data analysis from the Pew Hispanic Center. According to their report, "the most immediate result has been a substantial increase" in the number of US-born children growing up in poverty; they are nearly "twice as likely to be poor as the children of legal immigrants or native parents."[102] From origins into next generations, poverty accompanies most undocumented immigrants and their families.

The norms Farley derives from foundational autonomy and relationality—such as do no unjust harm, free consent, mutuality, and equality—squarely condemn the sexual exploitation of women on the move by *coyotes* or *polleros* (smugglers), other migrants, and employers. As she explicitly argues, "the buying and selling of women, by whatever cultural disguise, violates the dignity of women who are all ends in themselves."[103] Implicitly, Farley's norms condemn not only the rape or assault of women on the move, but also the widespread practice of women's assumption of protection in the form of an agreement with another male traveler or her use of contraception. Anthropologist Olivia Ruiz Marrujo notes that insofar as *coyotes* have almost "exclusive control over the people who have paid them to go north," they "often gain access to the bodies of women migrants." Women, aware that *coyotes* may deny her passage or abandon her midway if she refuses their advances, "and seeking to avoid a confrontation and possibly greater violence, may 'agree' from the beginning of her negotiations with a *coyote* to have sex with him in exchange for his 'help' or 'protection.'"[104] Genuine agency and relationality are compromised even for those who escape physical violation. An estimated 700,000 to 2 million people fall victim to human trafficking annually, the majority of whom begin as economic migrants or refugees seeking "safer or more economically viable alternatives for themselves and their families." Persons believed to be smugglers, employment contractors, even friends or relatives deceive would-be migrants. Women and unaccompanied children face a heightened risk of trafficking with attendant sexual abuse and violence, and upon escape, further stigmatization "upon return to their communities of origin."[105] Chapter 3 further explores the particular threats facing women and families.

Immigrants' Agency amid Constraint

The recurrent term "dehumanize" underscores how basic and thoroughgoing are the threats facing many irregular migrants. Yet such migrants also exhibit courage, integrity, and resilience, and with little agency accomplish big things.[106] An exclusive focus on constrained agency of migrants misses crucial aspects of their experience. Latin American liberation theologians remind us that in the poor we encounter life where we do not expect it. As Farley prompts, we are called to attend not only to persons' needs but also their beauty. Just as punitive or market-based approaches obscure the humanity of migrants, an abstract focus upon human rights violations can overlook the agency *expressed* in migrants' struggles.

Migrants become active subjects both through public events and in *lo cotidiano,* or their daily lives.[107] For example, migrant women are not just victims of globalizing trends, unscrupulous employers, and vicious predators; they are also agents of significant change for their families and their communities. Migrant women are agents of transformation for their communities in spite of the threats and constraints many face. Many are instrumental in cultivating social relationships in new settings, through informal kinship networks, home-town associations, or ecclesial base communities.[108] In terms of "would-be migrants," the majority of CRS's microfinance programs strategically target women, as studies indicate they are more likely to use their income to benefit their families by investing in their businesses and meeting household needs. Although women typically control the fewest resources in impoverished communities, CRS reports that they tend to purchase more and better quality food, improve family health care and housing, pay children's school fees, and save for emergencies with loan monies.[109] Through CRS microcredit enterprises in the Mexican border region, women have formed solidarity groups. These loans foster business and conflict resolution skills alike on a holistic model of integral human development. The groups even improve mental health for members, who report that the hope and support provided combat widespread depression.[110]

Migrant women have also employed creative strategies for disrupting oppressive constraints via grassroots involvement, contested spaces, and direct action. For example, women and children were very active in Los Angeles with the Justice for Janitors campaigns. Their participation helped make visible the needs for a living wage and family health insurance for the striking workers. As Latin American feminist theologians emphasize, the woman is both subject and object of the option for the poor, representing the power of survival and resistance.[111] María Pilar Aquino has highlighted the impact of Latin American women's resistance efforts through political demonstrations, popular projects, and intellectual renewal.[112] Whether through transnational mothering or sociopolitical engagement, these significant expressions of agency remind us that while Christians remain tasked with taking the crucified down from the cross, we must not miss the Easter among us.

Roberto Goizueta and Justo González have written about the border as a meeting place for the interaction of cultures and a category defining a human community and its encounter with God there:

> A border need not function as a frontier that only expands and excludes; it need not function as a safeguard for the illusory purity of one side. Even if too often denied in practice, an alternative understanding of the border is implicit in the *mestizo* history of Latin America: "A border is the place at which two realities, two worldviews, two cultures, meet and interact. . . . at the border growth takes place by encounter, by mutual enrichment. A true border, a true place of encounter, is by nature permeable. It is not like medieval armor, but rather like skin. Our skin does set a limit to where our body begins and where it ends. Our skin also sets certain limits to our give-and-take with our environment, keeping out certain germs, helping us to select that in our environment which we are ready to absorb. But if we ever close up our skin, we die."[113]

Understanding the border not simply as scar or frontier but as seedbed alerts us to migrants' agency and resurrection possibilities, as well.[114] Attending to migrants' humanity itself as "on the border" attunes us to the ways in which the fundamental humanity of irregular immigrants is at once deeply compromised and yet profoundly resilient. Chapter 5 explores the challenge that migrants' expressions of creative and risk-laden agency pose to reigning ethical models.

Conclusions

The dominant economic, security, and cultural frameworks governing contemporary migration serve to mask and distract from human costs. From the perspective of Christian ethics, deep commitments about what it means to be human call us to reconsider these habitual perspectives and harmful tendencies. The dehumanization pervading undocumented immigration—from the rhetorical, practical, ideological, and legal dimensions explored herein, to the surrogacy of immigration for other social problems and our criminalization of humanitarian aid to undocumented immigrants—underscores the urgency of bringing the defense of the person to the center of future considerations.[115] The threats outlined indicate the deficiencies of an immigration paradigm centered on expediency, national interest, or economic efficiency. A human-centered approach that values migrants' agency impels basic changes to systems and rhetoric that abet and disguise immigrants' exploitation and death. Fundamentally, it demands enhanced human rights protections and an expansion of the reigning paradigm's scope. Whereas the basic human rights required by Farley's obligating features and presupposed in Catholic social thought are universal in theory, in contemporary practice their exercise depends on legally sanctioned membership in a political community.[116] The practices that violate the human rights of the irregular immigrants examined herein not only threaten human life, bodily integrity, and family unity, but also undermine the rule of law and its legitimacy.

A focus on human rights also highlights the inadequacy of a Westphalian sovereignty model for immigration considerations more broadly considered.[117] Chapter 4 considers how understanding not only human rights as transcendent of citizenship, but also immigration dynamics as related to unjust international political and economic divides, demands an expansion of responsibility beyond the confines of national communities.[118] Reorienting the immigration paradigm in terms of transnational human rights does not readily resolve tensions between conflicting rights or obligations. The remaining chapters consider ways in which reform efforts might better integrate trade, development, labor, border security, detention, and family unification policies to begin to approach the intersecting considerations from a more comprehensive if not yet transnational perspective. Nonetheless, the prudential judgment proper to discerning best methods to attain needed reforms cannot justify indifference to border-crossing deaths.[119]

Moving forward, Farley's insights prod us to bring the needs and gifts of all persons to the center of immigration considerations. A Christian ethic of immigration must concretely protect the right not to have to migrate as well as those who have little choice but to do so.[120] Niebuhr's caveats regarding collective egotism caution us to heed his political thought concerning the continual need to restrain selfishness, honestly evaluate competing interests, and maintain a balance of power. Despite this realism, Niebuhr's insistence that love is the form of justice offers hope that an immigration ethic that centers on human rights can leaven existing legal arrangements to better approximate genuine kinship.

Notes

The epigraph is reprinted with permission of Martín Espada.

1. Data from Mexico's National Human Rights Commission and the ACLU of San Diego and Imperial Counties in California reports confirm this rate. Mexico foreign ministry/media sources bolster the estimate of 5,607 deaths from 1994 to 2008, and DHS reports 4,111, not counting those reported first to local authorities. Human rights groups report that US [and Mexican] agencies typically undercount deaths due to inconsistent classification standards. Human rights and civil liberties groups from both countries interpret the rising fatality rates as signaling "an escalating humanitarian crisis that is not going away and requires more effective governmental responses." Spencer S. Hsu, "Border Deaths Are Increasing: Rise Is Despite Fewer Crossers, U.S. and Mexican Groups Say," *The Washington Post* (September 30, 2009), available at www.washingtonpost.com/wp-dyn/content/article/2009/09/29/AR2009092903212 .html (accessed November 25, 2009).

2. Jeremy Slack and Scott Whiteford, "Violence and Migration on the Arizona–Sonora Border," 11. The Border Patrol's Tucson sector alone witnessed a ten-year low in apprehensions in fiscal year 2009, yet the bodies of suspected border crossers found in the region (213) marked the third highest ever, indicating the risk of dying had escalated to twice as high compared with five years prior, and nearly 30 times greater than in 1998. Brady McCombs, "No Signs of Letup in Entrant Deaths," *Arizona Daily Star* (December 27, 2009), available at www.azstarnet.com/allheadlines/322885 (accessed January 5, 2010). McCombs cites the number of apprehensions in the region in FY 2009 as 241,600 and compares the 213 bodies of suspected illegal border crossers found in the Tucson Sector to 230 in 2005 and 223 in 2007, according to the *Arizona Daily Star*'s border-death database. He writes, "There were 88 known deaths per 100,000 apprehensions in the area covered in the U.S. Border Patrol's Tucson Sector in fiscal year 2009, which ended on Sept. 30 . . . up from 39 known deaths per 100,000 apprehensions in 2004 and three per 100,000 apprehensions in 1998." See also Jacqueline Maria Hagan, "The Church vs. the State: Borders, Migrants and Human Rights," in *Religion and Social Justice for Immigrants*, ed. Pierrette Hondagneu-Sotelo (New Brunswick, NJ: Rutgers University Press, 2007), 93–103, at 94.

3. Gloria Anzaldúa, *Borderlands La Frontera*, 25.

4. As of January 2010, 10.8 million unauthorized immigrants lived in the United States, down from 11.8 million in January 2009. From 2000 to 2010 the unauthorized population living in the United States grew by 27 percent; 6.6 million (or 62 percent) of the unauthorized population came from Mexico, while the next leading countries of origin were El Salvador (620,000), Guatemala (520,000), Honduras (330,000), and the Philipines (280,000). Michael

Hoeffer, Nancy Rytina, and Bryan C. Baker, "Estimates of the Unauthorized Immigrant Population," 1, 4, 5.

5. Eliseo Pérez-Álvarez, "The Tortilla Curtain," 19.

6. Mary DeLorey reports, "There is a shelter specifically for 'mutilated' migrants who have fallen from trains in southern Mexico." Mary DeLorey, "International Migration," 48.

7. Forty-three percent of total irregular immigrants in 2010 were female, including 53 percent of the 45 and older age group. Hoeffer, Rytina, and Baker, "Estimates of the Unauthorized Immigrant Population Residing in the United States," 5. Miguel A. De La Torre, *Trails of Hope and Terror*, 15.

8. McCombs elaborates: "There are now 3,300 agents, more than 200 miles of fences and vehicle barriers, and 40 agents assigned to the agency's search, rescue and trauma team, Borstar, yet illegal immigrants are still dying while trying to cross the Border Patrol's 262-mile-long Tucson Sector. Border-county law enforcement, Mexican Consulate officials, Tohono O'odham tribal officials and humanitarian groups say the increase in fencing, technology and agents has caused illegal border crossers to walk longer distances in more treacherous terrain, increasing the likelihood that people will get hurt or fatigued and left behind to die." McCombs, "No Signs of Letup in Entrant Deaths."

9. John Fife, "Civil Initiative," in De La Torre, *Trails of Hope and Terror*, 170–75, at 174.

10. Gioacchino Campese, "¿Cuantos Más?," in Groody and Campese, eds., *A Promised Land*, 278.

11. According to the Global exchange, "a resolution passed by Amnesty International-USA in 2000 noted that the Gatekeeper strategy is an abuse of the right to control the border 'in that it maximizes, rather than minimizes, the risk to life." Global Exchange (www.globalexchange.org/countries/americas/unitedstates/california) as cited by De La Torre, *Trails of Hope and Terror*, 15.

12. Gustavo Gútierrez, *On Job*, as cited in David Tracy, "The Christian Option for the Poor," 119.

13. Kerwin, "Rights, the Common Good, and Sovereignty in Service of the Human Person," in Kerwin and Gerschutz, eds., *And You Welcomed Me*, 93–122, at 98. An in-depth discussion of NAFTA's dynamics and impact follows in chapter 4.

14. Erica Dahl-Bredine, Mexico Country Manager, Catholic Relief Services, as cited in DeLorey, "International Migration," in Kerwin and Gerschutz, eds., *And You Welcomed Me*, 37.

15. The Pontifical Council for the Pastoral Care of Migrants and Itinerant People *Erga Migrantes Caritas Christi (The Love of Christ Towards Migrants)* 9 (2004) as cited in Mary DeLorey, "International Migration," 32.

16. Mary DeLorey, "International Migration," in Kerwin and Gerschutz, eds., *And You Welcomed Me*, 31–54, at 37.

17. Benedict XVI, *Caritas in veritate*, no. 62.

18. The Catholic articulation of human rights encompasses civil and political liberties as well as social and economic rights such as housing, health care, education, and employment. The social anthropology grounding Catholic thought indicates that human rights are primarily realized in community, and rights are matched by corresponding duties to contribute to the common good.

19. Pope Pius XII, *Exsul familia (On the Spiritual Care to Migrants)* (September 30, 1952) in *The Church's Magna Charta for Migrants*, ed. Giulivo Tessarolo; Pope John XXIII, *Pacem in terris* (April 11, 1963) www.vatican.va/holy_father/john_xxiii/encyclicals/documents/hf_j-xxiii_enc_11041963_pacem_en.html); Pope Paul VI, *Populorum progressio* (March 26, 1967)

www.vatican.va/holy_father/paul_vi/encyclicals/documents/hf_p-vi_enc_e26031967_populor um_en.html.

20. Michael J. Himes and Kenneth R. Himes, O.F.M., *Fullness of Faith*, 46.

21. National Council of Catholic Bishops, "Economic Justice for All: Pastoral Letter on Catholic Social Teaching and the U.S. Economy" (Washington, DC: National Conference of Catholic Bishops, 1986), no. 1, 14.

22. John Paul II, *Laborem exercens*, no. 23.

23. John Paul II's *Ecclesia in America* highlights the rights of migrants and their families and the respect for human dignity "even in cases of non-legal immigration." *Ecclesia in America* (Washington, DC: USCCB, 1999), no. 65. Over recent decades social encyclicals have enumerated migrant rights to life and a means of livelihood, decent housing, education of their children, humane working conditions, public profession of religion, and to have such rights recognized and respected by host government policies. See 1969 Vatican Instruction on Pastoral Care (no. 7); 1978 Letter to Episcopal Conferences from the Pontifical Commission for the Pastoral Care of Migrant and Itinerant peoples (no. 3); Pope Paul VI, *Octogesima adveniens* (no. 17); Pope John XIII, *Pacem en terris* (no. 106); National Council of Catholic Bishops, *Resolution on the Pastoral Concern of the Church for People on the Move* (Washington, DC: USCC 1976) and endorsed by Paul VI (Christiansen, 93–94); and United States Conference of Catholic Bishops and *Conferencia del Episcopado Mexicano*, "Strangers No Longer: Together on the Journey of Hope" (Washington, DC: USCCB, 2003), no 38. The tradition insists that the church must remain a vigilant advocate on behalf of the rights of migrants and their families without documentation, from John Paul II's *Ecclesia in America* to the Mexican and US Bishops "Strangers no Longer" to the ongoing advocacy of the US Catholic Church on local, national, and international levels.

24. Pope John Paul II, *Laborem exercens*, no. 9.

25. For an analysis of day labor abuses in terms of Catholic social thought and social sin, see Kristin Heyer, "Strangers in Our Midst," 425–53.

26. Pope Paul VI, *Populorum progressio*, no. 28.

27. Oscar Romero, *The Violence of Love*, 24. Reprinted here with permission from Orbis Books, Maryknoll, NY.

28. John J. Hoeffner and Michele R. Pistone, "But the Laborers Are . . . Many? Catholic Social Teaching on Business, Labor and Economic Migration," in Kerwin and Gerschutz, eds., *And You Welcomed Me*, 55–92, at 71.

29. Pope Benedict XVI, *Caritas in Veritate* (June 29, 2009), available at www.vatican.va/holy_father/benedict_xvi/encyclicals/documents/hf_ben-xvi_enc_20090629_caritas-in-veritate_en.html (accessed December 10, 2009), no. 25.

30. Human services imperiled include regulation in energy sector, health care, education, and water resources. As Kenneth Weare notes, "free trade [often] means freedom from any democratically established laws [that protect human rights or the environment] that in any way hinder the maximization of profit for international corporations." Democratic laws that protect human rights or the environment may be struck down as nontariff barriers. See Kenneth Weare, "Globalization and Free Trade Agreements," in Linda Hogan, ed., *Applied Ethics in a World Church*, 39–45, at 41.

31. *Caritas in veritate*, no. 25, emphasis in original.

32. Ibid., no. 32.

33. Randy Capps, Michael Fix, Jeffrey S. Passel, Jason Ost and Dan Perez-Lopez, "A Profile of the Low-Wage Immigrant Workforce," 68.

34. Remarks made by Bishop John C. Wester of Salt Lake City, chairman of the US bishops' Committee on Migration, to the Vatican's World Congress on the Pastoral Care of Migrants and Refugees. See Cindy Wooden, "Migrants in Detention Have a Right to Spiritual Care, Speakers Say," *Catholic News Service* (November 12, 2009), available at www.catholicnews .com/data/stories/cns/0905031.htm (accessed July 1, 2011).

35. Anil Kalhan, "Rethinking Immigration Detention," 110 COLUM. L. REV. SIDEBAR (2010), 42–48, at 44–45. I take up the "immigration industrial complex" further in chapter 5 of this volume.

36. *Dying to Live* (2005), documentary produced by Groody River Films.

37. "Massacre in Tamaulipas Editorial," *New York Times* (August 29, 2010), available at www.nytimes.com/2010/08/30/opinion/30mon3.html (accessed August 29, 2010).

38. Reinhold Niebuhr, *The Nature and Destiny of Man*, Vol. 1, 179.

39. Ibid., 181.

40. Ibid., 182. Consequently guilt "represents the objective and historical consequences of sin," for which the sinner is held responsible; guilt represents "the actual corruption of the plan of creation and providence in the historical world," 222.

41. Ibid., 208.

42. Ibid., 209. Niebuhr describes group egotism in terms of the egotism of racial, national, and socioeconomic groups.

43. Ibid., 213.

44. Ibid., 226.

45. Many predict continued demographic challenges will sustain a demand for greater low-wage labor output than native workers can accommodate: native-born fertility rates are falling, the workforce is aging and becoming better educated, and the labor force participation rate is flattening, yet the economy is creating a large number of less-skilled jobs. See American Immigration Lawyers Association (AILA), "Making the Case for Comprehensive Immigration Reform: Resource Guide," available at www.aila.org/resourceguide (accessed February 27, 2008), 18.

46. Yen Le Espiritu, *Home Bound: Filipino American Lives across Cultures, Communities and Countries* (Berkeley: University of California Press, 2003), 207 as cited in Campese, "¿Cuantos Más?," 279.

47. De La Torre laments that "For over a century . . . the U.S. military protected U.S. corporations as they built roads in developing countries throughout Latin America to extract, by brute force if necessary, their natural resources and make use of cheap labor." He concludes that "[US] foreign policy has created an economic situation in [migrants'] home countries in which they are unable to feed their families." De La Torre, *Trails of Hope and Terror*, 16.

48. Niebuhr, *Nature and Destiny of Man*, Vol. 1, 190–91.

49. Whereas Aquinas supported private ownership as a means for distributing material goods, the principle ensuring the basic needs of all are met trumps private ownership. David Hollenbach, "The Market and Catholic Social Teaching," in Dietmar Mieth and Marciano Vidal, eds., *Outside the Market No Salvation?*, 67–76, at 72.

50. Donald Kerwin, "Toward a Catholic Vision of Nationality," 204.

51. Niebuhr, *Nature and Destiny of Man*, Vol. 1, 213.

52. See Yvette Flores-Ortiz, "*La Mujer y la Violencia*: A Culturally Based Model for Understanding and Treatment of Domestic Violence in Chicana/Latina Communities," in ed. Norma Alarcón et al., *Chicana Critical Issues* (Berkeley, CA: Third Woman Press, 1993), as cited in Segura and Zavella, eds., *Women and Migration*, 16.

53. Whereas crime rates in El Paso are dramatically lower than those in the murder capital of Juárez just over the line, "outlaw gangs terrorize local populations on both sides of the border. Most of the criminals along the border smuggle narcotics to satisfy the insatiable American appetite for drugs, but many also deal in human traffic and other contraband." Ben Daniel, *Neighbor*, 11.

54. *New York Times* editorial, "Massacre in Tamaulipas."

55. Amnesty International, "Invisible Victims."

56. Spencer S. Hsu, "Hate Crimes Rise as Immigration Debate Heats Up," *Washington Post* (June 16, 2009).

57. William O'Neill, response to "The Last Judgment: Christian Ethics in a Legal Culture," Sixty-sixth annual convention of the Catholic Theological Society of America, San Jose, CA (June 11, 2011), unpublished notes. The comments were made in the context of the US criminal justice system blurring the distinction between retribution and vengeance.

58. Mae M. Ngai, *Impossible Subjects*, 2.

59. Gioacchino Campese, "¿Cuantos Más?," 279.

60. De La Torre also characterizes governmental rhetoric as rife with contradictions, with recent administrations trumpeting a "'culture of life' while legislating immigration policies that cause death." De La Torre, *Trails of Hope and Terror*, 181. Emma Lazarus penned the sonnet "The New Colossus" in 1883, later inscribed on the pedestal of the Statue of Liberty. She characterizes the "Mother of Exiles" as illuminating a welcome haven for "tired . . . poor . . . huddled masses yearning to breathe free." Near the end of her life, Lazarus became an advocate for disenfranchised immigrants, arriving by the thousands at the turn of the century. Emma Lazarus, *The Poems of Emma Lazarus*, 2.

61. De La Torre, *Trails of Hope and Terror*, 181. He adds that the memory of Jim Crow laws illuminates the normalization of "the deaths of people of a particular race or ethnicity" in contemporary policies and mainstream culture" (16).

62. Virgilio Elizondo, "Analysis of Racism," in Dietmar Mieth and Lisa Sowle Cahill, *Migrants and Refugees*, 52–59.

63. As Carmen Nanko-Fernández points out, the association of im/migrants with disease-bearers in an age of pandemics "harkens back to Nazi rhetoric about Jews and others deemed detrimental to the state, and recalls images of braceros in a cloud of DDT being fumigated prior to entering the United States to work." Carmen Nanko-Fernández, "Beyond Hospitality," 57.

64. See Otto Santa Ana in *Brown Tide Rising*, 78, 86, sections 3 and 5, respectively.

65. Ibid., 253. Santa Ana continues, "as people live their lives, they enact the discourse practices associated with their subject positions. In doing so, they tend to accept the ideology of the standing social order, namely, the institutional practices that sustain and legitimize repressive power relations" (254). Writing analogously on an end to southern racism in the 1960s, Niebuhr focused the relevant question as "simply whether we are prepared to treat our fellow man with the respect that his innate dignity as a human being requires and deserves." Richard Fox, "Reinhold Niebuhr—The Living of Christian Realism," in Richard Harries, ed., *Reinhold Niebuhr and the Issues of Our Time* , 9–23, at 14.

66. Ali Behdad, *A Forgetful Nation*, 8.

67. DeLorey, "International Migration," 38.

68. Niebuhr, *Irony of American History*, 6, 8.

69. He names the FBI, the INS, and the Border Patrol, which he traces back to the Immigration Act of 1891. He notes that the Immigration Act of 1891 enabled the federal government to build the administrative machinery to control immigration at Ellis Island. He also laments the fact that the increasingly routine subjection of "brown skinned immigrants and citizens"

to "surveillance, interrogation, incarceration, and deportation as the perception of the foreigner as a threat to democracy" has become normalized by new laws, e.g., the USA Patriot Act, signed into law on October 26, 2001. Behdad, *A Forgetful Nation*, 10.

70. Ibid., 10.

71. Ibid., 146.

72. As reflected in the short-lived Alien and Sedition Act of 1798 imposed by the Federalist administration of John Adams, the representation of the foreigner as a political and social menace has been a fundamental element of American nationalism since the founding. Behdad, *A Forgetful Nation*, 10.

73. For an historical overview of the US deportation system's exclusionary practices as methods of immigration management as well as social control, see Daniel Kanstroom, *Deportation Nation*.

74. Behdad, *A Forgetful Nation*, 11–12.

75. Ibid., 117.

76. Other ethicists, theologians, and social scientists have described similar dynamics in terms of nonvoluntary social sin, scotosis or false consciousness, suggestive of ways in which we are susceptible to a captivating environment or cultural blinders that prevent us from seeing rightly. I take up an analysis of social sin and immigration in this vein in chapter 2.

77. Huntington feared the sheer volume and birth rates of concentrated Latin American immigrants would split the US into two de facto nations and their "identity politics" assaulted the revered tradition of individualism. Samuel Huntington, *Who Are We?*, 180. Jack Citrin, Amy Lerman, Michael Murakami, and Kathyn Pearson, "Testing Huntington," 31–32.

78. Citrin, Lerman, Murakami, and Pearson, "Testing Huntington," 32. See also Wilfred M. McClay, "The Continuing Irony of American History," *First Things* (February 2002), available at www.firstthings.com/article/2007/06/001-the-continuing-irony-of-american-history-36 (accessed December 16, 2009).

79. Donald Kerwin, "America's Children," 13.

80. Kerwin, "Rights, the Common Good and Sovereignty," 99.

81. Raul Fornet-Betancourt, "Hermeneutics and Politics of Strangers: A Philosophical Contribution on the Challenge of *Convivencia* in Multicultural Societies," in Groody and Campese, eds., *A Promised Land*, 210–25, at 217.

82. Ibid., 217.

83. Stephen J. Pope, "Catholic Social Thought and the American Experience," in Margaret O'Brien Steinfels, ed., *American Catholics & Civic Engagement*, 26–41, at 27.

84. Margaret A. Farley, "A Feminist Version of Respect for Persons," 185. Emphasis in original.

85. Although the treatment of migrants is not among the many areas to which Farley has applied her consequent anthropological and ethical insights, I argue herein that they illuminate patterns of migrants' exploitation in helpful ways.

86. Margaret Farley, *Just Love*, 212. Emphasis in original.

87. Ibid., 212.

88. Farley, *Just Love*, 212, and "A Feminist Version of Respect for Persons," 187.

89. Farley, *Just Love*, 212–13.

90. Ibid., 214.

91. Farley, "A Feminist Version of Respect for Persons," 198.

92. Farley, *Just Love*, 214. Farley's sexual ethics norms go on to specify the meanings of these features of personhood as they satisfy their demands (do no unjust harm, free consent, mutuality, equality, commitment, fruitfulness, social justice).

93. Farley, "A Feminist Version of Respect for Persons," 187.

94. Ibid., 195.

95. Farley, *Just Love,* 212.

96. Farley, "A Feminist Version of Respect for Persons," 198.

97. Practices that treat undocumented immigrants as imminent threats to national security and therefore disproportionately threaten or use force, unjust treatment in detention facilities, or the practice of depositing deportees in inconvenient and often unknown locales as a deterrent fall into this category. Local governments' attempts to "curb illegal migration through measures that deny housing, employment, health care" and other services. Donald Kerwin, "Rights, the Common Good, and Sovereignty," 101.

98. Gustavo Gutiérrez, "Poverty, Migration and the Option for the Poor," in Groody and Campese, eds., *Promised Land,* 76–88, at 84.

99. Ibid., 84.

100. Farley, *Just Love,* 214.

101. Kerwin, "Rights, the Common Good, and Sovereignty," 112. Kerwin adds that an estimated 4.9 million persons (2.2 million of whom reside in the US) have been approved for family-based visas but have not received them, as of February 2009.

102. The report attributes this discrepancy to the fact that undocumented immigrants tend to have low levels of education and because their immigration status makes it harder to move up the job ladder. See N.C. Aizenman, "An Undesirable Inheritance: U.S.-Born Kids of Illegal Immigrants Twice as Likely as Others to Face Poverty," *The Washington Post* (December 9, 2009), available at www.washingtonpost.com/wp-dyn/content/article/2009/12/08/AR2009120 804446.html?hpid = artslot (accessed December 10, 2009).

103. Farley, "A Feminist Version of Respect for Persons," 195.

104. Olivia Ruiz Marrujo, "The Gender of Risk: Sexual Violence against Undocumented Women," in Groody and Campese, eds., *A Promised Land,* 225–42, at 229.

105. DeLorey, "International Migration," 49.

106. I am grateful to Bob Lassalle-Klein for initially suggesting this direction.

107. Gioacchino Campese, "Beyond Ethnic and National Imagination: Toward a Catholic Theology of U.S. Immigration," in Pierrette Hondagneu-Sotelo, ed., *Religion and Social Justice for Immigrants,* 175–90, at 182. Ada Maria Isasi-Díaz writes about *lo cotidiano* in, for example, *La Lucha Continues.*

108. Gemma Tulud Cruz, "Between Identity and Security," 362.

109. "Microfinance," Catholic Relief Services (2011), available at http://crs.org/micro finance/ (accessed July 9, 2011).

110. See Jeffrey Odel Korgen, *Solidarity Will Transform the World,* chapter 1.

111. Ivonne Gebara, "La opción por el pobre como opción por la mujer pobre," *Concilium* 214: 463–72, at 468 (1987) as cited in Elina Vuola, *Limits of Liberation,* 142.

112. Marla Pilar Aquino, *Our Cry for Life,* 104–5.

113. Roberto S. Goizueta, "Beyond the Frontier Myth," 157. Goizueta is citing Justo González, *Santa Biblia,* 86–87.

114. Goizueta, "Beyond the Frontier Myth," 158.

115. In this country a good Samaritan risks receiving a twenty-year prison sentence for transporting a dying immigrant to the closest hospital. De La Torre, *Trails of Hope and Terror,* 179.

116. See, e.g., William O'Neill, "Rights of Passage," 113–36.

117. Scholars typically trace norms of state sovereignty (or political authority within a territory) to the 1648 Peace of Westphalia, which ended the Thirty Years' War and consolidated

Europe's transition to a system of sovereign states (spreading across the globe in the three centuries following, culminating in the decline of the European colonial empires). With Wesphalia, states became established as the sole form of constitutional authority, and the Holy Roman Empire no longer had the power to challenge state authority (states' intervention with one another on matters of religion was also brought to an end). The prominence of sovereignty in political thought at the time (Machiavelli, Luther, Hobbes) also contributed to these practical shifts. See Dan Philpott, "Sovereignty." Today the Charter of the United Nations protects norms of sovereignty in its articles enshrining political self-determination and nonintervention (Articles 1–2).

118. Graziano Battistella, "Migration and Human Dignity: From Policies of Exclusion to Policies Based on Human Rights," in Groody and Campese, eds., *A Promised Land,* 177–91, at 186.

119. Kerwin, "Rights, the Common Good, and Sovereignty," 114.

120. DeLorey, "International Migration," 31.

CHAPTER TWO

Social Sin and Inhospitality to Immigrants

This is the year that the hands
pulling tomatoes from the vine
uproot the deed to the earth that sprouts the vine,
the hands canning tomatoes
are named in the will
that owns the bedlam of the cannery;

—MARTÍN ESPADA, "Imagine the Angels of Bread"

A S CHAPTER 1'S EXAMPLES ILLUSTRATE, casualties of unjust immigration policies and practices include a significant increase in border deaths and smuggling networks, prolonged family separation, and the creation of an underclass.[1] By contrast, commitments to welcoming the vulnerable and fostering solidarity in light of common human dignity ground a Christian immigration ethic, manifest in pastoral care and social services for immigrant populations and advocacy for humane immigration reform. As the discussion of nativism and more subtle forms of nationalism highlights, many US citizens, Christians included, remain ambivalent about—if not resistant to—an ethic that urges hospitality and mercy for those who cross or remain within their borders through extralegal avenues.[2] Without dismissing concerns about the complex relationship between law and morality or the political involvement of churches, fierce resistance to an ethic of hospitality and justice may suggest Christian citizens' susceptibility to secular disvalues.

The etymology of conscience—knowing together with—highlights the social dimension of moral knowledge, for "convictions of conscience are shaped, and moral obligations are learned, within the communities that influence us."[3] Adherents' divergent positions on social and political issues within religious communities raise questions not only about the adequacy of ecclesial teaching on evolving moral issues, but also about spheres of influence and discernment.[4] Recent research on Catholic voting patterns suggests that increasingly, religious affiliation does not significantly influence voting behavior. In the privacy of the voting booth, one's tax bracket, cultural assumptions, or party loyalty may take priority over religious or moral formation on social issues.[5] As Mark O'Keefe has written, "constituted in part by his or her social relationships, the person generally will appropriate uncritically the prevailing values of a culture—even though from an objective standpoint an outsider may see quite readily that the prevailing hierarchy of values is seriously disordered."[6] Hence the cultural forces that perpetuate myths about immigrants and that consistently elevate economic and security concerns above moral ones may wield significant influence. This use of anti-immigrant sentiment as a smokescreen to divert attention from needed reforms and the scapegoating of undocumented immigrants for economic and security woes threaten to deafen citizen-disciples to gospel calls for hospitality and justice. Such phenomena elucidate the many fences, both physical and ideological, that US citizens construct to exclude and protect but that impact immigrant populations.[7] Increasingly within US communities, legal, social, and cultural borders have become fault lines that jeopardize common welfare.

In articulating a theology of migration, Gioacchino Campese suggests that theology must "read the reality of migration," privileging the perspective of undocumented migrants, and "uncover the presence of God within that reality."[8] Chapter 2 considers sinful practices that both characterize the realities of migration and at the same time conceal the face of God, as these practices impede our grasp of authentic values.[9] Whereas Reinhold Niebuhr's Christian realism and the social gospel movement that preceded it developed social categories of sin in the early to mid-twentieth century, subsequent Catholic elaborations of social sin further reveal how socioeconomic, legal, and political structures that foster irregular immigration are related to ideological blinders that contribute to inhospitality to undocumented immigrants.[10] We encountered in chapter 1 how efforts to escape insecurity can impact migrants' vulnerability at institutional and ideological levels. Chapter 2 presents an analysis of social sin that accounts for its personal, institutional, and nonvoluntary dimensions to illuminate the relationship between such structural injustice and legitimating ideologies. Tracing the development of the theological category, particularly its articulations by Pope John Paul II and Latin American liberation theologians, helps yield this comprehensive and dialectical conception of social sin.

Because social sin demands both personal conversion and social transformation, the chapter concludes with an ecclesial model of response to undocumented immigration that exemplifies a multidimensional approach.

Social Sin and Immigration: An Overview

In its broadest sense social sin encompasses the unjust structures, distorted consciousness, and collective actions and inaction that facilitate injustice and dehumanization.[11] According to Peter Henriot, social sin attempts to identify and interpret structural injustice. Such systemic sinfulness may take the form of structures that violate human dignity, stifle freedom, or impose gross inequality; situations that promote or facilitate individual selfishness; or "the complicity of silent acquiescence in social injustice."[12] Hence Kenneth Himes has characterized social sin as "the disvalue . . . embedded in a pattern of societal organization and cultural understanding," such as systemic racism, sexism, or imperialism.[13] Christian theologians differ on the precise scope of social sin, from limiting it to the effects or embodiment of personal sin, to an expansive sense of all sin as primarily social, with personal sins as mere manifestations of social sin.[14] The discussion of social sin herein relies upon a distinction between personal or actual sin, understood as free and conscious acts that oppose moral norms, God's law, and conscience, and sin of the world, understood as a synthesis of the consequences of original sin over time throughout human history, including the imprint of sin on human hearts, structures, and environments.[15]

As we have seen, a fundamentally social anthropology and the covenantal context of sin were not novel theological developments at the advent of Catholic articulations of social sin around the time of Vatican II. Biblical scholarship on sin in John and Paul has long understood sin more as a state or condition than as an act of transgression. In his Gospel John uses the "world" to describe, as Himes puts it, "that hard-hearted state of existence within which one becomes enmeshed upon entrance into life, life that is lived in darkness rather than the light."[16] Moreover, the social situation of original sin essentially constitutes a state that facilitates individual sinfulness.[17] Yet until recent decades, the Catholic moral tradition has neglected, if not resisted, a social understanding of sin due in part to an individualistic, act-oriented approach in traditional moral theology and a legalistic approach to questions of social justice.[18] During the 1960s Latin American liberation theology and German political theology criticized the traditional focus on private virtue in light of the social dimension of the Christian message.[19] Examining the subsequent development of social sin in magisterial teachings and Latin American liberation theology sheds light upon a fuller understanding of how the concept illuminates receptivity to a Christian immigration ethic.

A MAGISTERIAL UNDERSTANDING OF SOCIAL SIN: THE LEGACY OF JOHN PAUL II

According to post-Vatican II magisterial teaching, social sin is primarily understood as the sum total of personal choices toward evil. Pope John Paul II's development of the category of social sin during his papacy broadened and enriched the Church's moral teaching and equipped the Church to better name and respond to societal injustices. A brief overview of his use of the concept indicates his emphasis on the derivative nature of social sin and his interest in theologically circumscribing its meaning; he holds that a situation or structure, although it can be unjust, cannot in itself sin, since it lacks personal free will and thus moral agency.

John Paul II's development of the category from his introduction of a deprivatized notion of sin in *Reconciliatio et paenitentia* (1984) through later social encyclicals departs from the individualistic conceptions of sin pervasive in the neo-Scholastic moral theology manuals.[20] Nevertheless, he consistently seeks to circumscribe social sin theologically due to a concern that social sin risks diminishing individual accountability and an insistence that the category may only be understood as sin analogously, since structures cannot sin or accrue guilt. As John Langan puts it, "it is clear that for John Paul II personal sin remains the fundamental category, and the notion of structures of sin is secondary and derivative both in terms of our thinking about our situation and our actions to transform it."[21] The pope's "wary openness" to the idea of social sin becomes clear even as his Apostolic Exhortation *Reconciliatio et paenitentia* introduces the "most detailed recognition of the concept extant to the time," its first explicit use in a document "bearing authoritative weight for the whole church" and representing "a significant exercise of the ordinary universal magisterium."[22] Here John Paul articulates three understandings of social sin: first, due to human solidarity each individual's actions impact others, hence "every sin can undoubtedly be considered as social sin"; second, some sins "by their very matter constitute a direct attack on one's neighbor," whether sins of commission or omission; and third, "social sin refers to the relationships between the various human communities."[23]

Even as he grounds this concept of sin in a social anthropology, the pope emphasizes a primarily personal conception of sin, stressing that, while an individual may be conditioned by external factors or habits, "sin, in the proper sense, is always a personal act, since it is an act of freedom on the part of an individual person and not properly of a group or community"; at base "there is nothing so personal and untransferable in each individual as merit for virtue or responsibility for sin."[24] When he moves to the third dimension of social sin (that of communities' relationships), the pope remains at pains to emphasize personal accountability and the analogical nature of social sin, cautioning that even analogically sinful social phenomena "must not cause us to underestimate the responsibility of the individuals involved." His language constraining the concept's legitimate use is pointed:

> Having said this in the clearest and most unequivocal way, one must add at once that there is one meaning sometimes given to social sin that is not legitimate or acceptable even though it is very common in certain quarters today. This usage contrasts social sin and personal sin, not without ambiguity, in a way that leads more or less unconsciously to the *watering down and almost the abolition of personal sin*, with the recognition only of social guilt and responsibilities. . . . Whenever the church speaks of situations of sin or when she condemns as social sins certain situations or the collective behavior of certain social groups, big or small, or even of whole nations and blocs of nations, she knows and she proclaims that such cases of social sin are the result of the accumulation and concentration of many personal sins. . . . The real responsibility, then, lies with individuals.[25]

For John Paul, social sin remains fundamentally personal because a situation or institution is not properly the subject of moral acts. Hence, underscoring the ineffectiveness of structural transformation (via law or force) without personal conversion, he stresses his contention that "at the heart of every situation of sin are always to be found sinful people."[26]

Margaret Pfeil rightly points out that the aim of the texts issued by the Congregation for the Doctrine of the Faith (CDF) on either side of *Reconciliatio et paenitentia* is to circumscribe the use of social sin theologically, rather than "to explore the pastoral dimensions which gave rise to the language of social sin."[27] For example, in the first CDF instruction addressing Latin American liberation theology in light of its perceived appropriation of Marxist elements, the CDF stresses the consequential rather than causal nature of structures: "To be sure, there are structures which are evil and which cause evil and which we must have the courage to change. Structures, whether they are good or bad, are the result of man's actions. . . . The root of evil, then, lies in free and responsible persons."[28] Likewise, John Paul emphasizes social sin's analogical nature since it is impossible to "delimit the component personal sins" in social sin to "apportion responsibility and guilt."[29] The second CDF instruction (in 1986) does acknowledge the "fixed and fossilized" nature of some institutions and practices that harm human dignity.[30] Nevertheless, Norbert Rigali notes that "nowhere in John Paul's theology is the social character of sin separated from personal responsibility." Rigali goes on to observe that "without denying that social sins, in derivative senses, are aggregates of personal sins, one can ask whether they are not also particular expressions of the mysterious communion of sin in which all humanity is united."[31]

The following year, in *Sollicitudo rei socialis* (1987), John Paul gives more attention to structural realities, yet reemphasizes their rootedness in concrete individual acts.[32] Whereas his statements that imperialistic ideologies give the impression of creating personal and institutional obstacles demonstrate some recognition of such ideologies' "blinding effects" and "the almost automatic operation of economic and political institutions," his acknowledgment of this nonvoluntary dimension of social sin remains in tension with his significant emphasis on personal responsibility.[33] In the encyclical structural sins denote institutional realities that "create an unjust distribution of wealth, power, and recognition, and thus push a section of the population to the margin of society where their well-being or even their life is in danger."[34] When the pope identifies the absolutizing human attitudes of "the all-consuming desire for profit" and "the thirst for power, with the intention of imposing one's will upon others" to which nations and blocs are prone, his articulation holds potential for expanding beyond a derivative notion of social sin. He writes: "If certain forms of modern 'imperialism' were considered in the light of these moral criteria, we would see that hidden behind certain decisions, apparently inspired only by economics or politics, are real forms of idolatry: of money, ideology, class, technology."[35]

Acknowledgment of the more nonvoluntary aspects of social sin—for example, the impact ideologies have on personal agency—also surfaces in John Paul's references in subsequent encyclicals to humans' social conditioning: He identifies the ways structures of sin impede full human development (although "decisions" create such environments) through, for example, a "culture of death" that forms the context for individual responsibility with respect to abortion and other sins.[36] In *Evangelium vitae* the pope discusses four particular roots of the culture of death, two of which signify a more expansive understanding of social sin: The "eclipse of the sense of God and of man inevitably leads to a practical materialism, individualism, utilitarianism, and hedonism," and the "darkening of the human conscience both individually and in society—a confusion about good and evil that encourages the culture of death and consolidates structures of sin."[37] Given these indications, the pope's emphasis on personal agency should also be understood within the context of his appreciation of the power that culture exerts, as evident in his description of the dramatic conflict between a "culture of life" and a "culture of death" in *Evangelium vitae.*[38]

In the *Compendium of the Social Doctrine of the Church,* the Pontifical Council for Justice and Peace reiterates John Paul II's primary understanding that "at the bottom of every situation of sin there is always the individual who sins," since "in its true sense, sin is always an act of the person because it is the free act of an individual person and not properly speaking of a group or community."[39] Hence the pope advances the concept of social sin and elaborates its meaning over his corpus, yet his theological circumscription of the category to underscore individual responsibility reflected in contemporary magisterial articulations constrains its value for uncovering the subtle social dynamics that impact personal agency. His retention of the individual's role in sustaining sinful structures is significant and valuable for a consideration of subjective inhospitality to immigrants, yet the primacy of this personal dimension remains incomplete. In part his gradual expansion of the term's scope and meaning results from his indebtedness to the experience and theologies arising out of the church of Latin America, as I delineate below.

Social sin as elaborated by John Paul II holds potential for identifying structures of injustice that contribute to contemporary patterns of undocumented migration and opportunistic interdependence among neighboring nations in the Americas. Lawmakers and industry lobbyists make concrete decisions that shape visa caps and commodity subsidies with harmful effects. Yet the magisterial constraint of social sin limits efforts to fully unmask nonvoluntary dimensions of opposition to immigration teaching. In recent years moral theologians have increasingly called into question the isolation of personal acts and spheres of morality from their social contexts.[40] Whereas social sin may not directly *cause* personal sin or a reversal of one's fundamental option, it "creates an environment in which it becomes more difficult to make good choices," heightening the tendency "present because of original sin to turn away from God."[41] Hence as Lisa Sowle Cahill cautioned, "all moral theology must take into account not only individual choices but the practices and institutions in which agency takes shape."[42]

Magisterial understandings of social sin both benefit from and are defined against Latin American liberation theological articulations of the concept.

Gregory Baum points out that John Paul's discussion of social sin remains less sensitive than the Medellín teachings to the unconscious dimension of social sin and the impact unjust structures have on personal agency. The blindness produced by the very patterns the pope identifies has relevance for an adequate understanding of the scope and responsibility for sin; such blindness can prevent recognition, since exploitative institutions and structures both are sustained by the appearance of legitimacy and "tend to create a culture of conformity and passivity." Hence, as long as ignorance, nonrecognition, and ideological prisons hold sway, "there is no critical freedom and hence no personal sin in the strict sense."[43] My own concern in this instance lies less with the viability of institutional culpability or vincible ignorance per se, and more with the ways the category of social sin helps us consider the connections between the structural injustices John Paul identifies and more nonvoluntary, ideological influences that abet and result from communal actions. Baum has helpfully distinguished between "guilt by personal implication" and "guilt by common heritage" in terms of the relative levels of freedom with which people participate in structural sin and thereby incur guilt.[44] The nonvoluntary dimension of social sin holds considerable potential for unmasking the ideological and subconscious dynamics at play in resisting hospitality to immigrants.[45]

LIBERATION THEOLOGY AND SOCIAL SIN: INSTITUTIONALIZED VIOLENCE AND IDEOLOGICAL BLINDNESS

Latin American liberation theology articulates a framework that explicitly addresses both voluntary and nonvoluntary dimensions of social sin; in the case of immigration, it thus incorporates both the reality of the unjust institutions that contribute to border crossings and ideologies and symbolic systems that perpetuate blindness to such realities. Without downplaying the personal dimensions of sin that magisterial articulations emphasize, liberation theologians employ structural sin more expansively to describe "cultural and political patterns inherited from the colonial past, or economic and social practices resulting from Latin America's role in global capitalism."[46] In contrast to the magisterial approach, liberation theologians have been concerned less with safeguarding continuity with the theological tradition and write out of a primarily pastoral concern for distinctive contexts.[47]

The adoption of the language of social sin in liberation theology emerged with the 1968 Medellín, Colombia, conference where the Latin American bishops explicitly identified their reality as a sinful situation of institutionalized violence rooted in "the oppressive structures that come from the abuse of ownership and of power and from exploitation of workers or from unjust transactions."[48] For example, the historical concentration of nearly all arable land, wealth, and political power into the hands of the Fourteen Families in El Salvador (and similar oligarchies in other countries) created structures of sin that resulted in *campesinos'* utter disenfranchisement. The exploitation of indigenous populations throughout Latin America (and in Mexico in particular) forced to work in gold and silver mines during the colonial era, or more recent efforts to lure foreign investors to the region via free-trade zones, have resulted in structures of violence distinguished by poverty wages, dire working conditions, environmental exploitation, and anti-union business practices.

The 1979 gathering of Latin American bishops (Consejo Episcopal Latino-americano or CELAM) at Puebla, Mexico, underscored the Medellín assessment while attending more to the relationship between personal and structural sin. Here the bishops discussed ways in which personal sin gets mirrored in unjust interpersonal relations and situations that enslave and diminish freedom.[49] As José Ignacio González Faus summarizes the distinctive teaching of the two CELAM assemblies on the subject: "When human beings sin, they create structures of sin, which, in their turn, make human beings sin."[50] This conception presents a more expansive understanding of social sin than one that remains only derivatively social. Whereas some liberation theologians employ a social theory that focuses disproportionately on one sense of sin to the detriment of the other, the norm consists in a more balanced approach, in which the powerful external forces shaping and obstructing the path to personal conversion are emphasized without excluding Christian hope in transformation.

This approach is rooted in a communitarian social theory that underscores the multiple institutions that simultaneously implicate and influence individuals, whether familial, professional, economic, civic, religious, or otherwise. As a result of persons' participation in these complex interrelationships, the community and its governing structures more readily engender a series of situations that necessitate behaviors that favor and multiply individual greed. Hence "the human community is always more than the sum of individual human beings," and "evil, like the human being, is never just personal, although it is personal."[51] Liberation theologians root their analysis of sin in this social theory, particularly sin as they see it manifested in the grave injustice of their historical context. At base a Catholic theological anthropology that counters a view of humans as autonomous cells unconditioned by their interactive experiences—reflecting the intrinsic relationality emphasized by

Margaret Farley in chapter 1—challenges an insistence that sin be considered chiefly from the narrow perspective of an autonomous will.

Hence, on this view, both institutions and ideologies created and sustained by persons *and* people shaped by institutions and ideologies are guilty of sin and therefore in need of transformation. The structural inequality between the United States and its Latin American neighbors, in its historical roots and maintenance in laws and institutions, constitutes objective sin. Conversely, subjective sin resides in the choice, once aware of this inequality and its dehumanization, to refuse hospitality to its victims or to continue to opt for lifestyles and political programs that maintain an unjust disequilibrium. As Jon Sobrino notes, from the time of the Spanish and Portuguese conquests, the relationship between North and South has not substantially changed: "The poor countries are only important for what they can provide or—if there's no alternative—for what can be plundered from them: raw materials and cheap labor."[52]

Whereas John Paul II was concerned that structures not be understood as "committing sin," Ignacio Ellacuría insists that structures do, however, "manifest and actualize the power of sin, thereby causing sin, by making it exceedingly difficult for men and women to lead the life that is rightfully theirs as daughters and sons of God.[53] As Ellacuría notes, the sin of the world is "fundamentally historical and structural, communitarian and objective, at once the fruit and the cause of many other personal and collective sins, and its propagation and consolidation as the ongoing negation of the Reign of God."[54] It is witness to this realm of the Johannine sin of the world or "hamartiosphere" that leads Sobrino to speak of structural, objective sin as "the negative element of history," or of the "idols of death" that draw persons to their worship and away from worship of the authentic God of life.[55] As the theoretical dialectic makes clear, however, objective sin cannot exist only in systems and structures; "these idols have particular agents who cause particular offenses."[56] Idols and their adherents seek legitimization; the unjust act or situation is always accompanied by the lie, collective or individual, that seeks to offer its own self-serving logic and so obscure its reality as sin. Pervasive exploitation of undocumented laborers rests on a lie that humans are replaceable and not inherently worthy. In Sobrino's words, "sin and concealment go together, both personally and socially. And the size of that concealment is a measure of the sin."[57]

If the magisterial understanding of social sin remains primarily personal or interpersonal, sin as blindness denotes a transpersonal sense of sin: "We live in sin as a people, and our collective sin is more than the sum of individual sins."[58] Himes characterizes sin as collective blindness both in terms of "the ways in which our personal sin becomes incarnated in unjust social practices and institutions, as well as the power that these structures, having come into existence, exert upon us as heirs to the sins of those who have gone before us. We are inheritors of their faulty social arrangements."[59] This nonvoluntary dimension of social sin, also understood in terms of scotosis or false consciousness, is suggestive not only of the darkness of the state of original sin humans enter but also of the ways we are susceptible to a captivating environment or cultural blinders that prevent us from seeing rightly.[60] Whereas some debate the extent to which such blindness necessarily mitigates individual culpability, cultivated ignorance of the plight of others, the impact of our actions, or the effects of ideology cannot be summarily dismissed as outside the realm of moral responsibility.[61]

Finally, a situation of social sinfulness continues to describe the countries of origin for most Latino immigrants in the contemporary United States (81 percent of undocumented immigrants hail from Mexico, Central and South America).[62] The elements identified by CELAM in 1979, such as a lack of adequate housing, starvation wages, unemployment and underemployment, and compulsory mass migrations remain "a scandal and a contradiction to Christian existence" today.[63] The new norm of democratic governance that has emerged in subsequent decades, while improving upon military dictatorship, has done little to substantially alleviate the scarcity that confronts the poorest of the region. In El Salvador, for example, a country of nearly seven million people with four hundred attempting to depart for the United States daily, the share of national income received by the poorest 20 percent dropped from 3 percent in 1991, the last full year of the twelve-year civil year, to a mere 2.8 percent in 2002.[64] This reality reveals "the fact of the poor," for whom "living is a slow approach to death because of unjust and oppressive economic and social structures."[65] The bishops of Latin America identify this reality as sin and the product of sin; as such, a Catholic immigration stance must engage enduring root causes and a global perspective rather than political expediency or narrow nationalism.

Social Sin as Institutional and Ideological: Implications for Immigration

A more robust understanding of social sin emerges, which highlights the relationship between personal and structural sin and suggests the interrelated nature of its structural and ideological dimensions. John Paul II's legacy underscores the significance of carefully incorporating novel theological categories into the tradition and guards against downplaying individual culpability in sinful situations. Latin American liberation theology elucidates how personal will and culpability are interconnected with social injustice and institutional sin. Whereas magisterial documents have emphasized the voluntary aspect of social sin, Latin American liberation theology has stressed its nonvoluntary dimensions.[66] Rather than succumbing to either the fear that social sin risks downplaying personal responsibility or the idea that virtually all sin is social and that personal sin is simply a manifestation of this primarily social form of sin, the accounts traced above help elucidate more of a dialectical relationship between personal and social sin: Structures are both consequential and causal in nature, and persons are subjectively responsible for sinful situations yet remain subject to external influences. This more holistic understanding has significant bearing on the topic of receptivity to an ethic of hospitality and justice: That is, the socioeconomic, legal, and political structures that lead to undocumented immigration are connected to the ideological blinders that obstruct hospitality to immigrants.

Building upon sociological understandings of internalized structures, several theologians have articulated stages of social sin that shed light on the relationship between its voluntary and nonvoluntary dimensions.[67] For example, Baum outlines four levels of social sin: (1) unjust institutions and dehumanizing trends built into various institutions which embody people's collective life; (2) operative cultural and religious ideologies or symbolic systems fostered by society that legitimate unjust situations and intensify harm; (3) the level of false consciousness or blindness created by these institutions or ideologies that convince people their actions are good and lead to collective destructive action (I would include at this level what Henriot has characterized as the complicity of silent acquiescence); and (4) collective decisions made by distorted consciousness that increases injustice and intensifies dehumanizing trends.[68]

In light of this multilayered understanding of social sin we can begin to perceive the complex dynamics at play in resistance to a Catholic immigration ethic. Given the relationship between the United States and sending countries in geographic, economic, and political terms, US citizens may be willfully negligent of or indirectly responsible for the conditions that give rise to undocumented migration across their borders. Following Baum's four levels, for example, the factors propelling undocumented migration include the impact of an immigration system whose discrepancy between labor needs and legal avenues for work in certain sectors, outmoded family visa caps, and focus on symptoms rather than causes have increased the volume and danger of extra-legal flows over the first decade of the twenty-first century.[69] The primacy of deterrence has institutionalized (ill-founded) security concerns rather than concerns for human rights or family unity in US immigration laws, and the nation's economic interests have been institutionalized in uneven free-trade agreements.[70] Commodification trends are apparent in the asymmetry of Southwestern border fortification, on the one hand, and negligible surveillance of containers entering US ports and the free flow of capital on the other; in the workplace raid practices that reduce family members to economic units; and in proposed "point systems."[71] Such trends are also evident in the development of highly organized and profitable human trafficking networks. Hence as O'Keefe notes regarding Baum's Level 1, "the injustices and dehumanizing trends within these structural relationships indicate that the inherent value of certain persons and some of the values that are essential to authentic human development have been hidden, masked, or skewed in society."[72]

A consideration of operative ideologies that shape social trends and legitimate institutions suggests that media portrayals of immigrants as freeloaders (or worse) are at least as influential as religious rhetoric championing human rights of undocumented immigrants. As noted in chapter 1, when concerns about undocumented immigrants as economically or socially threatening get amplified or distorted by xenophobia, ethnocultural nationalism, or fear, anti-immigrant sentiment has led to increasingly acceptable demonization of populations of color. Amid a climate of anti-immigrant sentiment, buzzwords such as "national security" and "illegal alien" can serve as idols to conceal a sinful reality and provoke demonization. Whereas no terrorists have been caught along the Southwestern border, fear mongering and scapegoating of undocumented immigrants is on the rise. Sinful actions sustain such potent myths when news commentators exaggerate with impunity claims from immigrant tax evasion to violent crime and foster myths regarding the North American Union or a *reconquista*, or when Minutemen consider it their patriotic duty to intimidate and harass "illegals."[73]

At a more subtle level, a consumerist ideology shapes citizens' willingness to underpay or mistreat undocumented persons either directly or through indirect demand for inexpensive goods and services. Describing Level 2, O'Keefe remarks that "symbols are the vessels in which values are enshrined and the avenue by which values enter the human imagination, self-understanding and worldview. When cultural or religious symbols mask or hide values, they support the structural relationships that perpetuate injustice and that hinder authentic human development."[74] We encountered in chapter

1 the historical use of lofty and celebratory rhetoric to obscure exclusionary ends in this manner. Cultural ideologies have been highlighted here, but we also must assess the power of religious symbols, given Christian resistance to hospitality alluded to at the outset: how, for example, individualistic penitential rituals reinforce limited conceptions of sin, or the perception of how a single- or narrow-issue political agenda obscures the imperative of "defend[ing] life after birth and before death."[75]

These ideologically anchored structures of injustice then produce the scotosis or blindness that lulls US Catholics, among others, into equating "law-abiding" with "just" or into apathetic acquiescence. Social manifestations of these ideologies (such as a priority given to possessions or capital over persons) may aggregate to "large-scale hardness of heart."[76] Hence to remain ignorant of the plight of small farmers in Mexico, the fatal realities of the border, or the treatment of undocumented immigrants in detention centers, in an age of globalized technology and media, arguably enters the realm of culpable ignorance. When the comfortable allow themselves thus to remain unaware of the plight of the poor, we are able to "cherish the illusions" that keep us in a privileged position.[77] Hence internalized fears, tribalism, or callous greed can directly lead to silent acquiescence or indolence (Level 3). Internalized ideologies and distorted consciousness can also then lead to collective unjust decisions and actions. Recent years have witnessed the passage of punitive local ordinances, a sharp increase in workplace raids without proportionate employer accountability, the failure of comprehensive legislative reform, and the escalated abuse of undocumented persons (Level 4).

These various levels also intersect and interrelate in complex manners. Pervasive, internalized ideologies make us susceptible to myths; operative understandings influence our actions or inaction. When bias hides or skews values, it becomes more difficult to choose authentic values over those that prevail in society, a tendency already present because of original sin. As O'Keefe puts it, with social sin "the disordered sense of value from outside meets the internal tendency to choose the lesser value in situations of choice or to act for mere satisfaction rather than value."[78] Whether in the form of nationalism, expediency, or profit, social inducements to personal sin in the immigration context abound.

Hence the many fences, both physical and ideological, that North Americans construct to exclude and protect harm vulnerable immigrant populations and hinder hospitality. These entrenched, intertwined patterns of social sin require repentance from sustaining harmful myths out of fear or bias, from the greed of consumerism, and from indifference to the plight of the marginalized south of the US border and on its street corners. From repentance and conscientization US Catholics are called to conversion toward interdependence in solidarity.[79] As the US and Mexican bishops indicate, "part of the process of conversion of mind and heart deals with confronting attitudes of cultural superiority, indifference, and racism; accepting migrants not as foreboding aliens, terrorists or economic threats, but as persons with dignity and rights, revealing the presence of Christ; and recognizing migrants as bearers of deep cultural values and rich faith traditions."[80] As noted above, such nonvoluntary dimensions are directly related to structural reform. John Glaser argues that "policy change grows out of moral, public transformation," such that a foundational vision and the structures needed to realize and sustain it must precede concrete policy programs.[81] At the broader systemic level, nations must understand themselves as collectively responsible for the shared challenges posed by migration patterns. Such international conversion requires "a transformation of the present, often opportunistic interdependency among nations into something that grows out of a moral commitment to the global common good."[82]

Many US Christians remain too far removed from such realities to be attuned to such an invitation and its demands. Yet against these challenges stands the hope for personal conversion and social change that liberation theology and magisterial teaching alike hold out, acknowledging that a change of mind must be precipitated by a change of heart. Such metanoia, or conversion, can occur through personal encounters and relationships that provoke new perspectives and receptivity.

From Social Sin to Solidarity: A Paradigm for Pastoral Action

While my emphasis on the influence of social contexts should not be misunderstood as deterministic, and persons are called to critique and transcend prevailing cultural trends and ideologies, "the ultimate durability of any personal conversion and the ability of others to convert will require that authentic values be recognized and chosen within their social context."[83] How then can the Church better institutionally embody such values and facilitate personal and social conversion? In his work on social sin, Himes identifies a community's ability to shape its members' imagination through word and symbol as "an unparalleled resource for providing a vision to those who are blind."[84] The US Church has undertaken pastoral outreach and political advocacy on behalf of just and humane immigration reform, yet the laity remains divided on the issue. As Carmen Nanko-Fernández remarks of its immigration efforts, "the inability of ecclesial leadership to communicate this profound tradition of social justice in a concrete manner that makes sense to the grassroots remains an obstacle to the task of justice."[85] It bears consideration, then, how the Church might build on its existing commitment to invite conversion in word and witness.

Whereas the Church has appropriated prophetic and New Testament texts demanding justice and hospitality for the sojourner, explicitly naming the sinful realities surrounding migration will continue to sharpen the Church's prophetic potential. This entails identifying subjective participation in the exploitative structures and ideologies traced above as "sinful," as well as publicly underscoring their dehumanizing impact. As merely one example, Catholic Relief Services–Mexico (and other humanitarian organizations) estimate that more than 70 percent of women attempting to cross the border are sexually exploited en route. Such conscientization—the development of a critical, liberating consciousness—can begin to heal a collective imagination that absolutizes "limited goods, such as nationalism and sovereignty, over against truly absolute goods, such as the interdependence and solidarity of the human family."[86]

Given the complexity of responsibility in situations of social sin and of immigration matters, conscientization should also entail experiential strategies to uncover persons' passive support for attitudes and institutions that help maintain structural injustice. Dean Brackley helpfully posits that the cognitive liberation that broadens our limited horizons (which both interpret and distort reality) demands experiential engagement; he rejects the idea that reason alone can accomplish such transformation, since affectivity and commitment are central to the problem of distortion and thus remain crucial to its "hygiene."[87] As a community that ministers to protectionist and undocumented alike, the Church is well poised to help move its members beyond episodic encounters in which they remain confirmed in their viewpoints or unwilling to generalize beyond one trustworthy worker or goodhearted parent. This first step of overcoming blindness is essential, notes Himes, for "until a person moves beyond the stage of uncritical naïveté to the threshold of critical consciousness it is not possible to enter into the world of mature moral reflection."[88]

Given that social sin entails the distinct dimensions discussed here and requires both personal conversion and social transformation, a case study of an ecclesial model that attempts a holistic approach to its immigration out-reach and witness may illuminate a way forward. The work of Dolores Mission Parish in East Los Angeles embodies a hybrid response that integrates the conversion of hearts and institutions in ways particularly relevant to the multi-leveled barriers to receptivity explored above.[89]

This Jesuit parish engages in a range of dynamic outreach efforts, including provision of services to recent immigrants through its Guadalupe Homeless project. Every evening for nearly twenty-five years, the church has opened its doors to the homeless and the day laborers of Los Angeles. Many of these are undocumented immigrants seeking a safe place to eat, shower, and sleep; cots are set up between the pews and alongside the altar, and "sanctuary" takes on all of its many meanings. When the church first opened its doors and extended the notion of political sanctuary in the 1980s to include providing haven for economic migrants, a not uncontroversial decision at the time, then-pastor Gregory Boyle reflected that the community dissolved the notion of "us vs. them" that frequently characterizes debates about undocumented immigrants. This move was central to cultivating what Boyle describes as kinship, a virtue fundamental to the Catholic ethic regarding migration and reception.[90]

Jon Sobrino's reflections on the original sanctuary movement remain rele-vant for the contemporary context: "Sanctuary does not have to become a political movement but it cannot ignore its political connotations and conse-quences if it is going to defend the life of the poor. . . . It has to confront the contradictions and unmask the politics that support death rather than life for Central Americans," and, by extension, contemporary Latin American migrants.[91] Beyond meeting the immediate needs of a vulnerable population, the Dolores Mission community's mobilization in response to proposed immigration legislation in recent years has embodied nuanced Christian social witness that confounds typical categories that remain primarily spiritual or political. For example, just prior to Lent 2006, as a shared spiritual exercise the parish undertook a month-long communal fast for justice for immigrants engaging personal and social dimensions not unlike the sin dialectic outlined above. Participants conceived of the fast as both prayer (in terms of the desire to empty ourselves of what distracts us from knowledge of God's love) and as an act of solidarity (a bond of sympathy with those who, like so many immi-grants, suffer physical, spiritual, and emotional hunger). The prayer and fast-ing were coupled with prophetic preaching and consistent legislative advocacy and voter education on behalf of comprehensive and humane immigration reform.[92] At the end of the Lenten season, the practice of undocumented men

having their feet washed on Holy Thursday by Bishop Gabino Zavala power-
fully conveyed the parish's embracing posture.

On Good Friday 2008, the community undertook a Way of the Cross pro-
cession through the city culminating at the federal building downtown. The
parishioners united their own sufferings with Christ's passion; public devo-
tionals at each station focused on issues such as poverty, families torn apart
by Immigration and Customs Enforcement (ICE) raids, and exploitative labor
practices. The extensive media coverage of participants' witness to Jesus crucified in the undocumented person and efforts to illuminate hearts and minds
in favor of just and humane reform presents a countersign to vitriolic anti-
immigrant messaging in news and opinion media. The parish's multidimensional approach well represents the elements Henriot identifies as constitutive
of the Church's social mission: prophetic word, symbolic witness, and political
action.[93]

Hence Dolores Mission's sustained immigration response embodies a
hybrid pastoral model appropriate to countering the interrelated levels of
social sin and resistance outlined above. It incorporates methods that surface
Christian duties to resist unjust social structures, respond to the needy in their
midst who have fallen victim to institutional violence, and negotiate tensions
between discipleship and citizenship.[94] Such a paradigm can offer guidance
for US Christians wrestling with faithful discipleship regarding issues beyond
immigration alone. Siding with the so-called strangers in their midst who in
fact comprise an integral part of this community, parishioners bear countercultural witness to dominant ideologies like cultural superiority. By integrating
Christian practices of prayer, charity, solidarity, and collaborative advocacy,
this parish-based response begins to counter the matrix of social sins that
conceal and oppress.

In terms of replicating its general approach, it is useful to note Dolores
Mission's engagement of a "see, judge, act" methodology as it proceeds from
encounter, to reflection, to multipronged action. The continual presence of
undocumented immigrants through the Guadalupe Homeless Project keeps
alive the memory of community members' roots and does not allow the
human experience of suffering to become abstract. Hence initiatives that bring
parishioners face-to-face with immigrant communities (in the United States
or in countries of origin) can help foster hospitality and correct personal and
collective outlooks that remain obscured at the level of ideology. Next within
its base communities, members take seriously biblical exhortations and continually critique social issues like immigration through the lens of Catholic
social teaching in order to reveal the sinfulness of political structures and other

obstacles. This model commends churches to link education, outreach, and liturgical efforts, integrating structural and historical realities with the illumination of scriptural and magisterial teaching, and naming the sinfulness of realities—rather than assiduously avoiding any perception of politicized faith.

Finally, as noted, Dolores Mission moves from encounter and analysis into opportunities for compassionate political action seamlessly integrated into the spiritual life of the parish, combining communal fasts with legislative advocacy, reflective prayer with direct service, and routinely incorporating undocumented persons' *testimonios* into liturgical and advocacy settings alike. Parish leaders participate in citywide interfaith immigration reform networks and advocate on Capitol Hill. Empowerment and relationship-building also constitute key elements: The parish has formed a group of *promotores*—including some Guadalupe Homeless Project residents—whom they train to inform immigrant residents about their rights. Families of mixed status or vulnerable workers are educated on concrete steps to follow if caught in a raid, and parish-based community organizers have set up structures to help undocumented residents designate custody of their children so they do not end up in the care of the state. Ecclesial models like Dolores Mission's can assist US Catholics' formation for conversion amid a complex web of social sins on matters of undocumented immigration as well as other symptoms of social injustice.[95]

More broadly, such processes of communal conversion coupled with public repentance hold the potential to reframe public debate about immigration. Given the nonvoluntary dimensions of social sin, love and good will alone are insufficient to expose sinful structures. Rather, as Baum observers, "It is through moments of interruption, disturbing events that shatter our perceptions, that we discover the human damage done by our taken-for-granted world."[96] Any public witness to an ethic of hospitality and justice in the US Catholic context must entail repentance from complicity in patterns of imperialism and neocolonialism as well as from the sin of exceptionalism engrained in the nation's social psyche.[97] Each of these Christian and American social sins directly bears on immigration, and credible witness cannot ensue without such repentance.

Whereas determining the precise implications of such atonement in terms of culpability or reparations entails complex considerations, Baum helpfully identifies "readiness to mourn" and a "keener sense of personal responsibility" as proper spiritual responses to social sin. Shared grieving and assumption of the "burden of collective transgressions by spiritual solidarity" prepare participants for "social renewal and political action."[98] In terms of sacramental practice, the Church can facilitate and embody conscientization through communal examinations of conscience and penitential liturgies.[99] As James Cross has argued, "in the very gathering at a communal penitential liturgy, the Church is more obviously and more meaningfully symbolizing its conversion as well as the conversion from unjust habits and practices that human persons generally desire and pursue."[100] Religious and civic bodies' public repentance for past cooperation with the forms of social sin articulated herein could begin to convert communities away from amnesic entitlement and toward solidarity with those on the underside of such histories. Identification with the dispossessed and movements toward their emancipation, flowing from a spirit of repentance, can help end our subjective participation in social injustices.[101]

It is not enough for a Christian immigration ethic to call for the defense of human dignity or hospitality to strangers without attending to the complex structures and ideologies that abet blindness and complicity, preventing justice for reluctant migrants. Viewing immigration through the lens of individual culpability alone—whether reducing irregular migration to the actions of willful lawbreakers or blaming inhospitality on militant nationalists—obscures the multileveled, subtle dynamics at play. The following chapters counter this tendency through an examination of immigration in light of the family and the wider global community, each spheres that manifest and summon kinship across borders.

Notes

The epigraph is reprinted with permission of Martín Espada.

1. An earlier version of this chapter appeared as "Social Sin and Immigration," 410–36.

2. A recent study conducted by Pew Research Center for the People and the Press and the Pew Hispanic Center shows that despite the strong pro-immigrant statements issued by prominent religious leaders, large segments of the public—including many Catholics—harbor serious concerns about immigrants and immigration. The study concludes that while white Christians, including Catholics, are generally slightly less pro-immigrant than secular counterparts (but similar to the population at large), those more regularly attending church are more likely to agree with church leaders' more hospitable positions. See Pew Research Center for the People and the Press, "America's Immigration Quandary."

3. Richard M. Gula, "The Moral Conscience," in Conscience, ed. Charles E. Curran, 51–64, at 54–55.

4. For a thoughtful discussion on the topic of the reception of Catholic moral teachings and the Spirit's "grace of self-doubt" as essential to all co-believers' participation in moral discernment, see Margaret A. Farley, "Ethics, Ecclesiology, and the Grace of Self-Doubt," in A Call to Fidelity, ed. James J. Walter, Timothy E. O'Connell, and Thomas A. Shannon, 55–76. With respect to Catholic teaching on immigration in particular, as William O'Neill rightly points out, it is "far from a panacea." Its commitment to human rights "leaves many questions

unresolved" yet does offer "considerable wisdom" in the face of present practices and rhetoric. See O'Neill, "A Little Common Sense," 12.

5. See, e.g., Matthew Streb and Brian Fredericks, "The Myth of a Distinct Catholic Vote," and Mark M. Gray and Mary E. Bendyna, "Between Church, Party, and Conscience: Attitudes Concerning Protecting Life and Promoting Social Justice among U.S. Catholics," in *Catholics and Politics*, ed. Kristin Heyer, Mark Rozell, and Michael Genovese, 93–112 and 75–92.

6. Mark O'Keefe, "Social Sin and Fundamental Option," in *Christian Freedom*, ed. Clayton N. Jefford, 131–43, at 135.

7. In this chapter I use "ideology" in the sense of a dominant cultural ideology, a framing vision that claims objectivity and potentially distorts perceptions of reality. For a discussion of a more neutral sense of the term and its relationship to faith, see Juan Luis Segundo, *Faith and Ideologies*.

8. Gioacchino Campese, "Beyond Ethnic and National Imagination: Toward a Catholic Theology of U.S. Immigration," in *Religion and Social Justice for Immigrants*, ed. Pierrette Hondagneu-Sotelo, 175–90, at 181.

9. O'Keefe, "Social Sin and Fundamental Option," 141.

10. See Walter Rauschenbusch, *A Theology for the Social Gospel*.

11. While the focus of this chapter's inquiry is Roman Catholic theological understandings of social sin, given its objective of clarifying Catholic resistance to ecclesial teaching on immigration, Protestant parallels in concepts like Walter Rauschenbusch's structures of evil or Reinhold Niebuhr's collective egotism remain relevant as well.

12. Peter J. Henriot, "Social Sin: The Recovery of a Christian Tradition," in *Method in Ministry*, ed. James D. Whitehead and Evelyn Easton Whitehead, 127–44, at 128–29.

13. Kenneth R. Himes, "Social Sin and the Role of the Individual," 184.

14. For an overview of this range of understandings see Mark O'Keefe, *What Are They Saying about Social Sin?*

15. John Paul II discusses these traditional distinctions in his "The Sin of Man and the Sin of the World," General Audience of November 5, 1986.

16. Kenneth R. Himes, "Human Failing: The Meanings and Metaphors of Sin," in *Moral Theology*, ed. James Keating, 145–61, at 153.

17. Henriot, "Social Sin," 132.

18. Ibid. 135. For a valuable analysis tracing this historical development, see James F. Keenan, *History of Catholic Moral Theology*.

19. Gregory Baum, "Structures of Sin," in *The Logic of Solidarity*, ed. Gregory Baum and Robert Ellsberg, 110–26, at 111.

20. Norbert Rigali, "Human Solidarity and Sin," 339.

21. John Langan, S.J., "Personal Responsibility and the Common Good in John Paul II," in *Ethics, Religion and the Good Society*, ed. Joseph Runzo, 132–52, at 135.

22. Adam A. J. Deville, "The Development of the Doctrine of 'Structural Sin,'" 309; Margaret Pfeil, "Doctrinal Implications," 141.

23. John Paul II, *Reconciliatio et paenitentia*, Apostolic Exhortation of December 2, 1984, no. 16.

24. Ibid.

25. Ibid. (emphasis added).

26. Ibid. no. 16.

27. Pfeil, "Doctrinal Implications," 141.

28. CDF, "Instruction on Certain Aspects of the Theology of Liberation," no. 15, *Origins* 14 (1984): 194–204.

29. As the pope notes, "If one may and must speak in an analogical sense about social sin, and also about structural sin—since sin is properly an act of the person—for us, as pastors and theologians, the following problem arises: Which penance and which social reconciliation must correspond to this *analogical* sin?" John Paul II, "The Value of This Collegial Body," *Synod of Bishops: Penance and Reconciliation in the Mission of the Church* (Washington: US Catholic Conference, 1984), 65, emphasis in original; cited in Pfeil, "Doctrinal Implications" 139.

30. "These are sets of institutions and practices which people find already existing or which they create, on the national and international level, and which orient or organize economic, social and political life. Being necessary in themselves, they often tend to become fixed and fossilized as mechanisms relatively independent of the human will, thereby paralyzing or distorting social development and causing injustice." CDF, *Libertatis conscientia*, Instruction on Christian Freedom and Liberation, no. 74.

31. Rigali, "Human Solidarity and Sin," 341, 344.

32. See John Paul II, *Sollicitudo rei socialis* (December 30, 1987), no. 36.

33. Pfeil, "Doctrinal Implications," 143, relying upon Baum, "Structures of Sin," 115. John Paul II suggests the dominant ideologies of "liberal capitalism" and "Marxist collectivism" blinds participants from recognizing the faults of their own systems. See Gregory Baum, *Essays in Critical Theology*, 193. Charles Curran rightly points out that the pope's emphasis on personal moral agency as contributing to social sin reflects his entire philosophical and theological approach of personalism, with its emphasis on "the primacy of the subject over the object, labor over capital, and the need for all to participate responsibly in economic and political institutions and structures" (*The Moral Theology of Pope John Paul II*, 83).

34. Baum, "Structures of Sin," 112.

35. John Paul II, *Sollicitudo rei socialis*, no. 37. Nevertheless his emphasis remains on the side of individual responsibility even as structural injustice and ideologies receive greater attention. Baum concludes that John Paul was "aware of the unconscious, nonvoluntary, quasi-automatic dimension of social sin," that he recognized "the power of ideology" yet "the greater emphasis in his analysis of social sin lies on personal responsibility" (Baum, "Structures of Sin," 115).

36. John Paul II, *Centesimus annus* (May 1, 1991), no. 38; John Paul II, *Evangelium vitae* (March 25, 1995), no. 12.

37. Ibid. nos. 23–24; see also Curran, *Moral Theology of Pope John Paul II*, 14–15.

38. John Paul II, *Evangelium vitae* no. 50; see also Curran, *Moral Theology of Pope John Paul II*, 85.

39. Pontifical Council for Justice and Peace, *Compendium of the Social Doctrine of the Church* (Washington: US Conference of Catholic Bishops, 2004), no. 117. *The Catechism of the Catholic Church* (New York: Bantam Double Day, 1995), no. 1869, puts it this way: "'Structures of sin' are the expression and effect of personal sins. They lead their victims to do evil in their turn. In an analogous sense, they constitute a 'social sin.'"

40. Christine Gudorf rightly suggests that the complex relationship of social structures to individuals casts doubt on the adequacy of traditional understandings of human behavior that focus on the interaction between a predisposition to sin and the strength of the individual will or mind: "Many persons have come to see how inevitably and decisively humans are anchored in the concrete material world, how complex are the levels, structures and systems affecting interaction in that world, and how influential those structures and systems seem to be in human behavior" ("Admonishing Sinners: Owning Structural Sin," in *Rethinking the Spiritual*

Works of Mercy, ed. Francis A. Eigo, , 1–29, at 3). Below I return to the influence of sociological understandings of the nature and role of structures on a comprehensive view of social sin.

41. O'Keefe, "Social Sin and Fundamental Option," 142.

42. Lisa Sowle Cahill, "Moral Theology: From Evolutionary to Revolutionary Change," in *Catholic Theological Ethics in the World Church*, ed. James F. Keenan, 221–27, at 222.

43. Baum, "Structures of Sin," 113–14.

44. Gregory Baum, *Essays in Critical Theology*, 198–201.

45. John Paul II's elaboration of social sin ensued in tandem with and, in some instances, in direct response to the development of the category by Latin American liberation theologians. The two conceptions are not presented here in any chronological order but rather indicate distinct theoretical frameworks and contexts developed within recent Catholic tradition.

46. Kenneth R. Himes, "Liberation Theology and Catholic Social Teaching," in *Hope and Solidarity*, ed. Stephen J. Pope, 228–41, at 237.

47. Latin American bishops did not intend to undermine the significance of this theological tradition (such as the role of personal agency in formal sin), but were concerned to highlight the connections between sin and structural injustice in their context(s). See Pfeil, "Doctrinal Implications," 137–38. Also, it is worth acknowledging that references to social sin by John Paul II and the CDF were in part precisely aimed at responding to perceived or potential misuse by Latin American liberation theologians.

48. Consejo Episcopal Latinoamericano (CELAM), "The Church in the Present-Day Transformation of Latin America in Light of the Council" (Washington: US Catholic Conference, 1973), 78, 49.

49. CELAM, "Evangelization at Present and in the Future of Latin America" (Washington: National Conference of Catholic Bishops, 1979), 328. In their words, "sin, a force making for breakdown and rupture, will always pose obstacles to growth in love and communion. It will always be operative, both within the hearts of human beings, and within the various structures which they have created and on which they have left the destructive imprint of their sinfulness" (281).

50. José Ignacio González Faus, "Sin," in *Mysterium Liberationis*, ed. Ignacio Ellacuría and Jon Sobrino, 537.

51. Ibid. 536.

52. Jon Sobrino, "Five Hundred Years: Structural Sin and Structural Grace," in *The Principle of Mercy*, 69–82, at 73.

53. John Paul II maintains that institutions themselves cannot sin, as we have seen, yet his prophetic articulation of solidarity as a virtue for institutions suggests the potential for institutional vice or sinfulness in some sense, at least. Ignacio Ellacuría, "Aporte de la teología de la liberación a las religionas abrahámicas en la superación del individualismo y del positivismo," manuscript of an address to the Congress of Abrahamic Religions held at Córdoba, Spain, in February 1987, as cited by Sobrino, "Central Position of the Reign of God in Liberation Theology," in *Mysterium Liberationis*, 355.

54. Ibid.

55. José Maria González Ruiz understands "the 'hamartiosphere,' the sphere of sin [as] 'a kind of parameter or structure which objectively conditions the progress of human history itself.'" See Gustavo Gutiérrez, *Essential Writings*, 194–95. Sobrino elaborates this concept in, among other of his writings, *The True Church and the Poor*, trans. Matthew J. O'Connell (Maryknoll, N.Y.: Orbis, 1984), 165–67; and "Latin America: Place of Sin and Place of Forgiveness," in *The Principle of Mercy*, 58–68, at 58–60.

56. Sobrino adds, "The great sin takes particular sin in these forms, and the idols are personalized in torturers and murderers" (Sobrino, "Latin America," in *Principle of Mercy*, 62).

57. Sobrino, *Where Is God?*, 41.

58. Himes, "Human Failing," 158.

59. Ibid. 159.

60. See O'Keefe for an overview of several scholars' discussion of this dimension of social sin as "knowing ignorance," including Bernard Lonergan's understanding of scotosis as an unconscious blocking of understanding and Bernard Häring's identification of sin as *skotos* or "darkness." O'Keefe, *What Are They Saying About Social Sin?*, 36. See also Himes, "Human Failing," 159. Elsewhere he asserts: "Only with the removal of the ignorance which accompanies the blindness of social sin do we enter a world of moral responsibility" (Himes, "Social Sin," 213–14).

61. Here the traditional categories of vincible ignorance or culpable loss of freedom similarly indicate the responsibility to overturn rather than perpetuate social sins. See O'Keefe, "Social Sin and Fundamental Option," 140.

62. Jeffrey S. Passel and D'Vera Cohn, "Unauthorized Immigrant Population."

63. CELAM, "Evangelization at Present and in the Future of Latin America," 29.

64. US Agency for International Development, "USAID Budget: El Salvador" (FY 2005) available at www.usaid.gov/policy/budget/cbj2005/lac/sv.html (accessed January 21, 2010).

65. Jon Sobrino, "Sanctuary," 165. The phenomenon of poverty as structural violence is evident in a variety of global contexts, yet the reality remains equally urgent in the Latin American context and hence for the majority of recent immigrant arrivals to the United States.

66. Baum, "Structures of Sin," 116–17.

67. See Peter L. Berger and Thomas Luckmann, *The Social Construction of Reality*, on the external objectification and internalization processes that indicate the objective and historical fact of social institutions and their idea that such structures embody value relationships, operating not only outside of persons, but also within them. See also Piet Schoonenberg's description of being "situated" in sin: "Modern individual and social psychology makes us realize to what extent the decision of our will is influenced by our way of seeing concrete reality . . . [and] by our whole former education and present environment. All of this constitutes the ground on which, and the raw materials with which, our free decision takes shape" (*Man and Sin*, 111). Finally, Bernard Häring emphasizes the impact of one's environment, which includes more than people whom we directly or indirectly come into contact with: "our cultural heritage, the world in which we live, civilized nature, the conditions of economic and professional life with its organizations and groupings, the complex reality of political life and legislation, of off-time entertainment, particularly, however, of public opinion which approaches us through thousands of channels" (*What Does Christ Want?*, 206).

68. Gregory Baum, *Religion and Alienation*, 200–03. In a similar manner Stephen Duffy's fourfold typology incorporates the embodiment of social sin in (1) dehumanizing behavior, (2) cultural and religious symbols that ignite the heart and imagination to reinforce unjust institutional arrangements, (3) false consciousness "created by institutions and ideologies that allow people to participate in a network of oppression with self-righteousness," and (4) resulting collective decisions and consent. Stephen J. Duffy, "Sin," 901.

69. Recent figures indicate US immigration laws supply only 5,000 low skilled permanent residency visas, whereas the labor market demands an estimated 500,000 full-time low-skilled service jobs per year. Whereas the irregular immigration population surged from an estimated 8.4 million in 2000 to a peak of 12.0 million in 2007, in the subsequent three years it has

declined and leveled off at around 11 million. See Passel and Cohn, "Unauthorized Immigrant Population," 9.

70. Whereas the aggregate impact of NAFTA or CAFTA is complex, most agree they have taken a negative toll on the most vulnerable populations in Latin America, who rely more than ever on remittances sent home by family members who migrate to the United States. In 2008 the bishops of Mexico directly linked the recent surge in immigration to the United States to the effects of NAFTA on small rural communities whose farmers are unable to compete with heavily subsidized producers north of their border. Chapter 4 considers this issue in further detail.

71. In contrast to increased border fortification, only 2 percent of containers entering US ports are checked, highlighting this priority of capital to persons in related policy considerations.

72. O'Keefe, "Social Sin and Fundamental Option," 137.

73. See Media Matters Action Network's "Fear and Loathing in Prime Time: Immigration Myths and Cable News" (May 21, 2008) for a study documenting the rhetoric surrounding immigration on cable news with particular attention to common myths and urban legends regarding undocumented immigrants. Available at Document3http://mediamattersaction.org/static/pdfs/fear-and-loathing.pdf.

74. O'Keefe, "Social Sin and Fundamental Option," 137.

75. As Dean Brackley recently put it, this imperative "is the condition of credibility today for anyone who speaks about eternal life." Dean Brackley, "The Church and the Crucified Peoples," May 20, 2007, St. Ignatius Church, San Francisco Calif., available at www.usfca.edu/lanecenter/pdf/Brackley5.20.07.pdf (accessed January 21, 2010).

76. As Henriot suggests, "the act orientation of traditional moral theology does not provide much assistance in guiding individual Christian consciences [in the case of large-scale hardness of heart.]" Henriot, "Social Sin," 134.

77. See Patrick Kerans, *Sinful Social Structures*, 83–104, for his Lonerganian understanding of "knowing ignorance."

78. O'Keefe, "Social Sin and Fundamental Option," 138.

79. I use the term "conscientization" to refer more broadly to the process by which all sectors of society, particularly privileged ones, become newly aware of the presence of injustice and the demands of justice, rather than a Freirian notion of liberative education for oppressed populations. See Paulo Freire, *Pedagogy of the Oppressed*. In John Paul II's words, "these attitudes and 'structures of sin' are only conquered—presupposing the help of divine grace—by a diametrically opposed attitude: a commitment to the good of one's neighbor with the readiness, in the gospel sense, to 'lose oneself' for the sake of the other instead of exploiting him, and to 'serve him' instead of oppressing him for one's own advantage" (*Sollicitudo rei socialis* no. 38 [see Mt 10:40–42; 20:25; Mk 10:42–45; Lk 22:25–27]).

80. US Conference of Catholic Bishops and *Conferencia del Episcopado Mexicano*, "Strangers No Longer: Together on the Journey of Hope," no 40, www.usccb.org/mrs/stranger.shtml.

81. John W. Glaser, "Health Care Reform as Public Conscience Work."

82. Christopher Steck, "Solidarity, Citizenship, and Globalization," 164.

83. O'Keefe, "Social Sin and Fundamental Option," 143.

84. Himes, "Social Sin and the Role of the Individual," 214.

85. Nanko-Fernández, "Beyond Hospitality," 55.

86. J. Bryan Hehir, "With No Vision, People Perish," in *All Come Bearing Gifts*, Proceedings of the National Migration Conference (Washington: US Conference of Catholic Bishops, 2003) as cited in Campese, "Beyond Ethnic and National Imagination," 187.

87. Dean Brackley, "Higher Standards for Higher Education."

88. Himes, "Social Sin and the Role of the Individual," 193.

89. As a disclaimer, I was a parishioner of Dolores Mission parish from 2005 to 2009. Sean Carroll, Michael Kennedy, and Arturo Lopez were interviewed for this section by Charles Bergman and me.

90. For a helpful discussion of how the overlapping virtues of solidarity, compassion, and hospitality link matters of social justice (including undocumented immigration) to moral formation, see Christopher Vogt, "Fostering a Catholic Commitment to the Common Good."

91. Sobrino, "Sanctuary: A Theological Analysis," 168.

92. The community's efforts included letter-writing campaigns and visits to state senators, several marches and protests outside City Hall and the offices of the Democratic and Republican National Committees, sustained collaboration with immigration reform coalitions across the city, and peaceful civil disobedience.

93. See Henriot, "Social Sin and Conversion," 122–30.

94. I analyze such hybridity in terms of the mutual clarification of "radicalist" and "public" approaches to Christian social responsibility in "Bridging the Divide in Contemporary U.S. Catholic Social Ethics."

95. The interfaith new sanctuary movement as well as the haven that St. Bridget's Roman Catholic Church in Postville, Iowa, offered following that town's large-scale raid (similarly combining sanctuary, outreach and spirituality) offer additional models. For information on the New Sanctuary Movement, see www.newsanctuarymovement.org/. For information on St. Bridget's efforts (the parish opened its doors to 400, offering sanctuary from *la migra*, food distribution, commemorative liturgical services and symbols), see Samuel G. Freedman, "Immigrants Find Solace after Storm of Arrests," *New York Times* (July 12, 2008), www.nytimes.com/2008/07/12/us/12religion.html?_r = 1&oref = slogin.

96. Baum, *Essays in Critical Theology*, 203.

97. I am grateful to Jonathan Y. Tan for drawing my attention to these significant elements, including counterexamples of repentance in Asian and Canadian contexts.

98. Baum, *Essays in Critical Theology*, 200–1.

99. James T. Cross, "Communal Penance and Public Life: On the Church's Becoming a Sign of Conversion from Social Sin," in *Faith in Public Life*, ed. William J. Collinge, 284–97, at 289–90.

100. Ibid. 290–1.

101. Gregory Baum, "Critical Theology," in *Conversion*, ed. Walter E. Conn, 281–95, at 294.

CHAPTER THREE

Domestic Church and Threats Facing Immigrant Families

this is the year that the eyes
stinging from the poison that purifies toilets
awaken at last to the sight
of a rooster-loud hillside,
pilgrimage of immigrant birth;
—Martín Espada, "Imagine the Angels of Bread"

WHEREAS SCHOLARS AND POLITICIANS frequently frame immigration as a security or economic issue, families and households confront and channel the diverse impacts of migration.[1] Chapter 3 draws upon Christian social ethics and feminist ethics to illuminate immigration as a family issue, indicating how a backlash in family-based immigration policies, traumatic enforcement mechanisms, and gender-based assault threaten families' well-being with social consequences. The impact of immigration policies and procedures on women, children, and families exposes ways in which unjust structures—aggravated by facilitating ideologies, as suggested in chapter 2—undermine the sanctity of the family and endanger the common good. Reflecting the commodification we have witnessed as operative across many immigration and trade considerations, policies that prevent immigrant workers from attaining or maintaining family unity treat them as economic units rather than recognizing their full humanity as parents and children. Christian family ethics offers key resources for critiquing harmful patterns that both enduring gendered experiences of poverty and newer globalized forms and migration enforcement mechanisms sustain: Its profoundly relational anthropology and its integration of a family's intimate communion with its charge to mutually engage the broader social good contest the practices a market ethos engenders. The experiences of migrant family members contextualize and critique dominant notions of the ideal family and Christian family ethics as well.

Migrant Women's Vulnerabilities: En Route and on the Job

The struggles of migrant women and families expose the inhuman costs and human consequences of flawed immigration and trade policies. Recent decades have witnessed the increasing feminization of global migration, with women now constituting half the international migrant population and in some countries, 70 to 80 percent.[2] While global economic shifts directly influence migratory patterns, the circumstances compelling and accompanying most migrant women are marked by the enduring feminization of poverty: Half of the world's population, women continue to perform nearly two-thirds of the world's work, receive one-tenth of the world's income, and own less than one percent of the world's property. In the US context, the heightened border enforcement since the mid-1990s has contributed to this feminization trend; as it has become more difficult to cross without documents or travel back and forth seasonally, many male migrants have extended their stays and arranged for their families to join them.[3] Significantly more women are migrating on their own or as heads of households today than in the past, as well.[4]

Women on the move face particular threats, from sexual assault by smugglers and officials, to abuse on the job, to manipulation in detention facilities.[5] As noted in chapter 1, the majority of annual victims of human trafficking begin as economic migrants or refugees, and trafficked women become vulnerable to sexual violence and sexually transmitted infections, yet have little access to medical or legal services.[6] According to the US attorney general, an estimated 14,500–17,500 people are trafficked into the United States each year, and more than 20,000 Mexican children are victims of sex trafficking annually, particularly in tourist and border areas. Given that migrant women frequently work in gender-segregated, unregulated sectors of the economy such as low-status, low-wage production and service jobs, exposure to exploitation and abuse persists for those who survive perilous journeys.[7]

Fully half of the 215 million international migrants in 2010 were female, and women and girls likewise represented half of those of concern to the United Nations' refugee agency (refugees, asylum-seekers, internally displaced persons and returnees).[8] Yet women are less likely to fit existing visa and asylum categories (entrepreneurs and political dissidents, for example) and there exist no gender-based or gender-specific categories. Women seeking asylum must show that they have "suffered legally cognizable persecution and that their persecutory treatment was on account of one of five enumerated categories: race, nationality, religion, political opinion, or membership of a particular social group." Gender is not a category; some claim it is understood in terms of the existing five, others that it should constitute a sixth category (either gender-specific or gender-based).[9]

Many women who migrate to the United States undergo oppression from interlocking structures of discrimination due to gender, class, race, ethnicity, and citizenship status. The increasingly multinational character of women's work complicates these deeply embedded social and economic trends.[10] As Shawn Copeland puts it, globalization "cannibalizes the bodies, the labor and creativity, and the sexuality and generativity of global 'others.'"[11] Global cities have witnessed shifts from manufacturing to service-dominated economies and the relocation of standardized work arrangements to more informal settings.[12] The resulting "hegemony of flexibility" characterizes the majority of employment opportunities for migrant women, with the flexibility of capital exerting "downward pressure" on conditions of employment.[13]

Less likely to qualify for employment-based immigration than men, the majority of migrant women work in unregulated jobs in these contingent contexts (the informal sector), with the flexibility of capital exerting downward pressure on the conditions of their employment. Domestic work, for example, long considered unproductive by economic measures, uniquely occurs within homes and in close proximity to employers such that migrant women are regularly victim to exploitation through long hours, isolation, and low wages. Those who undertake paid caregiving work are disproportionately women of color, and are among the lowest-paid workers in the workforce.[14]

In a recent study by the Southern Poverty Law Center of 150 women across various sectors of the food industry who have spent time in the United States without documents, respondents overwhelmingly reported "feeling like they were seen by the employers as disposable workers with no lasting value, to be squeezed of every last drop of sweat and labor before being cast aside."[15] Women working in the fields are repeatedly exposed to toxic chemicals in pesticides; those in plants and fields alike report denial of access to bathrooms, lack of allowances for tending to emergencies, and illegal discrimination due to pregnancy.[16] Fear of reprisals—including family separation via deportation—deters resistance to poor treatment, unjust conditions, and rampant wage theft.[17] Intensified enforcement of immigration law has made undocumented workers more vulnerable to workplace exploitation, pushing them further underground and further depressing wages (for immigrant and native-born low skill workers alike).[18] Whereas undocumented workers earn lower wages than citizens in the same jobs, women routinely earn less than their male counterparts.[19]

Such commodification of migrant women is also readily apparent in the widespread sexual violence committed against women on the move from origins to destinations. Sexual violence experienced by women and girls while traveling is difficult to track, but estimates in studies of Central Americans traveling to and through Mexico, and Mexican and Central Americans traveling to the United States, suggest from 60 to 90 percent are subject to such abuse.[20] As noted in chapter 1, the demeaning practice of assuming various modes of contraceptive protection has become routine among women on the move, as they are increasingly vulnerable to sexual assault by *coyotes* or other migrants. Women farm workers hide their gender with baggy clothing and bandanas to deter sexual assault, whereas women who work in border zone factories are subject to regular pregnancy tests. Eighty percent of Mexican women (and women of Mexican descent) working in California's Central Valley surveyed in 2010 reported experiencing some form of sexual harassment (as compared to 50 percent of all women in the workforce who experience at least one incident).[21] Such women frequently fear—with good reason—that reporting abuses will risk job loss and deportation, leading to separation from their children.[22] Beyond such fears, they face multiple barriers to speaking out against such wrongdoings: poverty, lack of access to legal resources, language barriers, shame, and cultural pressures.[23] Hence, undocumented women are often perceived by predators as perfect victims: they remain isolated, uninformed about their rights, and are presumed to lack credibility.[24]

In instances of harassment and assault, women are victimized both by individuals' debasing actions and by harmful attitudes and practices that facilitate these patterns. Mexican anthropologist Olivia Ruiz Marrujo's research on women in the Soconusco region reveals how gender relations heighten susceptibility to sexual misconduct on the move.[25] She writes, "in daily conversation [women in southern Mexico] refer to sexual relations with their partners as '*cuando hace uso de mí*'—'when he makes use of me,'" and local emergency rooms "attend daily to women who arrive unconscious" as a result of domestic violence.[26] Influential transnational postures of sexism (*machismo*) and violence, as well as more culturally specific norms like *marianismo*, shape women's and men's expectations and behaviors in ways that heighten vulnerability.[27] As a result, for example, "an undocumented Central American woman for whom sexual relations has rarely, if ever, been consensual, may consider a *coyote* or supervisor's demand for sex expected male behavior."[28] Such practices reflect social and cultural expressions of a reductive vision of (indigenous) women as means rather than ends. As detailed in chapter 1, respect for universal dignity realized in community is antithetical to the widespread exploitation and commodification of migrant women's bodies and their labor. The examination of social sin in chapter 2 likewise interrogates ideologies that facilitate such dehumanizing practices; Cynthia Crysdale notes that to the degree that group bias or quests for power distort conditions for promoting life, "survival of the fittest means that some, literally, survive at the expense of others. Perhaps more profoundly, some claim personhood, meaning and self-value at the expense of others' dignity."[29] These threats to women's well-being—physical, economic, psychological—frequently also threaten families on both sides of the border.

Alienating Families: Barriers to Unification

Whereas most irregular male migrants state they come to the United States out of economic necessity, female migrants more frequently cite family reunification.[30] Many undocumented women serve as the linchpin that binds transnational families and as breadwinner once they arrive in the United States. Family members' material needs in immigrants' countries of origin frequently compel migration, and in receiving countries immigrants must negotiate familial separation, including prolonged waiting periods for reunification and fear of deportation as they attempt to provide for their families. While family members migrate and work tirelessly abroad to support one another's survival, fear of deportation sends hardworking laborers into the shadows of society. The vulnerability of families threatens children's welfare, the health of communities, and social cohesion. Whereas discussion of threats to family values in the US context frequently focuses upon marital and sexual norms, families of mixed immigration status face acute threats to their well-being. The sections that follow offer an overview of the impact of immigration policies and workplace raids on children and families to expose how current practices undermine human dignity and the sanctity of the family and endanger the common good.

Family reunification has been a cornerstone of the US immigration system in recent decades, yet new restrictions, growing backlogs, and backlash against family preference contribute to the realities of prolonged family separation and the undocumented migration that results. The Immigration Reform and Control Act of 1986 (IRCA), the last large-scale bill that legalized undocumented immigrants in the United States, failed to provide status to family members of IRCA's beneficiaries, and the surge in petitions has contributed to long backlogs: 3.4 million whose family-based petitions have been approved currently wait to receive their visas. The number of visas available annually continues to remain far fewer than the number of prospective immigrants who await visas. At present backlogs persist in all categories of family-based immigration (except the spouses/children/parents of US citizens for whom there are no per-country or category ceilings). For example, a spouse or child of a US lawful permanent resident must wait almost five years before receiving a visa (for as long as ten years if coming from Mexico), while citizens petitioning for a sibling can expect to wait ten to twenty years. Backlogs are so long that immigrants sometimes switch categories and move from one long line to another while they wait as they age or get married.

The 1996 Illegal Immigration Reform and Immigrant Responsibility Act (IIRIRA) facilitated a large-scale removal of legal resident immigrants, increased income requirements for immigrant sponsorship, and increased border enforcement resources (further beefed up by the 2006 Secure Fence Act). IIRIRA introduced provisions that made it harder for poor immigrants to enter the country to join their families and easier for the government to deport noncitizens. Its provision requiring citizens and legal permanent residents to earn 125 percent of the federal poverty level prevents legal immigration for many Mexican and Central American applicants, and likewise thwarts the reunification of many families along the US–Mexico border.[31]

Ceilings on the number of immigrants the United States allows from any one country (no more than 7 percent of the worldwide quota of visas) limit both family-based and employment-based immigration. The current quota system's category and per-country limits on family-based immigration fail to facilitate family unification.[32] To the inevitable question of why immigrants don't get in line to reunite with family members or have a chance at more dignified wages, the answer for most Mexicans is that there is no line to join. According to the Pew Hispanic Center, of the 5,000 permanent visas the United States offers annually for unskilled laborers worldwide, in 2005 *two* went to Mexican legal immigrants. That year about 500,000 unskilled Mexican workers crossed the border to work without documents, and most found willing employers.[33] In 2009 the Council on Foreign Relations' Task Force on US Immigration Policy concluded that the trend over the first decade of the twenty-first century of approximately 800,000 total undocumented immigrants arriving per year with the large majority finding employment indicates that the legal migration system "has not remotely reflected market demand."[34]

A backlash against a family-based immigration system has persisted in recent decades, which underlies these restrictive procedures. According to legal scholar Bill Ong Hing, as Asian and Latino immigrants began to take advantage of the family-based immigration system in the 1970s and 1980s, policymakers began to attack family reunification categories, arguing that a point system would better bring in skilled immigrants and a system based on family ties risks nepotism. By the late 1980s, nearly 90 percent of all immigration to the United States occurred through the kinship categories; by the 1990s, the large majority of these immigrants hailed from Asia and Latin America.[35] Critics in the 1980s and 1990s charged that unassimilated immigrants jeopardized cohesion, and thinly veiled racism and xenophobia were reflected in concerns raised in congressional testimony about the "environmental and social costs" to the American "quality of life" by mostly nonwhite immigrants.[36] Contemporary proponents of an ethnic or ethno-cultural nationalism likewise target family-based immigration as the cause of the "admission of large numbers of immigrants who threaten to dilute, if not overwhelm, US 'Western' culture," reminiscent of US nativist attacks on immigrant waves in the late nineteenth and early twentieth centuries whose countries of origin (Southern and Eastern Europe) or (Catholic) religion was deemed "incompatible with democratic values."[37] Such nativists often term family-based immigration "chain" migration, which they oppose less because of the numbers being admitted than their attributes.[38]

Nearly 14 million people in the United States live in mixed-status families with some members, typically US-born children, having citizenship or legal residency but with a parent or spouse who does not. Under US immigration law, undocumented parents of US-citizen children must prove that their departure from the United States will lead to "exceptional and extremely unusual hardship" for the children; typically only life-threatening medical conditions or unusually urgent circumstances qualify, not economic loss, inadequate medical care, or low quality of education.[39] Undocumented single parents who have worked in the United States for a decade or longer are regularly deported because they can rarely meet this criterion. Of the roughly four million US-citizen children who have at least one parent residing in the United States without a regular immigration status, tens of thousands undergo the deportation of a parent annually.[40] Legal scholars point out that little discussion is given to what citizenship means for a child, particularly when many rights (voting, jury service, candidacy for public office) are denied them; "children's interests in terms of immigration policy as other public policy are sometimes ignored."[41]

The prolonged family separation facilitated by these policies and ideologies risks negative consequences for the social fabric within the United States as well as immigrants' countries of origin. Family unity promotes the stability, health, and economic productivity of family members, each with social consequences. Hing notes that family structures promote economic productivity after resettlement in the United States at least as significantly as particular skills brought.[42] By contrast, family separation can have enduring detrimental effects. In many families children grow up without knowing one or more parent. Loneliness and isolation cause stress that can also lead to family disintegration and even pose public health risks. For example, 40 to 60 percent of single and married immigrant men have used sex workers while in the United States, increasing risk for STD transmission.[43] The United States then exports such diseases as it deports infected migrants across the border to Mexican communities in increasing numbers; AIDS cases in rural Mexican communities have increased from 3.7 percent in 1994 to 6 percent in 2000 with "33 percent of [all] AIDS cases in Mexico [coming] from those states that export the highest number of migrants to the United States."[44] Many rural dwellers cannot reach cities where antiretroviral drugs are dispensed, and the wives of returning men are particularly vulnerable given cultural norms about gender and sex that hinder their ability to protect themselves from infection.[45] US deportation of immigrants to border towns where they frequently have no social contacts or means of survival similarly risk sexual and other exploitation.

As noted in chapter 1, apart from family separation, the mixed status of an intact family impacts children's education, future work experience, and social integration. The marginalization of children growing up in families of mixed status also threatens the common good. The US Congress' repeated failure to enact the DREAM Act betrays a lack of recognition of the connection between children and families' well-being and the wider social order.[46] In the 1982 *Plyer v. Doe* decision on the right of undocumented children to public education through high school, the Supreme Court noted: "It is difficult to understand precisely what the State hopes to achieve by promoting the creation and perpetuation of a sub-class of illiterates within our boundaries, surely adding to the problems and costs of unemployment, welfare and crime . . .Whatever savings might be achieved by denying these children an education, they are wholly insubstantial in light of the costs involved to these children, the State and the nation."[47] Hence the creation of an underclass reflects neither US values nor its interests as a nation, yet attempts to extend opportunities to young people after high school or draw upon international law to protect rights to family life and children's best interests have not garnered sufficient political will or legal precedent.[48]

Enforcement Mechanisms and Familial Fallout

The detrimental impact of family separation has been poignantly evident in the enforcement mechanisms that have escalated in recent years, in the form of workplace raids under President George W. Bush, the expansion of 287(g) programs under President Barack Obama, and state and local measures.[49] The surge in workplace and door-to-door arrests poses risks of family separation, economic hardship, and psychological trauma. Not only are children emotionally, developmentally, and financially dependent upon their parents, many of the children at risk are well integrated into their schools and communities in the only nation they have known as home.[50] Enforcement raids abruptly divide family units and divert attention from comprehensive reform and resources from genuine criminal threats to security.

Since its creation in 2003, Immigration and Customs Enforcement (ICE) has dramatically enhanced its efforts to combat unlawful immigrant employment, increasing worksite administrative arrests more than sevenfold.[51] In December 2006, for example, ICE arrested over 1,000 workers in six Swift and Company meatpacking plants. Framed as criminal identity thieves, workers in a Greeley, Colorado, plant were met by agents dressed in SWAT uniforms carrying one hundred pairs of handcuffs into the plant. For every two immigrants apprehended in such workplace raids, one child is left without proper care or support, which suggests that potentially thousands of children have been separated from their parents as a result of such raids. Fully two-thirds of affected children were US citizens or legal residents, and the large majority of those affected were infants, toddlers, and preschoolers.[52] Whereas immigration raids are ostensibly intended to deter undocumented adults from working, an Urban Institute study on those raids indicates they have adverse effects on families ranging from sudden poverty to the psychological effects of trauma. The arrests also resulted in wider community tensions, primarily marked by polarization between Latino immigrants and other residents. Enforcement mechanisms continue to dismantle trust between immigrant and law enforcement communities, risking unreported crimes.[53]

Whereas the Obama administration's approach has replaced the large-scale employee targeted ambushes with company audits, by the fall of 2011 it had deported approximately 1.1 million immigrants.[54] Its Secure Communities program (SCOMM) "uses the fingerprints of people in custody for other reasons to identify deportable immigrants"; thus far, "the administration has expanded the system to 437 jails and prisons from 14 and aims to extend it to 'every law enforcement jurisdiction' by 2013."[55] An early 2010 study by the Migration Policy Institute indicated that roughly half of 287(g) activity involved noncitizens arrested for misdemeanors or traffic offenses.[56] A study in late 2010 by the Center for Investigative Reporting found that to reach its unofficial quota of 400,000 deportations that year, ICE fast-tracked deportations of those persons with and without serious criminal backgrounds, including many mothers with children who then remained in the United States.[57] Concurrently, government statistics indicate that immigration judges are challenging an increasing number of deportation orders in court on grounds that "many immigrants up for deportation have civil violations like a lack of documentation, and no criminal record."[58]

ICE processing and detention procedures make it difficult to arrange for child care when parents are arrested, given the limited access to telephones, the isolation of detainees, and parents' fear of putting their children at risk by divulging their existence.[59] A 2011 investigation found that there are at least 5,100 children living in foster care who are prevented from being unified with their detained or deported parents.[60] Detained mothers separated from their breastfeeding children, or ugly custody battles such as the one under consideration by the Missouri Supreme Court over a five-year-old boy raised in Missouri by a couple whose rights to adoption during his birth mother's detention remain in question, make visible the heart-wrenching stakes of inadequate policies.[61] More mundane examples abound, given ICE's practice of entering homes in the middle of the night, with mounting reports documenting those caught for (mere) misdemeanors or while lodging domestic dispute complaints. In the immediate aftermath of detention or deportation, families face major economic instability, and they are reluctant to seek assistance from public and private agencies. The loss of a parent increases instability in the home environment, and the associated fear and stigma have led to depression, anger, and social isolation among affected children. These factors together "have a profound impact on child development and well-being."[62] Whereas nondeportability persists as one of the most significant entitlements of citizens (regardless of criminal acts committed, even treason), if a child's parents are deported, the child is often de facto deported or they suffer "constructive deportation."[63] Christians understand all children to be gifts of creation, thereby deserving of love and care in stewardship.[64] More broadly, the harmful impact of raids on children violates fundamental norms protecting human dignity and care for the vulnerable.

Market Logic and the Family

The policies and practices traced above that prevent immigrant workers from attaining or maintaining family unity obscure their full humanity as spouses, parents, and children. The pervasive market logic operative across many immigration and trade considerations helps foster the dehumanizing conditions that generate economic refugees and exploit undocumented immigrant workers.[65] From Pope Paul VI's initial concern for the survival of children and well-being of families in light of international development, through Pope Benedict XVI's more recent critique of global economic threats to integral human development in *Caritas in veritate*, Catholic social thought decries systems that deny basic goods to families in the name of development or free trade.[66] Ecumenical voices in Christian ethics likewise point out how neoliberal economic policies sanctify profits over family ties. As we have seen through our treatment of the objectification of migrant laborers in chapter 1 and complicity in harmful ideologies and structures in chapter 2, the operative value hierarchy prioritizing capital to persons is diametrically opposed to Christian values and is as subtly formative as it is harmful to families.

Immigration attorney Thomas Greene argues that economics has become the "source and summit" of US immigration law and policy: "Economics has shaped the allotment of visas, the immigration court system, the judiciary and the deportation industry with the result that immigrants are now treated more as economic units than human beings."[67] He cites legal anthropologists who assert that the predominant economic vulgate today prompts one to view humans as a cost to be reduced, or, at best, as "human capital" to be managed, given that economic science controls globalization discourse and interests.[68] The visa system in particular offers prima facie evidence that family ties or values are "not afforded the same priority as economic gain."[69] The US State Department's monthly visa bulletins indicate the waiting period for those who wish to obtain documents for entry, divided by employment-based and family-based categories, and further subdivided based on skill or earning capacity and proximity of relationship.[70] Whereas only two of the eight categories of employment-based visas have waiting periods (visas remain available for those with significant earning potential like physicians and professional athletes), visas remain largely unavailable for waiting family members. In the spring of 2012, the government was processing 1993 applications of Mexican adult children of US citizens and 1989 applications of Filipino siblings of US citizens.[71]

The ethos characterizing structures and attitudes on a more macro level directly impacts migrant families, as well. Pope Paul VI framed the impact of international consumption and economic competition patterns in stark terms in *Populorum progressio:* "At stake are the survival of so many innocent children and, for so many families overcome by misery, the access to conditions fit for human beings; at stake are the peace of the world and the future of civilization."[72] Christian social ethicists have subsequently critiqued the impact that the institutions and ideology of a free-market economy have on the family with respect to issues like wage and welfare policy.[73] Immigration practices similarly reveal the detrimental effects of the priority of market logic to social solidarity; as Gemma Cruz puts it, migrants have become "contemporary globalization's flexible, expendable and disposable capital."[74] The considerations shaping broader globalization trends favor small government and trade liberalization, which elevate outcomes and values that can detrimentally impact families. As Gloria Albrecht notes,

> Neoliberalism, with its mantra of "small government," celebrates the reduction of government funding for programs that support families and that could even lift families out of poverty. With its mantra of "free trade," neoliberalism celebrates the globalization of the labor market, the weakening of labor unions, the erosion of the real value of the minimum wage, and every reduction in the cost of labor. We have seen the benefits of economic growth and worker productivity being siphoned from most US families into the hands of a few. But some families, especially low-income families, single mothers and disproportionately families of color, are faced with truly tragic choices: take care of your children or lose your job; work overtime . . . take a pay cut . . . leave your oldest in charge of the youngest . . . work a different shift than your spouse/partner so that your children are not alone or lose your job.[75]

Whereas her work focuses primarily on female US citizens, Albrecht's analysis well characterizes the bind faced by migrant families in their countries of origin and destination alike. The dominant power of economic interests in migration and trade considerations effaces the impact of decisions on spouses and children.[76] Moreover, the reigning political economy that thwarts families' basic goods—be it under the guise of trade liberalization or family values in the developed world, or via development and progress in developing contexts—destroys the foundation of human welfare.[77] Consequences mount for families' physical and moral well-being alike. For threatened as they feel by social forces beyond their control, "families rich, poor and in-between hunker down [and turn inward in a way] that shrivels their ability to care about others. Threatened by a harsh and unjust political economy, they take adaptive reactions, not all of which will be successful."[78] These realities shape the moral choices of desperate migrant families and those who scapegoat them. Hence as these economic forces and a market ethos sever religious, familial, and even political ties, globalization's rhetoric of the increased freedom and interconnection in fact conceals bondage and displacement.[79]

Christian Family Ethics: Resources for Retrieval

Beyond this critique of economic idolatry, the sanctity and social mission of the family developed in Christian family ethics further reorient the stakes away from deportation quotas or fiscal bottom line. Anthropological, social, and scriptural teachings on the family and immigration strongly challenge these patterns of commodification. Hebrew and Christian scriptures are not only replete with injunctions regarding hospitality to strangers, but also with examples of families uprooted and migrating: Abraham is called forth from his homeland to establish a great nation of peoples in the Promised Land; Jacob's family migrates from Israel to Egypt due to the great famine; Moses leads the Israelites' exodus from Egypt in search of religious and political freedom; and Mary and Joseph flee their home in Palestine into Egypt seeking asylum from religious and political oppression. These scriptural examples reveal a pattern not unlike what economic refugees face today: "Families are forced to uproot themselves, leaving behind their homes, their relatives and friends, the security of their lands and their provisions, the familiarity of their language and support of their communities."[80] In his 2007 World Day of Migrants and Refugees address, "The Migrant Family," Pope Benedict connects the drama of the Family of Nazareth to the humiliation, poverty, and fragility of the modern migrant family. He grounds the urgency for measures to ensure the re/unification of the family in its mission as "the cradle of life and the primary context where the human person is welcomed and educated."[81] A Christian family ethic offers several significant resources for reorienting the immigration paradigm in several constructive ways: (1) its profoundly relational anthropology; (2) the family as "domestic church," that is, a basic cell of society, school of deeper humanity, and mediator of covenantal love; and (3) the family's social mission, central to an "integral family humanism."

RELATIONAL ANTHROPOLOGY

As stated from the book's outset, Christian anthropology has grounded my critique of dehumanizing immigration practices, considering the person as the subject of migration rather than as its object.[82] The centrality of human dignity and agency in Christian ethics challenges trade and enforcement practices that unduly prolong familial separation. The relationship between freedom and relationality emphasized in chapter 1 underscores the intrinsic nature of family relationships to personhood.[83] In contrast to the unfettered *homo economicus*, a Christian understanding of humans imaged in a Trinitiarian God necessitates that personhood entails relationship. As noted in chapter 1, families comprise our most intimate relationships such that protracted separation threatens our very human subjectivity. If, as Pope Benedict emphasizes in his recent social encyclical, humans find themselves through sincere gift of themselves, impeding family unity and provision amounts to impeding self-determination.[84] Because we realize our very selves through love, we are "deprived of human freedom (the most basic human right) when [we] cannot completely give of self."[85] Certainly most people risk migration for the sake of their family or children; the long hours of work and self-sacrifice that go into sending remittances, for example, signal the gift of self that immigrants make for family members.[86] The policies and underlying rationales profiled here that undermine family unity frustrate this core relationally.

Despite intermittent family values rhetoric on US political and religious scenes, a relational anthropology confronts a culture with a primarily individualistic ethos that does not value caregiving labor. The credo in *el Norte* that we pull up our bootstraps and make our own fate is perhaps as entrenched as it is incompatible with a solidaristic idea that we share each other's fate. Whereas a Christian anthropology does not compromise autonomy, its understanding of humans as interdependent, at turns more dependent and more interdependent, offers a significant contribution to discussions of migrant family members' identities and contributions.[87] As Ada María Isasi-Díaz puts it, the importance of family life frames ethical responsibility, nurturing members in "a world where one *is* because one is in relationship to others."[88] This relational anthropology critiques exploitation of migrant labor at the personal levels, at the policy and procedural levels, and it contextualizes our sense of migrant integration at wider cultural levels.

My colleague William O'Neill has reflected on his work at a women's prison ministering to mostly Mexican and Central American women for whom motherhood is so central to their identity that separation induced by mandatory sentences can be devastating. This intrinsically familial identity could hardly be further removed from the language of "illegal alien," he has mused. The levels of shame piled upon these imprisoned migrant women (most of whom are Mexican and Central American women without a high school education, convicted of drug-related offenses) constitute the "inverse of solidarity," he notes; the induced family separation—with children routinely farmed out to an overburdened foster care system as wards of the state—fails to register as a question of justice in the criminal justice system.[89] Isasi-Díaz characterizes la familia as the central institution in Latina/o culture: It functions as a duty, a support system, a responsibility, and a primary identity marker.[90] Hence for those migrant women whose agency is caught up in motherhood, separation or failure due to imprisonment, deportation, or inability to provide for or reunite with children can fracture their integrity and identity in profound ways.

A Christian notion of the lifegiving context of family also stands in sharp contrast to rhetorical and practical assaults on childbearing and family unity. Recent attacks on birthright citizenship tend to portray migrant women solely as "breeders" and are first and foremost attacks on existing rights of citizen children.[91] Whereas birthright citizenship has been supported on rule of law grounds, immigration attorney Donald Kerwin points out that it in fact offends the rule of law to treat the Fourteenth Amendment as an immigration loophole. Idiomatic differences are revealing, beginning with the image of "dropping anchor babies" increasingly employed by politicians that does violence to the idea of bringing life into the world. The Spanish language more aptly captures the sacred countersign: Dar a luz signifies that giving birth entails bringing light into the world and attunes us to migrants' children as irreducibly worthy of reverence rather than burdens incurred by the scheming.[92] I will turn below to the ways in which the cultural value of familismo interacts with globalizing trends and migrant experiences in more complex ways; on the whole, however, threats to migrants' relationality may be characterized as pervasive and inhibiting.

DOMESTIC CHURCH

Flowing from this social anthropology, Christian ethics defends the sanctity of the family as "domestic church," and its value as the "cradle of society that fosters the welfare of society."[93] Both personal and social development are closely connected to the health of the family, a school of deeper humanity. Catholic social thought on the family integrates a family's intimate communion with its charge to mutually engage the broader social good. If families serve as basic cells of civil society, social conditions must protect and ensure their participation in the demands and benefits of the common good. Deprivation of dignified labor opportunities and traumatic enforcement raids signify hostile social forces impeding social engagement and access to social goods. The defense of the family as a basic social cell has been reinforced in the US legal discourse and developed throughout the Catholic social tradition.[94] In the first social encyclical, Pope Leo XIII defends the person and the family as prior to the state, rejecting state interference with a worker's right to provide for his family and in cases of "exceeding distress" support for public aid to families.[95] At Vatican II, the council describes the family as "a kind of school of deeper humanity" in its pastoral constitution, one that requires the "joint deliberation of spouses, as well as the painstaking cooperation of parents in the education of their children" in order to flourish.[96] The council underscores the strength and power of the institutions of marriage and family in the face of economic, social, and psychological disturbances, and calls for public authorities to protect and promote family life, safeguarding parental rights and the protection of children.[97]

Since Pope John Paul II's 1981 publication of *Familiaris consortio*, the Catholic Church has witnessed a resurgence of the domestic church metaphor.[98] John Paul's vision of family as a domestic church echoes patristic thinkers like John Chrysostom and Augustine, who described the family as small church, church in miniature, and church of the home. The pope notes that the Christian family "constitutes a specific revelation of ecclesial communion, and for this reason too it can and should be called 'the domestic church.'"[99] The model connects the family's inner communion to its participation in the common good: "far from being closed in on itself, the family is by nature and vocation open to other families and to society."[100] Whereas its rapid development and parameters have been debated, some scholars note that the symbol helps counterbalance marriage as contract, helping to "reappropriate the notion that the [Christian family] participates in an ongoing sacramental reality, through which they are sanctified" and called to engage in the church's social mission.[101]

As families nurture their children and extend out beyond themselves, they educate next generations in the virtues of discipleship and social responsibility.

In this way families serve as our first school of justice. The family remains the primary social institution that not only meets the basic human need to be loved and valued, but also shapes moral character through daily, repetitive practices that influence how we perceive the world and live our lives: "sharing income, stretching food and clothes to meet the needs of each, giving care, feeling compassion, treating each person with equal respect."[102] Family practices are likewise critical to personal (and consequently societal) understandings of justice, fairness, and human rights.[103]

Hence families' formative roles connect to their broader social roles and responsibilities. Lisa Sowle Cahill characterizes modern Christian ethics as marked by a "socially transformative approach to family," noting that Pope John Paul II's emphasis on the family's social mission advances an "authentic family humanism," not just an evangelical ideal.[104] This assumption that all families have a right and duty to contribute to and benefit from the common good has significant implications for a consideration of migrant families.

FAMILIES' SOCIAL MISSION

In *Familiaris consortio* Pope John Paul II connects families' call to reveal love and bring children into and up through the world (procreation and education) to its vocation to practice hospitality, political engagement, and give witness through a preferential option for the poor.[105] This "intimate connection between family and society" demands that familial autonomy not simply be protected from undue interference by the state, but that families should not be "abandoned to hostile social forces or left without effective institutional links to the assets their society can offer."[106] Put positively, John Paul notes that "public authorities must do everything possible to ensure that families have all those aids—economic, social, educational, political and cultural assistance—that they need in order to face all their responsibilities in a human way."[107] In *Centesimus annus* a decade later, he characterizes the family as "a community of work and solidarity" whose countercultural witness requires robust social supports, including adequate resources for the tasks of child and elder care.[108] This connection between familial formation and public witness has remained underdeveloped in Christian social ethics. Julie Hanlon Rubio has written about the tendency for the field to neglect the role of middle associations like the family, arguing that social transformation "necessarily involves changes of the heart, ongoing conversion, and counter-cultural practices that can only begin in the home."[109]

Particularly in light of this social mission, the practical and rhetorical threats to the well-being of migrant families reviewed above jeopardize contemporary society's "fundamental task of respecting and fostering the family."[110] Policies and conditions that perpetuate family separation undermine human subjectivity and harm the common good. They impact the person, church, and society. The consequences of federal inaction on comprehensive immigration reform have been grave for families and communities, and an enforcement-only approach will remain practically ineffective, as well. So fundamental is the human desire for communion that failure to allow family members to re/unite will only continue to encourage undocumented immigration by family members. The conciliar conception of the family as generations helping one another to "harmonize personal rights with the other requirements of social life," offers a vision particularly well suited to more justly confronting the challenges posed by the human casualties of a global economy and forced migration.[111]

Christian Family Ethics: Caveats and Challenges

A brief and incomplete retrieval of the sanctity and social mission of the family in Christian family ethics thus poses profound critiques to harmful immigration practices. Migrants' own experiences also serve as a source for Christian ethics in ways that challenge and potentially develop dominant Christian family ethics. Space here does not permit an adequate analysis of the categories of domestic church or integral family humanism, such as treating concerns about whether and how diverse, finite, and sinful families can mediate sacramental love. The social contexts of migrant women's experiences explored suggest several caveats about traditional notions of the ideal family that shape Christian family ethics yet hinder familial flourishing—especially for migrant and otherwise vulnerable women and family members. These entail: (1) inadequate approaches to the work of social reproduction; (2) the multivalence of *familismo*; and (3) the manner in which idealized familial norms function to reinforce an unjust status quo. The constructive retrieval is coupled with this critique in the hopes that the inclusion of overlooked voices will contribute to a deeper critical awareness of family life that more effectively values families in practice and theory alike.[112]

THE WORK OF SOCIAL REPRODUCTION

Assumptions about the complementarity of the sexes that often lurk below Christian family ethics serve to bolster uneven burdens for the work of social reproduction with ontological status. The self-declared *papa feminista*, John Paul II supported women's equal access to social, economic, and political goods while emphasizing the "feminine genius" of motherhood as women's primary vocation.[113] This anthropological dualism confers an "equal but different" status that continues to hinder women's flourishing in work inside and outside the household alike.[114] Whereas Catholic social thought—and, as we have seen, the integral family humanism of John Paul II—emphasize the fact that social involvement is indispensable for full personalization, the separate spheres' ideology has helped sustain not only inequities in the workplace, but also a lack of mutual accountability in shared household and parenting responsibilities.[115] Feminist ethicists have long emphasized the tension that persists between Christian teachings on equal human dignity and affirmations of women's contributions in social and political life, on the one hand, and this emphasis on women's maternal function, familial vocation, and gender complementarity, on the other. Assumptions about the nature of women and caregiving work have conspired to make aspects of women's labor invisible, legitimize a "second shift"—felt most poignantly by women at the bottom economic rungs struggling for their own and their families' survival first and foremost—and increasingly pit women against one another in shouldering the work of social production.[116]

These assumptions about women's nature obscure the contributions and conditions of women's labor and the relationship of the work of production to that of reproduction.[117] What John Paul II termed the feminine "genius" burdens women with the pluriform caregiving and rearing duties rather than calling forth intergenerational solidarity marked by shared responsibility and adequate compensation.[118] Ways in which societies understand and organize the necessary work of social reproduction (such as dependent care, nurturance, and socialization) vis-à-vis the work of material production constitute a social justice issue.[119] Albrecht documents how "unjust structures of gender power, deepened by racism and economic exploitation, deny all women social equality."[120] The forces constraining migrant women and families likewise deny them and their offspring social equality—in many cases without the floor of citizenship on which to crouch. Critiques of gendered social roles and the economic system underlying the public-private and wage-labor framework are also relevant to migrant dynamics. For example, Christine Firer Hinze critiques ways in which the capitalist, free-market economy underpinning the notion of a family living wage ignores significant contributions to the common good not accounted for by the wage labor structure.[121] In contrast to the de facto liabilities women and caregivers face in the reigning economy and culture that assume an anthropology of isolated individualism, Albrecht argues that the "equality of women requires a political economy in which being an actual or potential mother, being in need of care, and being responsible for the care of others, *are* the human norm."[122]

A lack of shared responsibility for the daunting demands facing mothers in the low-wage workforce is frequently camouflaged by lip service given to a narrow construal of family values. Where family values language holds sway, conservative Christians across denominations fear feminism is destroying families and thereby undermining society, and some advocate a return to separate gendered tasks and spaces.[123] Much to the dismay of Latina/o groups that forged alliances with the evangelical parachurch organization Focus on the Family, for example, the organization's leadership has indicated that "while immigration and poverty are worthy issues, the focus must remain on abortion and homosexuality."[124] As theologians and bishops from developing countries have noted, by contrast, threats to the family from a "culture of death" include the forces that displace and uproot families and the poverty that haunts and demeans.[125]

Hence, whereas unequal work of social production hinders groups beyond undocumented women alone, the particular vulnerability they face underscores the urgency of these dynamics for moral consideration and redress. Moreover, the lack of sustained attention to the impact of the political economy on family and community well-being not only facilitates exploitative means to economic success examined above, it also masks "the actual connections between the deprivation of low-wage workers and the lifestyle of others."[126] For as upper- and middle-class women have been liberated from some of the work of social reproduction or other domestic tasks, in many cases this is accomplished by relying upon low-wage workers, thereby duplicating gendered labor or reinforcing traditional divisions of labor.[127] This dynamic frees "one class of women from the performance of some of this work while at the same time ensuring that the work remains women's work."[128] Anthropologist Jennifer Hirsch describes this "outsourcing of caring" in the developed world in vivid terms: "Now the changing of diapers of both the very young and the very old—as well as the cleaning of the toilets of those who are, however temporarily, between Huggies and Depends—is done largely by darker-skinned hands."[129] This problematic shift in the organization of social reproduction is largely excluded from discussions of citizenship and work and too often remains peripheral to ethical discourse on family life and economic justice.[130]

THE MULTIVALENCE OF *FAMILISMO*

The complex ways in which economic aspects of globalization have alternately undermined and reinforced structured class and gender inequalities are evident not only in the shifting responsibilities of women in receiving countries like the United States, but also in the ways in which cultural values such as *familismo* both impact and are altered by migrant experiences.[131] A brief consideration of how a Latin American understanding of family might tutor an individualistic ethic on one hand, and ways in which it is altered by migration and diaspora experiences on the other, offers insight into the way in which traditional Christian family ethics can both support and constrain women. These dimensions challenge Christian ethics to expand its notion of kinship networks, make more visible the oppression of women within the home, and expose inadequate construals of family values.

Familismo or familism typically refers to a strong value placed on family relationships and obligation, the value of children and community, and the importance of intergenerational kinship networks. Family serves as the primary organizing structure in most Latin American migrants' lives, for their social identity is relational rather than individual.[132] The traditional cultural value of *familismo* intensifies the connection of familial relationships to women's identity with motherhood constituting an integral part of the female gender role. Women play a central role in *familismo*, serving as the backbone that binds this unique cultural, economic, social, and often religious network of familial relationships. Migrant women are frequently accompanied by children or family members, whether at church, socializing, or even on the job if they can work it out. As the symbolic center of *la familia*, women's primary identity is formed and understood in relation to their web of kinship relationships.[133]

The inclusion of extended family and community within *familismo* contrasts with the dominant focus on the nuclear family in the United States. As my colleague Socorro Castañeda-Liles conveyed to me, because Latinos do not distinguish between their extended and nuclear family, many migrants encounter a shocking dissonance between the ideal nuclear family understood as including mother, father, children (and dog!) that they encounter here in the United States, due to the extensive and malleable understanding of kinship networks marking *familismo*.[134] Such networks extend laterally and vertically and include *compadres/comadres* (godparents) and *tias y tios* (aunts and uncles) whether or not they are blood relations; boundaries among members remain fluid and transcend genetics. A focus on the nuclear family evidenced in dominant Christian family ethics often overlooks the "extended family solidarities and caregiving activities" of such kinship groups.[135] This understanding of family life aims to offer a sense of belonging so that members may flourish in interdependent relationship.[136]

The value *familismo* places on unity and collective goals over individual well-being both challenges and is challenged by the autonomous ethos more predominant in the United States. Its kin networks "facilitate familistic reciprocity behavior," and studies indicate this social support provides "powerful protective effects on health and emotional well-being."[137] Across admittedly diverse Hispanic families' traits and self-understandings, social scientists identify certain familism indicators differentiating them from their white counterparts at risk as immigrants accept US norms that "tend to erode kinship patterns and traditional family behavior."[138] For example, US-born Mexican Americans have higher divorce rates than Mexican immigrants to the United States and third-generation Mexican children are 17 percent less likely to live with both parents than those of Mexican-born parents.[139] Studies have correlated high acculturation with Hispanics' declining health (US-born Hispanics report the worst health and greatest engagement in at-risk behaviors); such acculturation reduces familism across Hispanic generations by fostering individualism.[140]

On the other hand, it is also important to emphasize that, like mainstream configurations of family, women often face discrimination and marginalization within *familismo*. The experience of migration to the United States has in some cases liberated women from some of the social contexts and consequences that had previously constrained or harmed them (or their mothers). In her study of Mexican immigrant women who have been victims of sexual violence, sociologist Gloria González-López found that two sets of gendered dynamics emerged: "Family honor anchored in notions of female purity and motherhood; and fear of the repercussions associated with contesting male violence."[141] Participants who migrated from Jalisco and Mexico City alike reported altered childrearing practices reflective of new perspectives. For example, they became "passionate foes of coercive marriage" and critics of a legal system "that fails to protect rape survivors in Mexico."[142] In many Latin American nations, sexual assault and violence against women and sexual assault are legally framed "as crimes against the honor of the family, rather than as crimes against the personal, physical integrity and human rights of the woman victim."[143] One woman raped after migrating noted that "although she experienced emotional trauma after being raped, geographical distance from her family and a sense of anonymity in a foreign country protected her from potential family confrontations and conflict, and feelings of shame, guilt and moral prosecution." She noted she told no one so as not to shame her family, reflecting both the constraints of *familismo* and the different social consequences of sexual violence in her new setting.[144]

Hirsch's research on changing relational norms among Latin American migrant women and men suggests the complex nature of these influences. Her interviews of women and men in rural Mexico (Degollado and El Fuerte) and Atlanta indicate intergenerational shifts among Mexican transnational communities with respect to gender roles and relationships to which a variety of factors including migration to the United States contribute. In contrast to an older marital ideal where women earn respect "through complying with the gendered ideals for public and private behavior," Hirsch finds younger generations "more likely to make decisions jointly, to regard a spouse as a companion, to share the tasks of social reproduction, and to value sexual intimacy as a source of emotional closeness."[145] Whereas older generations emphasized "mutual fulfillment of gendered responsibilities" and wives' assent to husbands' opinions as essential signs of respect, younger women express ideals of mutuality (they share *el mando de la casa* or the decision making power of the home) and heterosociality ("erosion of gendered boundaries of space between the house and the street" and women and men sharing tasks and time together).[146] She documents a general "softening of a strictly gendered division of labor," yet notes that men continue to be judged by how well they support family and women by the cleanliness of their home and propriety of their children.[147] Significantly, women report they are no longer as easily pushed around as previous generations (*ya no somos tan dejados como las de antes*), with older women's focus on *respeto* (respect) being supplanted by younger women's focus on *confianza* (confidence).

Beyond evolving relationship dynamics, Hirsch notes several key areas of difference in sending and receiving immigrant communities with respect to women and family matters: the privacy and social organization of public space (noting that a sense of invisibility in receiving countries can be empowering for women); legal protections against domestic violence (willingness of government to intervene in receiving but not in sending countries); and economic opportunities for women (eroding *el mando*, as the power to give orders is no longer an "economically earned right" for men alone).[148] These differences— combined with the relative loss of masculine privilege experienced by Mexican men (especially those who remain undocumented)—offer Mexican women in the United States increased bargaining power.[149] On the other hand, a male household head's departure for work in the United States enhances a wife's autonomy and authority over daily decisions regarding family finances and discipline.[150] The portrait is more complex than one wherein US values on gender justice deserve praise or blame, but they do point to the multivalent nature of cultural (and religious) values related to family life and their malleability in light of migration experiences and economic necessity.[151] For example, Hirsch highlights the significance of "Mexican processes of social and economic transformation . . . lived experience of migration . . . and individual yearnings for modernity, coupled with the economic and political powerlessness of rural Mexicans" as factors that have also elevated love as a marital and life goal.[152] Whereas male domination persists for migrants as other women, gender inequality remains linked to racial denomination and economic exploitation: "Since work and family have rarely functioned as dichotomous spheres for women of color, examining racial ethnic women's experiences reveals how these two spheres actually are interwoven."[153] The impact of economic globalization and migration on family structure is an ambivalent and complex tale that must be more thoroughly incorporated into considerations of Christian family ethics.

Whereas the policies outlined at the chapter's outset have harmful concrete effects on family units and members, the discourse of broken families fails to capture the flexible configurations and strategies transnational families accomplish. Just as we must examine which social frameworks effectively value families, considering what forms of gendered practices best permit mutuality and flourishing may be more complicated than supposed. *Familismo* can perhaps broaden a dominant US Christian notion of kinship restricted by idealized nuclear family assumptions and underscore the ways in which solidarities can both connect and conceal, suggesting the importance of autonomy and interdependence alike. As González-López puts it, "Gender inequality resembles a puzzle scattered on both sides of the border, with migration serving as the social dynamic that connects women to a holistic critique of hitherto fragmented histories of violence and objectification. . . . In the midst of this transnational process, both women and men are gradually becoming more aware of how the dynamics of violence against women are produced and reproduced."[154] The expansive incorporation that *familismo* embraces signals the new kinship Jesus inaugurated. Mujerista perspectives rooted in the significance of *la familia* while rejecting patriarchal and authoritarian structures give witness to Jesus's inclusive and just kin-dom.[155]

THE LIMITS OF IDEALIZED NORMS

Observers have long challenged the ideology of "the monolithic family" that risks elevating any specific arrangement as "natural, biological or 'functional' in a timeless way."[156] Even feminist critiques often rely upon a middle-class model of a nuclear family, with a dichotomous split between a public and private sphere that does not always represent the experiences of migrant families (or other nondominant ethnic families).[157] As the cases of migrants' evolving familial norms indicate, distinct experiences and "structures of gender, generation, race and class result in widely varying experiences of family life," which the glorification of the *familismo* or the nuclear family as refuge serves to obscure.[158] In a similar vein, a criticism leveled at John Paul II's understanding of marriage concerns its "metaphysical and ultimately a-historical picture of human relationships detached from their concrete social, economic and cultural conditions," which results in "too idealistic an image of the conjugal union."[159] The subsequent emphasis upon the spousal meaning of body in terms of utter self-gift yields a marital sexual ethic that risks overlooking social forces that can abet sexual exploitation and violence. The conditions fostering "loneliness sex" among migrants, the exploitation of women on the move, or protracted family separation damage marital and family relationships. The iconic Christian symbol of motherhood of "the Virgin Mary peacefully cradling a newborn baby" does not fully speak to the experiences of many mothers who "must tirelessly labor to feed and protect their children."[160] Likewise, disproportionate emphasis on Our Lady of Guadalupe's innocent purity and compliant motherhood at *quinceañera* celebrations or liturgies celebrating her feast day (December 12) can fail to connect with women's felt concerns in harmful ways.

Idealized family norms not only miss significant realities and voices, but they serve to reinforce oppression. In Albrecht's critique of liberal Christianity's norm of the "new egalitarian family," a model she deems unrealistic for most working families, she notes such ideals "function to sustain an oppressive status quo."[161] Whether through this liberal egalitarian norm or a more conservative family values platform, families' presumably private choices become the locus of ethical concern or target for reform. To the extent that women and their contributions remain invisible within families, care for women risks being trumped by the family's claim to protection from the state on the grounds of privacy as well as by the family itself, which places women's needs behind all others.[162] Furthermore, absent economic analysis, "family distress and survival strategies tend to be explained in universalizing, psychological terms," without acknowledgment that "the ideal of a privileged few becomes social ideology."[163] As Cahill rightly notes, whereas a gospel identity should convert families to the hospitality and neighbor regard outlined above, "historically, the so-called Christian family has often been coopted by existing social structures, especially those that reproduce economic and gender inequities."[164] The task for Christian families to embody countercultural identities becomes more urgent, as she points out, yet migrants' experiences suggest that this may manifest in different ways for families without the luxury of responding in hospitality and justice per standard prescriptions.

The experiences migrant families endure should caution Christian ethics against universalizing Western families as Christian family norms.[165] Enrique Dussel points out that since an ideal Christian family cannot exist in perfect realization nor in empirical reality, "what we need to set about bringing into being is an actual family that is *better* than we have at present, that *will institutionalize* structures rebuilt on the counter-pretense demands of the gospel."[166] A Christian family ethic unduly attentive to the family dynamics and pressures of those in the peripheral world, including migrant family members living in shadow societies, neglects significant factors that impact the majority of the world's (vulnerable) family members and that complicate strict ideals.[167] The experiences traced herein may help us appreciate the violence, fragility, and cultural forces—beyond relativism or sexual libertarianism—that impact actual families' lives and temper or challenge harmful, idealized generalizations.

Cahill proposes that families "laboring under disadvantage to become participating members of American society" not only require social support but crucially that they "have a contribution to make in defining what family is, how families carry Christian identity, and how the church is built up in and through families."[168] What does this require? The experiences of migrant women suggest it demands social supports that concretely value caregiving work, economic and political policies that unite rather than divide families, and enforcement strategies that do not hinder family and community well-being. Also, the experiences of migrant women indicate that it demands that women earn a just wage for their work outside of the family, and that spousal, extended family, and sociopolitical support enable women to be economically productive members of a family. As Susan Moller Okin points out, families cannot school the next generation in practices and mentalities to challenge injustice without the support of social and economic policies.[169] Rather than uncritically denigrating or glorifying migrants' survival strategies or family networks and values, it is important to bear in mind ways in which they are shaped by the challenges of economic insecurity; this dynamic suggests that social policies must not focus on changing family behaviors alone, but also improve economic conditions and concretely support a range of existing family arrangements.[170]

Migrants' experiences and complex family dynamics alert us to the limitations of a Christian family ethic that remains insufficiently inclusive, liberative, and centrally binding. Albrecht offers a significant step in this direction: "Christian ethics supports social conversion to the family values of Jesus when it provides a social analysis that reveals our fundamental human interconnectedness, destroys the innocence of the privileged, and works to exhibit and establish the social power of relationship by which we can choose to co-create one another for the better."[171] She notes that reigning family values discourse assumes Christian values reflect neoliberal commitments to "economic growth, individualism, and the nuclear family." The foregoing contextual analysis of the experiences of migrant women and families reveals how a market logic undermines radical Christian values of women's equality and families' well-being. As Albrecht warns, "the ideals of the privileged should never be mistaken as Christian ideals."[172] The dominant norms risk reifying particular virtues or cultural models in isolation and can overlook significant barriers to familial flourishing. These considerations can augment existing emphases on families' inherently sacred and social dimensions toward more inclusive and reality-based norms for Christian families and communities.

Conclusions

Attending to women on the move and families in limbo entails taking in their resilience, as well as the human rights violations they continually endure. Migrant women's experiences of assault on the move and on the job, together with the disruption to family life that outdated visa policies and new enforcement procedures incur, reveal patterns at odds with Christian commitments to human rights and the sanctity of family life. In turn, the experiences of migrant women in the family and the workplace problematize idealized family and gender norms in fruitful ways. The shifting self-understandings of women and families over the course of migration and resettlement challenge dominant perceptions of immigration and ethics more broadly considered, as well. Migrant women's family ties remind us that migration decisions are rarely personal choices alone, and they highlight the inadequacy of approaches that flatly criminalize irregular migrants. The spectrum of migrant women's experiences broadens and "genders" notions of immigrant rights, signals great strides in the midst of formidable obstacles, and challenges dominant moral paradigms as well as piecemeal, punitive approaches to immigration. Efforts to highlight migrant women's needs would sharpen the churches' prophetic potential on matters of immigration. For example, although US Catholic bishops repeatedly testify before Congress on immigration reform, they typically remain silent on the sexual exploitation or other gender-specific threats that migrants face.

Familial patterns of distributive injustice across the double (or triple) shift, the trials of separated family members, and migrant women's persistent courage in the face of formidable barriers also highlight shortcomings of an ethical methodology that assumes agency without constraint.[173] Confronting the attitudes that shape our expectations and that facilitate the exploitation of persons on the move attunes us to how such patterns dehumanize the oppressors—those of us blindly complicit in cultures of violence, consumerism, leisure, or exceptionalism, not to mention unconscious racism and sexism. Explicitly calling out our own participation in such sinful realities surrounding migration sheds light on the ways in which unjust practices, in fact, harm permanent residents of receiving communities, as well.

Notes

The epigraph is reprinted with permission of Martín Espada.

1. Patricia R. Pessar, "Gender and Family," in Mary C. Waters and Reed Ueda, eds., *The New Americans*, 258–69, at 259.

2. UNFPA: United Nations Population Fund, "Linking Population, Poverty and Development; Migration: A World on the Move," available at www.unfpa.org/pds/migration.html (accessed July 12, 2010). United Nations. 2006. "Trends in Total Migrant Stock: 2005 Revision" (POP/DB/MIG/Rev.2005). Spreadsheet. New York: Population Division, Department of Economic and Social Affairs, United Nations. "Women and girls represented, on average, 49 per cent of persons of concern to UNHCR. They constituted 47 percent of refugees and asylum-seekers, and half of all IDPs and returnees (former refugees). Forty-one percent of refugees and asylum-seekers were children below 18 years of age." UNHCR: The UN Refugee Agency, "2009 Global Trends: Refugees, Asylum-seekers, Returnees, Internally Displaced and Stateless Persons," Country Data Sheets, June 15, 2010, available at www.unhcr.org/4c11f0be9.html (accessed July 11, 2010). By the end of 2009, women constituted of 47 percent refugees; 40 percent of asylum-seekers; 50 percent of IDPs protected/assisted by UNHCR; 51 percent of returnees (refugees); and 50 percent of stateless persons.

3. Wayne A. Cornelius and Jessa M. Lewis, eds., *Impacts of Border Enforcement on Mexican Migration*, chapter 6, "Gender Differences," by Elizabeth Valdez-Suiter, Nancy Rosas-Lopez, and Nayeli Pagaza, 97–114, at 97. They cite Katherine M. Donato and Evelyn Patterson,

"Women and Men on the Move: Undocumented Border Crossing," in *Crossing the Border*, ed. Jorge Durand and Douglas S. Massey, 111.

4. International Organization for Migration, World Migration Report 2010, The Future of Migration: Building Capacities for Change (Geneva, Switzerland, 2010), available at http://publications.iom.int/bookstore/index.php?main_page = product_info&products_id = 653 (accessed July 8, 2011).

5. Silvia Falcon, "Rape as a Weapon of War: Militarized Rape at the U.S.–Mexico Border," in *Women and Migration in the U.S.–Mexico Borderlands*, ed. Denise A. Segura and Patricia Zavella, 203–23.

6. UNFPA: United Nations Population Fund, "Linking Population, Poverty and Development Migration: A World on the Move," available at www.unfpa.org/pds/migration.html (accessed July 12, 2010).

7. UNFPA: United Nations Population Fund, "Linking Population, Poverty and Development Migration," and María Arcelia González Butron, "The Effects of Free-Market Globalization on Women's Lives," trans. Paul Burns, in *Globalization and Its Victims*, ed. Jon Sobrino and Felix Wilfred, 43–49, at 46.

8. UNHCR: The UN Refugee Agency, "2009 Global Trends: Refugees, Asylum-seekers, Returnees, Internally Displaced and Stateless Persons," Country Data Sheets, June 15, 2010, available at www.unhcr.org/4c11f0be9.html (accessed July 11, 2010).

9. Talia Inlender, "Status Quo or Sixth Ground? Adjudicating Gender Asylum Claims," in Benhabib and Resnik, *Migration and Mobilities*, 356–70.

10. Anne Carr, "Women, Work, and Poverty," in *The Power of Naming*, ed. Elisabeth Schüssler Fiorenza, 83–87, at 83.

11. Shawn Copeland, *Enfleshing Freedom*, 66.

12. Saskia Sassen, "Global Cities and Survival Circuits," in *Global Woman*, ed. Barbara Ehrenreich and Arlie Russell Hochschild, 254–73, at 261.

13. Cranford, "'¡Aquí estamos y no nos vamos!' Justice for Janitors in Los Angeles and New Citizenship Claims," in *Women and Migration*, ed. Segura and Zavella, 306–26, at 313–14. Cranford elaborates that amid the dominance of flexible production in a racialized and gendered service sector, significant connections persist between the overvalorization and profits of the corporate sector and undervaluing of the service sector. See also David Bacon, *Illegal People*, 76.

14. Gloria H. Albrecht, "For Families," in *To Do Justice*, ed. Rebecca Todd Peters and Elizabeth Hinson-Hasty, 12–20, at 17.

15. One hundred and fifty women were interviewed by Southern Poverty Law Center (SPLC) who worked in the US food industry in Arkansas, California, Florida, Iowa, New York, and North Carolina (all without documents at the time or at some point). The interviews were conducted from January to March of 2010. See Southern Poverty Law Center, "Injustice on Our Plates: Immigrant Women in the U.S. Food Industry," 23, 63.

16. Ibid., 23.

17. Many women interviewed by the SPLC reported their pay stubs routinely showed far fewer hours than actually worked. Ibid., 25.

18. J. David Brown, Julie L. Hotchkiss, and Myriam Quispe-Agnoli, "Undocumented Worker Employment and Firm Survivability," Working Paper 2008–28, Federal Reserve Bank of Atlanta, December 2008 (cited in SPLC "Injustice on our Plates," 24).

19. Randy Capps, Michael Fix, Jeffrey S. Passel, Jason Ost, and Dan Perez-Lopez, "A Profile of the Low-Wage Immigrant Workforce," Immigrant Families and Workers, Urban Institute, Brief No. 4, November 2003, as cited in SPLC "Injustice on our Plates," 24.

20. Amnesty International, "Invisible Victims: Migrants on the Move in Mexico," (London: Amnesty International Publications) 2010 (part 1 introduction), available at www.amnesty.org/en/news-and-updates/report/widespread-abuse-migrants-mexico-human-rights-crisis-2010-04-27 (accessed July 15, 2010).

21. Irma Morales Waugh, "Examining the Sexual Harassment Experiences of Mexican Immigrant Farmworking Women," *Violence against Women* (January 2010), 8, as cited in SPLC, "Injustice on Our Plates," 46. The study cited similar factors contributing to their vulnerability: extreme poverty, language barriers, isolated orchards, continuous stooping required, male controlled industry and discrimination based on race, class and gender.

22. SPLC, "Injustice on Our Plates," 41–42.

23. Ibid., 42.

24. Ibid.

25. The Soconusco region lies in the state of Chiapas along Mexico's southern border with Guatemala.

26. Olivia Ruiz Marrujo, "The Gender of Risk: Sexual Violence against Undocumented Women," in *A Promised Land*, ed. Daniel Groody and Gioacchino Campese, 225–42, at 232.

27. Very generally speaking, *machismo* is typically described as being dominant, virile, and independent, whereas *marianismo* emphasizes being submissive, chaste, and dependent.

28. Marrujo, "The Gender of Risk," 228.

29. Crysdale, "Making a Way by Walking," 54.

30. Valdez-Suiter, Rosas-Lopez, and Pagaza, "Gender Differences," in Cornelius and Lewis, eds., *Impacts of Border Enforcement*, 97–114, at 102. The authors also note that 61 percent of migrant women surveyed (603 returned migrants and potential first-time migrants to the United States in Jalisco and Zacatecas, Mexico) reported having their children with them in the United States during their most recent stay, whereas only 36 percent of the men surveyed indicated this (108).

31. Nestor Rodriguez and Jacqueline Maria Hagan, "Fractured Families and Communities," 331. They note that the "latter consequence affects lower-income border immigrants in a particularly severe manner because, in comparison to immigrants in the interior, these immigrants often depend on family unity for economic survival, given the precarious conditions of labor markets in border communities." Rodriguez and Hagan cite Augusta Dwyer, *On the Line*, for the border community impact, in particular.

32. Further, "the definition of 'family' in immigration regulations fails to reflect the broader network of cooperating kin who constitute the practical and moral family for many immigrant populations. This lack of fit often forces immigrants to engage in costly and dangerous legal, extralegal and illegal strategies aimed at uniting families." Pessar, "Gender and Family," 263.

33. Kevin Clarke, "These American Lives," 15. In California only 1 percent of its 650,000 farm laborers work on H-2A visas even though they comprise one third of the nation's agricultural workforce. See David Bacon, "Borrowed Hands: Does the H-2A Guest Worker Visa Program Make It Easy to Exploit Farm Workers?" *California Lawyer* (September 2011), available at www.callawyer.com/story.cfm?eid=917686&evid=1.

34. National Council on Foreign Relations (Jeb Bush and Thomas McLarty III, chairs, Edward Aldin, Project Director), *U.S. Immigration Policy*, Independent Task Force Report No. 53 (Washington, DC: National Council on Foreign Relations, 2009), 50.

35. Bill Ong Hing, *Deporting Our Souls*, 118–19.

36. Ibid., 120.

37. Donald Kerwin, "America's Children."

38. Donald Kerwin, "Toward a Catholic Vision of Nationality," 199.

39. Jacqueline Bhabha, "The 'Mere Fortuities of Birth'? Children, Mothers, Borders, and the Meaning of Citizenship," in Benhabib and Resnik, *Migrations and Mobilities*, 187–227 at 207. For a review of relevant case law and pending legislation to shift the "extraordinary circumstances" burden to the best interests of citizen children, given that few if any undocumented parents are able to prove that their deportation imposes extreme hardship upon their children under existing standards, see Satya Grace Kaskade, "Mothers without Borders."

40. A 2010 Pew Hispanic Center study indicated that "at least four million children born in the United States belong to undocumented parents," and that in 2009 "37 percent of adult undocumented immigrants were parents of U.S. citizen children." Alfonso Chardy, "Children at Center of Immigration Debate," *Miami Herald*, August 12, 2010. See also Bhabha, 189–90. Bhabha points out that little discussion is given to what citizenship means for a child, particularly when many rights (vote, jury service, candidacy for public office) are denied them; children's interests in terms of immigration policy as other public policy are sometimes ignored. Bhabha, "The 'Mere Fortuity of Birth'?" 190–91.

41. Ibid., 190–91.

42. Hing, *Deporting Our Souls*, 135.

43. Thomas M. Painter, "Connecting the Dots: When the Risks of HIV/STD Infection Appear High but the Burden of Infection Is Not Known: The Case of Male Latino Migrants in the Southern United States," *AIDS and Behavior* (November 2006), available at www.springer link.com/content/482255t623377868/ (accessed December 21, 2007). I am indebted to Elizabeth Shaw for originally bringing these data on migrants and HIV to my attention. Some migrant workers are forced into prostitution themselves out of desperation. At job sites in Los Angeles, "more than a third of the migrants . . . [have] been solicited for sex by men seeking partners. About a tenth of the men, desperate to earn a living, have agreed." See Marc Lacey, "Back from the U.S. and Spreading HIV: Migrants Take AIDS to Rural Mexico," *The International Herald Tribune* (July 17, 2007): 5.

44. Melissa Sanchez et. al., "The Epidemiology of HIV," 205.

45. Mexico provides antiretrovirals to even those poor migrants without health insurance (unlike the United States).

46. The DREAM Act stands for Development, Relief and Education for Alien Minors. It has been introduced repeatedly in the House and Senate from 2001–2011. The bill would provide conditional permanent residency to undocumented students who arrived in the country as minors and have been in the country continuously for at least five years (prior to the bill's enactment) who graduate from US high schools and demonstrate "good moral character," if they complete two years at a four-year institution of higher learning or two years in the military.

47. US Supreme Court, *Plyer v. Doe*, 457 US 202 (1982). Donald Kerwin rightly points out that the court here highlights the complementary nature of rights and the common good, a feature common to US law and Catholic social thought. Kerwin, "America's Children."

48. *Beharry v. Reno* deemed that "forcible separation of a non-citizen legal resident [of the United States] from his citizen child or spouse implicates this right to familial integrity," drawing upon international law protecting the right to family life and a child's interest, but it was reversed on appeal. Bhabha, "The 'Mere Fortuity of Birth'?" 209–10.

49. The Illegal Immigration Reform and Immigrant Responsibility Act (IIRIRA) of 1996 added Section 287(g) to the Immigration and Nationality Act (INA), authorizing the US Department of Homeland Security to enter into agreements with state and local law enforcement agencies, permitting designated officers to perform immigration law enforcement functions ["provided that the local law enforcement officers receive appropriate training and

function under the supervision of sworn US Immigration and Customs Enforcement (ICE) officers"]. See ICE's own description of this function at www.ice.gov/pi/news/factsheets/070622factsheet287gprogover.htm (accessed May 20, 2010). In 2006 ICE allocated $5 million to 287(g) efforts, and in 2010 it allocated $68 million to such delegation. Raha Jorjani, "The Real-time Effect of Cooperation between the Criminal Justice System and Immigration Enforcement," lecture at Santa Clara Law School, April 6, 2010.

50. Randy Capps, Rosa Maria Castaneda, Ajay Chaudry, and Robert Santos, "Paying the Price: The Impact of Immigration Raids on America's Children," A Report by The Urban Institute (National Council of La Raza: 2007), 1.

51. Ibid., 10.

52. Ibid., ii.

53. Police Chief Steve Lamken refused to help at the slaughterhouse raid in Grand Island, NE, explaining, "When this is all over, we're still here, and I have a significant part of my population that's fearful and won't call us, then that's not good for the community." David Bacon, "Justice Deported," 5.

54. The pace of company audits has roughly quadrupled since President George W. Bush's final year in office. The Obama administration has been moving away from using work-site raids to target employers. In August 2011 the administration introduced new guidelines for the use of prosecutorial discretion in deportation case review, potentially suspending deportation proceedings against those who pose little threat to national security or public safety.

55. See Porter Slevin, "Deportation of Illegal Immigrants."

56. See Randy Capps, Marc. C. Rosenblum, Cristina Rodríguez, and Muzaffar Chishti, "Delegation and Divergence: A Study of 287(g) State and Local Immigration Enforcement" (Washington, DC: Migration Policy Institute, 2011).

57. An expedited removal can be used in cases where persons attempt to enter the country without valid entry documents. At the time of attempted entry an inspector typically orders this type of removal; the individual is not permitted to consult legal counsel or present his or her claim before an immigration judge. Expedited removals accounted for more than 25 percent of all removals in 2009. Jeanne Batalova and Kristen McCabe, "Immigration Enforcement in the United States," *Migration Information Source* (Washington, DC: Migration Policy Institute, 2010), available at www.migrationinformation.org/USFocus/display.cfm?ID = 806#23 (accessed July 1, 2010).

58. Ruxandra Guidi (reporting from Tijuana, Mexico), "Border Separates Undocumented Mothers from Their Children," "The California Report," National Public Radio (KQED), Nina Thorsen producer/director, (Dec 29, 2010). Removals more than doubled between 2000 and 2009, with 393,289 total removals in 2009, the highest number in ten years. Jeanne Batalova and Kristen McCabe, "Immigration Enforcement in the United States," *Migration Information Source* (Washington, DC: Migration Policy Institute, 2010), available at www.migrationinformation.org/USFocus/display.cfm?ID = 806#23 (accessed July 1, 2010).

59. Women were separated from men in some cases; there was also movement across state lines due to ICE overcrowding.

60. Applied Research Center, "Shattered Families: The Perilous Intersection of Immigration Enforcement and the Child Welfare System," as reported by Amy Goodman, "Thousands of U.S.-born Kids Languish in Foster Care as Parents Detained, Deported," *Nation of Change* (November 10, 2011), available at www.nationofchange.org/thousands-us-born-kids-languish-foster-care-immigrant-parents-detained-deported-1320931831 (accessed November 22, 2011). I am grateful to Jean Molesky-Poz for bringing this report to my attention.

61. Mary Sanchez, "In Missouri, a Case That Would Stump Solomon," *Kansas City Star* (January 31, 2011). As Judge David C. Dally stated in this custody case (after the boy's birth mother, Encarnación Bail Romero, was not informed that Carlos' adoption had been expedited during her detention following a poultry plant raid), "her lifestyle, that of smuggling herself into the country illegally and committing crimes in this country, is not a lifestyle that can provide stability for a child." See De la Torre, *Trails of Hope and Terror*, 87. The would-be adoptive parents renamed Carlos as "Jameson."

62. Ibid., 41–42.

63. Bhahba, "The 'Mere Fortuity of Birth?'" 192, 201. The Fourteenth Amendment to the US Constitution states that "all persons, born, or naturalized in the United States, are citizens of the United States and of the State wherein they reside. No States shall make or enforce any law which shall abridge the privileges or immunities of citizens of the U.S."

64. Todd David Whitmore (with Winright), "Children: An Undeveloped Theme in Catholic Teaching," in *The Challenge of Global Stewardship*, ed. Maura Ryan and Todd David Whitmore, 161–85 at 176.

65. Linda Woodhead, "Faith, Feminism and the Family," in *The Family, Concilium*, eds. Lisa Sowle Cahill and Dietmar Mieth, 43–52 at 50.

66. Pope Paul VI, *Populorum progressio* (March 26, 1967) available at www.vatican.va/holy_father/paul_vi/encyclicals/documents/hf_p-vi_enc_26031967_populorum_en.html (accessed January 29, 2011), no. 80; Pope Benedict XVI, *Caritas in veritate* (June 29, 2009), available at http://www.vatican.va/holy_father/benedict_xvi/encyclicals/documents/hf_ben-xvi_enc_20090629_caritas-in-veritate_en.html (accessed January 29, 2011).

67. Thomas Greene, "Families and Social Order" panel presentation, Annual Meeting of the Society of Christian Ethics (January 4, 2008) Atlanta, GA.

68. Ibid., 86 relying upon Alain Supiot, *Homo Juridicus*, 74.

69. Greene, "Families and Social Order."

70. Visa bulletins are available at http://travel.state.gov/visa/bulletin/bulletin_3897.html (accessed March 30, 2011).

71. April 2012 Visa Bulletin, available at http://travel.state.gov/visa/bulletin/bulletin_5674.html (accessed April 13, 2012).

72. Pope Paul VI, *Populorum progressio* (March 26, 1967), available at www.vatican.va/holy_father/paul_vi/encyclicals/documents/hf_p-vi_enc_26031967_populorum_en.html (accessed March 22, 2011) no. 80.

73. See, e.g., Christine Firer Hinze, "Bridge Discourse on Wage Justice," 531–32. This essay first appeared in Harlan Beckley, ed., *The Annual of the Society of Christian Ethics*; see also Thomas J. Massaro, *United States Welfare Policy*.

74. Gemma Tulud Cruz, "Between Identity and Security," 363.

75. Albrecht, "For Families," 18.

76. Albrecht argues that "by sanctifying the primacy of competitive, self-interested economic activities," and relegating moral formation to family life, classical liberalism exempted them from moral considerations such as environmental and familial impact. Gloria H. Albrecht, *Hitting Home*, 141.

77. Albrecht, "For Families," 18.

78. Ibid., 18

79. Cruz, "Between Identity and Security," 372. Chapter 4 takes up these dynamics of globalization in greater detail.

80. Robert Fortune Sanchez, "Migration and the Family," 19–20.

81. Pope Benedict XVI, "The Migrant Family," World Day of Migrants and Refugees address, excerpted in "Migrant Families Can Help All of Humanity," in *L'Osservatore Romano* no. 3 (January 17 2007).

82. Bishop Nicholas DiMarzio, "John Paul II," 192.

83. Farley, *Just Love*, 214.

84. Pope Benedict XVI, *Caritas in veritate* (June 29, 2009), available at www.vatican.va/holy_father/benedict_xvi/encyclicals/documents/hf_ben-xvi_enc_20090629_caritas-in-veritate_en.html (accessed March 16, 2011).

85. Bhahba, "The 'Mere Fortuity of Birth'?" 197, 199. DiMarzio, "John Paul II," 200, referring to Pope John Paul II's remarks in Messori, ed., *Crossing the Threshold of Hope*.

86. DiMarzio, "John Paul II," 197.

87. I am indebted to a comment made by Mary Ann Dantuono on interdependency following her discussion "The Economic Issues That Migrant Women Encounter," Second Conference of Catholic Theological Ethics in the World Church, In the Currents of History: From Trent to the Future, Trento Italy (July 26, 2010).

88. Ada María Isasi-Díaz, "Kin-dom of God: A Mujerista Proposal," in *In Our Own Voices*, ed. Benjamín Valentín, 171–90 at 181.

89. Private discussion planning joint panel on migration presented at Second Conference of Catholic Theological Ethics in the World Church, In the Currents of History, Trento Italy, (July 26, 2010).

90. Isasi-Díaz, "Kin-dom of God," 181.

91. Bhahba, 197, 199.

92. Donald Kerwin, panel remarks at The Catholic Church and Immigration: Pastoral, Policy and Social Perspectives conference sponsored by The United States Conference of Catholic Bishops and the Catholic University of America (March 21, 2011), available online at http://live.cua.edu/ (accessed March 21, 2011).

93. Pope Leo XIII, *On Christian Citizenship (Sapientiae cristianae*, 1890), no. 42, in *The Church Speaks to the Modern World*, ed. Etienne Gilson.

94. The law defers to marriage, "one of the basic civil rights of man, fundamental to our very existence and survival" (*Loving v. Virginia*, 388 U.S. 1, 12 [1967]) in ways unique to other contracts. Its role is described as the "parent, not the child of civil society" (*Dalrymple v. Dalrymple* 2 Hag. Con 63 [1811]).

95. Pope Leo XIII, *Rerum novarum* (May 15, 1891) available at www.vatican.va/holy_father/leo_xiii/encyclicals/documents/hf_l-xiii_enc_15051891_rerum-novarum_en.html (accessed September 4, 2010) esp. no. 13, 14, 35.

96. Second Vatican Council, *Gaudium et spes,* no. 52.

97. Ibid., no. 47, 52.

98. For a discussion of the significance and development of the domestic church in Catholic tradition see Joseph C. Atkinson, "Family as Domestic Church"; Michael A. Fahey, "The Christian Family as Domestic Church at Vatican II," in Cahill and Mieth, eds., *The Family, Concilium*, 85–92; Florence Caffrey Bourg, "Domestic Church"; and Michael Lawler, *Family, American and Christian*, esp. 105–9.

99. Pope John Paul II, *Familiaris consortio*, no. 21.

100. "This happens where there is care and love for the little ones, the sick, the aged; where there is mutual service every day; where there is a sharing of goods, of joys and of sorrows." Ibid., no. 42.

101. Fahey, "The Christian Family as Domestic Church at Vatican II," 91.

102. Albrecht, "For Families," 12. Julie Hanlon Rubio's *Family Ethics* similarly profiles practices for Christian families.

103. Albrecht, "For Families," 12–13.

104. Lisa Sowle Cahill, *Family*, 85, 90. Pope John Paul II speaks of "authentic family humanism" in *Familiaris consortio* (1981) no. 7, available at www.vatican.va/holy_father/john_paul_ii/apost_exhortation s/documents/hf_jp-ii_exh_19811122_familiaris-consortio_en.html.

105. John Paul II, *Familiaris consortio*, no. 44, 47.

106. Ibid., no. 45; Cahill, *Family*, 91.

107. John Paul II, *Familiaris consortio*, 45.

108. Pope John Paul II, *Centesimus annus* (May 1, 1981) available at www.vatican.va/holy_father/john_paul_ii/encyclicals/documents/hf_jp-ii_enc_01051991_centesimus-annus_en.html (accessed March 22, 2011) no. 48.

109. Julie Hanlon Rubio, *Family Ethics: Practices for Christians* (Washington, DC: Georgetown University Press, 2010), 58.

110. John Paul II, *Familiaris consortio*, 45.

111. Second Vatican Council, *Gaudium et spes* (1965), no. 52, in David J. O'Brien and Thomas A. Shannon, *Catholic Social Thought*, 200.

112. Following a panel on "Women on the Move" at the Second Conference of Catholic Theological Ethics in the World Church, In the Currents of History (Trent Italy, July 26, 2010), attendees discussed the possibilities for cultivating such an awareness in arenas of home, church, and society. Gemma Tulud Cruz asked, for example, how we might reimagine the ideology of family and domesticity at play as a moral economy of kinship.

113. At the Vatican conference on Women's Health and Human Rights in 1998, Pope John Paul II declared *"Io sono il Papa feminista,"* "I am the feminist pope."

114. John Paul II, *Familiaris consortio*, no. 23.

115. See Christine Firer Hinze, "U.S. Catholic Thought, Gender, and Economic Livelihood" for a lucid assessment of these intersecting challenges.

116. See Arlie Russell Hochschild, *The Second Shift* and *The Time Bind.*

117. Barbara Hogan, "Feminism and Catholic Social Thought," in *The New Dictionary of Catholic Social Thought*, ed. Judith A. Dwyer, 394–98 at 397–98.

118. Pope John Paul II, *Mulieris dignitatem*, no. 30–31.

119. Albrecht, *Hitting Home*, 139. Karen Vierira Powers' analysis of gender parallelism and gender complementarity among Andean cultures prior to the Spanish invasion offers examples of more just constructions: "In gender-parallel societies women and men operate in two separate, but equivalent spheres, each enjoying autonomy in its own sphere." In Andean societies marked by gender complementary (in a distinct sense from the Christian use above), "women and men performed distinct social, political and economic roles, but roles that were perceived as equally important to the successful operation of society, whether performed by women or men." She shows how Spanish colonization and Christian evangelization ultimately all but destroyed these spheres in favor of patriarchal systems. Karen Vieira Powers, "Andeans and Spaniards," 511–12. I am grateful to Socorro Castañeda-Liles for this reference.

120. Albrecht, *Hitting Home*, 139.

121. Christine Firer Hinze, "Bridge Discourse on Wage Justice: Feminist and Roman Catholic Perspectives on the Family Living Wage," in *Feminist Ethics and the Catholic Moral Tradition*, ed. Curran, Farley, and McCormick, 511–40 at 531–32. This essay first appeared in *The Annual of the Society of Christian Ethics* in 1991.

122. Albrecht, *Hitting Home*, 148.

123. Ibid., 139, 142–43.

124. Tom Minnery, "Staying Focused: Why We Don't Address All the Issues," *Focus on the Family Magazine* (September 2007): 20–21 as cited in De La Torre, *Trails of Hope and Terror*, 83, 208.

125. See, e.g., the Peruvian Pastoral Conference, "The Family: Heart of the Civilization of Love," *Catholic International* 5 (June 1994): 270 as cited by Cahill, "Commentary on *Familiaris consortio*," 380.

126. Albrecht, *Hitting Home*, 141. Patricia Hill Collins has written about "racial ethnic women's motherwork," giving voice to the experiences of African-American, Native American, Hispanic and Asian-American women, which challenge white, middle class feminist assumptions. She describes its contradictory elements: "On the one hand, racial ethnic women's motherwork for individual and community survival has been essential . . . On the other hand, this work often extracts a high cost for large numbers of women. There is loss of individual autonomy and there is submersion of individual growth for the benefit of the group. While this dimension of motherwork remains essential, the question of women doing more than their share of such work for individual and community development merits open debate." See Patricia Hill Collins, "Shifting the Center: Race, Class, and Feminist Theorizing about Motherhood," in *American Families*, ed. Stephanie Coontz, Maya Parson, and Gabrielle Raley, 173–87 at 176.

127. Studies show that in the early 1990s families stood to gain $13,000–$20,000 by trading the services of a college-educated wife for a paid, full-time household employee. See Kathy A. Kaufman, "Outsourcing the Hearth: The Impact of Immigration on Labor Allocation in American Families," in *Immigration Research for a New Century*, ed. Nancy Foner, Ruben G. Rumbaut, and Steven J. Gold, 355.

128. Linda Bosniak, "Citizenship, Noncitizenship and the Transnationalism of Domestic Work," in *Migration and Mobilities*, ed. Seyla Benhabib and Judith Resnik, 127–56 at 133. As Jennifer Hirsch elaborates, "the precarious domestic bargains middle-class women and American women strike, our fragile progress toward domestic 'equality,' our own companionate marriages, are largely predicated on offloading work we consider unpleasant on women from the developing world." Hirsch, "'Love Makes a Family': Globalization, Companionate Marriage, and the Modernization of Gender Inequality," in *Love and Globalization*, ed. Mark B. Padilla, Jennifer S. Hirsch, Miguel Muñoz-Laboy, Robert E. Sember, and Richard G. Parker, 93–106 at 102.

129. Hirsch, "Love Makes a Family," 103.

130. Bosniak, "Citizenship, Noncitizenship," 131. The volumes resulting from the University of Delhi's international conference on Women and Migration in Asia offer a welcome exception. See an overview of the series in Meenakshi Thapan, "Series Introduction," 14–15.

131. Hirsch, "Love Makes a Family," 102.

132. Victoria Malkin, "Reproduction of Gender Relations in the Mexican Migrant Community of New Rochelle, New York," in Segura and Zavella, eds., *Women and Migration*, 415–35 at 426.

133. Malkin, "Reproduction of Gender Relations," 432, 434. An anthropologist, Malkin points out that "women negotiate and construct their gender identity within migrant networks, which most often remain bound to ideologies that continue to construct women within their familial roles" (433).

134. Castañeda-Liles herself migrated to California from Mexico.

135. Naomi Gerstel and Natalia Sarkisian, "The Color of Family Ties: Race, Class, Gender and Extended Family Involvement," in *American Families*, ed. Coontz, Parson, and Raley, 447–53 at 447.

136. Isasi-Díaz, "Kin-dom of God," 180–81.

137. William A. Vega, "The Study of Latino Families: A Point of Departure," in *Understanding Latino Families*, ed. Ruth E. Zambrana, 3–17 at 7, 14. Vega reports that familism "attenuates delinquency and drug use," and, in part, accounts for the "low use of health and mental health services by Latinos" (15).

138. The studies identity factors including large family households that include extended family members, higher than average fertility levels, and early childbearing, for example. Marta Tienda and Faith Mitchell, eds., *Mulitiple Origins*, 77–78.

139. Ibid., 79. They note that an increase in intermarriage of Hispanics among different nationalities and with non-Hispanics can "redefine or erode Hispanic familism over generations."

140. Ibid., 122.

141. Gloria González-López, "'Nunca he dejado de tener terror: Sexual Violence in the Lives of Mexican Women," in Segura and Zavella, *Women and Migration*, 224–48 at 228.

142. Ibid., 236.

143. The interpretation of gender violence as crimes against the honor of the family has lethal consequences for women, since Mexican laws still consider the honesty, honor, and good name of the woman to be relevant to the characterization of certain sexual crimes and to determine their punishment. Rosa Kinda Fregoso, "Toward a Planetary Civil Society," in Segura and Zavella, *Women and Migration*, 36–66 at 51 citing Fiona Macaulay, "Tackling Violence against Women in Brazil: Converting International Principles into Effective Local Policy," in *States of Conflict: Gender, Violence and Resistance,* eds., Susie Jacobs, Ruth Jacobson, and Jennifer Marchbank, 144–62 at 200, 149. Macaulay notes this is true for the penal codes of all Latin American countries excepting Cuba and Nicaragua.

144. Relevant to our discussion of migrant women's vulnerabilities, González-López notes, "the everyday life experiences of immigrant women living in an urban contexts often expose them to socioeconomic segregation, demanding work schedules, lack of transportation, unsafe neighborhoods, and unprotected work areas—all of which combine to create dangerous social spaces [making them] easy targets for sexual violence." González-López, "'Nunca he dejado de tener terror'" 236.

145. As she puts it, marriage is shifting from "a system for organizing social reproduction," to more of a "project for personal satisfaction." Hirsch, "Love Makes a Family," 94. See also Jennifer S. Hirsch, "'En El Norte la Mujer Manda': Gender, Generation and Geography in a Mexican Transnational Community," in Segura and Zavella, eds., *Women and Migration*, 438–55 at 441.

146. Hirsch, "Love Makes a Family," 94–95.

147. Ibid., 95; Hirsch, "'En El Norte la Mujer Manda,' 442–43.

148. Ibid., 446–50.

149. Hirsch, "'Love Makes a Family," 99.

150. Jorge Durand and Douglas S. Massey, "What We Learned from the Mexican Migration Project," in *Crossing the Border*, ed. Jorge Durand and Douglas S. Massey, 1–16 at 8.

151. For a discussion of faulty assumptions attributing changing familial structures solely to "acculturation or modernization" and failing to account for political familism, see Maxine Baca Zinn, "Political Familism."

152. Hirsch, "'Love Makes a Family," 96–97.

153. Patricia Hill Collins, "Shifting the Center," 174.

154. González-López, "'Nunca he dejado de tener terror'" 243.

155. Isasi-Díaz, "Kin-dom of God," 185–86. In her *Mujerista Theology*, Isasi-Díaz describes "mujerista" as denoting devotion to Latinas' liberation (61) and mujerista theology as rooted in the lived, ordinary experiences and struggles of Hispanic women (107, 129).

156. Barrie Thorne, "Feminism and the Family: Two Decades of Thought," in *Rethinking the Family*, ed. Thorne and Marilyn Yalom, 3–31 at 4.

157. Collins, "Shifting the Center," 173.

158. Thorne, "Feminism and the Family," 5.

159. Thomas Knieps-Port le Roi, "Innovation or Impasse?" 77.

160. Cathleen Kaveny, "Defining Feminism." Similarly, the failed women's pastoral (initiated in 1984) was indicative of divergence in perspective on what constitutes women's issues: American women favored the need for equal pay and child care and the Vatican insisted upon contraception, abortion and priesthood.

161. Don Browning and his collaborators propose as ideal "*the committed, intact, equal-regard, public-private family*," predicated on a model where both spouses work a thirty-hour workweek outside of the home and share childcare responsibilities. See Don S. Browning, Bonnie J. Miller-McLemore, Pamela D. Couture, K. Brynolf Lyon, and Robert M. Franklin, *From Culture Wars to Common Ground*, 2 (italics in original).

162. See Martha Craven Nussbaum, Women and Human Development, chapter 4. I am indebted to Maureen O'Connell for this suggestion.

163. Albrecht, *Hitting Home*, 146.

164. Cahill, *Family*: 83.

165. Enrique Dussel, "The Family in the 'Peripheral World," in Cahill and Mieth, *The Family, Concilium*, 53–65 at 53.

166. Ibid., 59.

167. Albrecht notes "Mainstream Christian ethics has long insisted, with little success, that the economy be subservient to ethical criteria that protect human dignity and livelihood," yet absent adequate analysis of socially constructed differences among humans, white male assumptions provide the context for defining dignity and livelihood, and the characteristics of "economic man" threaten American community and family life. Albrecht, *Hitting Home*, 140.

168. Cahill therefore calls for the ideal of family as domestic church to flow from three premises: "(1) Christian families structure their internal relations according to Christian ideals of spirituality and reciprocity; (2) Christian families serve others in society to build up the common good by transforming society itself; and (3) Christian families struggle, survive, and thrive together, despite economic, racial and ethnic differences or differences in family structure." Cahill, *Family*: 84.

169. See Susan Moller Okin, *Gender, Justice and the Family*.

170. Naomi Gerstel and Natalia Sarkisian, "The Color of Family Ties: Race, Class, Gender and Extended Family Involvement," in *American Families*, ed. Coontz, Parson, and Raley, 447–53 at 452.

171. Albrecht, *Hitting Home*, 154.

172. Ibid., 154.

173. I analyze these methodological implications in chapter 5.

CHAPTER FOUR

Global Solidarity and the Immigration Paradigm

> *this is the year*
> *that shawled refugees deport judges,*
> *who stare at the floor*
> *and their swollen feet*
> *as files are stamped with their destination;*
>
> —MARTÍN ESPADA, "Imagine the Angels of Bread"

THE EXPERIENCES PROFILED in chapter 3 bring to light the impact that unconstrained neoliberal policies and inadequate immigration procedures have on women and families, in particular. These mounting threats indicate the deficiencies of an immigration paradigm centered on national interest, expediency, or economic efficiency. Despite the migrant-centered locus of enforcement and common misconceptions about why people migrate outside of regular channels, undocumented migration is connected to complex global dynamics. Contextualizing immigration patterns in broader political and economic arenas sheds light on the transnational actors and international forces at play, including the roles those in the United States play in pushing and pulling migrants north across the Mexican border. Given the reach of exclusionary global dynamics, I analyze globalization in the terms utilized in chapter 2: interconnected structures and internalized ideologies. In light of the consequent inadequacy of both state-centered responses and migrant-focused enforcement, I introduce an understanding of solidarity to reframe migration as a shared international responsibility and cultivate conversion from pervasive idolatries.

Globalization and Migration

As we have glimpsed throughout, international trade, regional development, and labor markets rank among the most significant contributors to dislocation and migration.[1] Globalization implies an increase in the phenomenon of globalism, or the networks of interdependence across continents sustained through the flow and impact of capital and goods, information, ideas, people, and substances.[2] The increase in the density of these transnational modes of association takes many forms: interconnected political and economic networks, cultural homogenization and influence of consumerist hyperculture, the emergence of an international human rights regime and nongovernmental organizations, and threats that cross borders, whether public health risks or transnational gangs and terrorist networks. I was struck by the reach of economic and cultural globalization when my husband recounted his experience in the 1990s hiking La Isla del Sol, the remote and ancient island in Lake Titicaca that holds a central place Incan mythology, located at approximately 12,500 feet above sea level. Just below the peak of the highest point on the island (from which one can view the birthplace of the Sun and the Incan people), he came across a shack from which a person was selling Coca Cola and Twix bars to tourists.

Whereas in many cases this increased mobility of goods and services has helped feed those who are hungry and increase life expectancy, the dominant models of economic globalization have also served to substantially increase inequality. The expansion of postindustrial or neoliberal capitalism around the globe has been characterized by its operation across national boundaries, its ability to move capital rapidly, and its quest for short-term profit.[3] Polarized wealth and poverty have resulted, in large part, from this strategy that prioritizes maximizing revenue without necessarily committing long-term to local communities, thereby destroying many traditional and small-scale societies and economies.[4] By 2005 the wealthiest 20 percent of the world accounted for 76.6 percent of total private consumption, while the poorest fifth accounted for merely 1.5 percent.[5]

Whereas the world has witnessed increased access to communication and goods, the distribution has not reached everyone nor been equitable.[6] These exclusivist strains have contributed to environmental degradation, the disruption of cultural integrity and local labor markets, and the erosion of civil society. Jon Sobrino laments that despite positive developments and claims, globalization results not in "a planetary-wide family embrace but a cruel abyss between peoples."[7] His diagnosis of the "proliferation of triviality" is echoed in Adolfo Nicolás's meditation on the "globalization of superficiality."[8] Both call into question not only the material devastation global economic policies wreak but also the nature of what else gets globalized and toward what end: "one world or conquest?"[9] From the perspective of those on the underside, economic globalization is predominantly marked by structural and ideological sin; indeed many observers have characterized globalization as a continuation and intensification of colonialization.[10] I turn now to a discussion of its interrelated forms of injustice, particularly as they relate to migration in the North American contexts.

NEOLIBERAL GLOBALIZATION AND ECONOMIC POLARIZATION

The push for free-market economics in the West following the fall of the Soviet bloc promised to increase peace and economic prosperity globally, but the cyclical poverty that has resulted for many in the ensuing decades has fallen far short of such hopes. Increased movement of finance capital has not always increased the financial stability of every area, and in terms of commercial capital, the lowering of trade barriers has, in most cases, increased developing countries' vulnerability.[11] Neoliberalism, or economic globalization, denotes more than the extension of world trade or capitalism; rather, neoliberal globalization is a political economic theory *within* capitalism that assumes the ability of minimally regulated markets to achieve the best economic balance and solutions to social problems.[12] Income inequality between and within countries has increased as countries deregulate. Whereas economic globalization nearly always benefits trade, without government regulation of the economic flow, poverty and inequality increase.[13] Those with $5 million or more—who represent .1 percent of the population (among them Mexican Carlos Slim Helu)—controlled 22 percent of the world's wealth in 2011.[14]

Corporations have been around since the late sixteenth century, yet globalization has extended corporate power over world markets. Fifty-one percent of the world's one hundred wealthiest bodies are corporations, and about 13 percent of the world's population controls 25 percent of the world's financial assets.[15] In 2004 half of the world's one hundred largest economies were transnational corporations, whereas the 48 least-developed nations accounted for less than .3 percent of world trade.[16] At the turn of the last century, the top two hundred corporations governed over 25 percent of the world's economic activity, yet employed less than one percent of its workforce.[17] It is no wonder that some refer to economic globalization as corporate globalization, given the growing influence of a corporately determined model and business climate. Individual governments (whether democracies or dictatorships) play an increasingly weaker role in trade and planning for growth, whereas independent corporations whose operations are neither democratic nor transparent play an increasingly powerful one.[18] Even in the wake of the global financial crisis beginning in 2007, the influence of financial titans has only increased. The full impact of the 2010 US Supreme Court ruling permitting corporations unlimited financial influence over elections remains to be seen, but it is certainly another step toward increasing their power and influence.[19]

The structural adjustment policies (SAPs) required by the International Monetary Fund (IMF) and World Bank as a condition for receiving financial assistance in the wake of debt crises beginning in the 1980s have reoriented the entire economies of many developing countries from production for internal consumption to production for external consumption in other countries. World Bank statistics indicate that the poorer the country, the more likely that its "debt repayments are being extracted directly from people who neither contracted the loans nor received any of the money."[20] For every dollar in aid a developing country receives, over twenty-five dollars are spent on debt repayment.[21] Economist Stan Duncan argues that SAP repayment rules were more pivotal in integrating poor countries' markets, economies, and cultures into the rich countries' market fold than any other single event in the past two centuries: "In one generation the countries gutted centuries of production habits and became a piece of the international production-consumption process, and the effect that it had on their personalities and self-understandings as a race or people is profound."[22]

In addition to export-oriented production, the SAPs of the IMF and its partner institutions (which owned 80 percent of developing countries' debt by the end of the 1980s) entail public sector layoffs, the privatization of state-owned enterprises, spending reductions in basic social programs like education and health care, the abolition of price controls on basic foodstuffs, wage freezes and labor suppression, and devaluation of local currencies. Taken together, these policies have "contorted and stacked the decks of the financial machinery that runs the earth in such a way that it rewards the rich and extracts payments from the poor."[23] Since the start of the IMF-imposed policy on Mexico in 1982, the country cut its aid to farmers by more than 70 percent; this ultimately led to millions of farmers and their dependents fleeing the fields for the cities and more often for the United States in search of work. This pattern was intensified by the passage of the North American Free Trade Agreement (NAFTA) one decade later.

UNFREE TRADE IN THE AMERICAS: THE CASE OF NAFTA

Mexico's inability to repay its debt in the 1980s, coupled with these SAP conditions of its bailout packages amid dual economic crashes that decade, left it particularly well-poised to accept the terms of NAFTA. NAFTA's economic integration among Canada, the United States, and Mexico created the first large-scale trade agreement forged between developed and developing countries. The agreement preserved few protections for the weaker Mexican economy and the signatories had far more unequal economies and wage disparities than across the European Union (EU). These factors would further fuel pressures to migrate.[24]

At their introduction of NAFTA in 1994, establishing the largest free-trade zone in the world, presidents Bill Clinton and Carlos Salinas de Gortari conveyed optimism about its mutual benefits. Whereas the Mexican president framed it as a "choice between getting Mexican tomatoes or tomato pickers," Clinton predicted that it would not only create 200,000 jobs within its first two years but also curb irregular immigration, "because more Mexicans would be able to support their children by staying home."[25] In the same year that NAFTA was signed, Salinas modified Article 27 of the 1915 Constitution, lifting the ban on the privatization of *ejidos* (communal lands) and the foreign ownership of land by foreigners 100 km from the border and 50 km from the coasts. Mexico substantially cut tariffs on agricultural and livestock goods and virtually all US-manufactured products, reducing tariffs faster and more significantly than required by NAFTA.[26] As has become clear in earlier chapters, NAFTA has failed to deliver on promises of Mexican prosperity or migration reduction. Due to uneven agricultural subsidies that belie the term "free," one-sixth of Mexican farmers have been expelled from their fields and have been faced with the options of "emigration, delinquency, subemployment or starvation" since NAFTA's promulgation.[27]

When developing countries are required to lift their subsidies before wealthy trade partners follow suit, as in NAFTA or in the case of India with European imports, the result is, unsurprisingly, unfreedom for the economically weaker partner. Within a few years of NAFTA's enactment, Mexico's four-thousand-year culture of corn production was essentially dismantled.[28] With their own subsidies eliminated, indigenous farmers were unable to compete with highly subsidized US agribusiness farmers who were now dominating their market.[29] In the first two years following NAFTA alone, two million peasant farmers were forced off their land, and were unable to compete with the accelerated imports of cheap, subsidized US corn.[30]

As a result, migration is not simply a means of achieving the American Dream promised on the television sets that even families in poverty can often access, but a strategy for survival. Former Mexican tomato and onion farmer Alberto Gonzalez of San Cristobal de las Casas went from employing a dozen

people on ten acres of land, to becoming utterly dependent upon small remittances sent from his oldest son who migrated to San Diego and the generosity
of his uncle whose home became his family's own. Seventy-five percent of the
monies migrants annually remit to sending countries returns to the United
States to pay for food, as the cost of staples increased 125 percent from 1994
to 2000.[31] After NAFTA, Gonzalez could purchase produce more cheaply in
the local market than he could have once grown on his own land. He experiences the deal as a war that he and farmers like him lost: "For those people
with the big farms and the big tractor, those who know the big people, NAFTA
has been very good. But for the rest of us, those of us who worked hard but
were not already rich, it was a war, a bloody war. And we lost it."[32]

Additional factors in the years following NAFTA's implementation have
influenced Mexicans' plight and migration trends, including demographic
booms, the indifference of successive Mexican governments to the plight of
rural regions, and the devaluation of the peso in the wake of another financial
crisis in the mid-1990s. The Mexican government did not invest in the infrastructure needed to accommodate new factories, as promised. Powerful commercial corn and tortilla interests in Mexico also colluded to reap the profits
of a cheap influx of foreign corn, replacing hand-produced *masa* with mecha-
nized, mass-produced corn flour and edging out thousands of small-scale tortilla producers.[33] Historical migration patterns and the pull of employment
opportunities in the United States, particularly amid demographic shifts, also
contributed. Mexico's relative trade liberalization with other trading partners
played a role, although the World Trade Organization (WTO) has determined
that Mexico reduced its agricultural tariffs more significantly with the United
States. Perhaps most significantly, the entrance of China into the WTO in
1999 drew manufacturing and foreign investment from Mexico to China due
to its larger workforce, lower wages, fewer environmental and safety regulations, and undervaluation of its currency. By 2004 about 30 percent of the
jobs that had been created in the manufacturing plants or *maquiladoras* in the
1990s had been moved to Asian countries.[34] In globalization's race to the bottom, China rapidly edged out Mexico in the competition for US-based corporations' investment and outsourcing.[35] Nevertheless Mexico's agriculture
sector (which employed one-fifth of its population) lost 1.3 million jobs in the
ten years following NAFTA's passage, causing most to identify agricultural
trade liberalization linked to NAFTA as the chief factor in the loss of agricultural jobs there.[36]

Hence the agreement's asymmetry and selective implementation remains
the primary cause for an outcome quite different from that initially assured

by the nations' presidents: Fifteen years after the passage of NAFTA, Mexico exports 300,000 undocumented workers annually while importing $110 billion in staple food.[37] NAFTA's provisions require that the United States lower its subsidies to its own farmers to help level the playing field, yet more than fifteen years later it has not done so; by contrast, government subsidies to US commodity producers have increased. During a particularly difficult period from 1999 to 2004, for example, the prices Mexican corn farmers were paid fell by more than 50 percent, whereas the price of tortillas to Mexican consumers rose 380 percent. In the words of Mexican economist Miguel Picard, "Mexican farmers are not competing with US farmers; they are competing with subsidies paid by the US *taxpayers*."[38] It is also important to note that two-thirds of all US farmers do not receive any commodity payments; of those who do, the top ten percent receive two-thirds of the taxpayer-supported subsidies.[39]

Considering the relative positions of the countries entering into NAFTA, the procedural inequities, and the devastating consequences thus far, the characterization of structural injustice seems far more apt than that of free trade. I noted in chapter 2 ways in which the Latin American bishops have forged a path connecting institutionalized violence to the suffering of peoples throughout the region; their statements from Medellín, Puebla, and Santo Domingo have identified the legacy of colonialism, the debt crisis, development, and trade policies outlined above, first-world support for repressive governments, and forms of cultural imperialism as contributing factors.[40] The uneven subsidies and tariff rules flout Pope Leo XIII's early warnings against considering agreements between unequal partners just, simply because they were entered into by mutual consent.[41] The SAP-shackled deals better reflect what philosopher Michael Walzer has called "exchanges borne of desperation."[42] Pope Paul VI rejected the ability of the rule of free trade alone to govern international relations, given the unfair results produced by prices freely set in the market. He noted that too often the law of free competition alone "creates an economic dictatorship."[43] The case of NAFTA raises these broader considerations about the justice of a global trading system that enshrines the interests of the few, excludes the voices of the many, and prescribes rigid solutions to economic problems that mirror their initial causes. In sharp contrast to policies narrowly focused on maximizing economic growth, Catholic social thought's more holistic conception of integral development addresses basic human needs, just distribution, the participation of all community members, ecological and spiritual concerns, and respect for diverse cultures.[44]

THE RELIGION OF MODERN EMPIRE: IDEOLOGIES THAT CONCEAL AND ENSLAVE

Latin American liberation theologians and bishops have addressed the totalitarian nature of world markets as they cease to be sufficiently regulated in democratic ways with the effect of exacerbating misery.[45] Ignacio Ellacuría describes the dominant "civilization of capital" as the most basic form of structural violence, which crucifies four-fifths of humanity. Reflecting the interlocking modes of social sin explored in chapter 2, he indicates that the world's wealthy nations conceal their exploitative intention to defend their capitalistic interests by maintaining their intention to make developing countries "democratic" or "wealthy."[46] Whether rooted in self-deception or cunning malice, globalization's ability to evangelize the world to the gospel of consumerism serves to strengthen the dehumanizing structural trends outlined above.

Chapter 3 began to make clear how globalization's effective bondage and displacement are masked by rhetorical promises of freedom and interconnection.[47] Many migrants and would-be migrants experience bondage precisely as a result of trade liberalization. As Timothy Gorringe puts it, "free trade is the flag of convenience under which the ship of capitalism sails." As we encountered in the case of NAFTA, the United States is, in reality, highly protectionist. Gorringe calls unjust trade in the form of exclusions of products from free-trade schemes and discrimination against basic commodities by the European Union and United States the strongest weapon against poor countries, noting their considerable exacerbation of environmental degradation, as well.[48] Even at the level of consumer agency, the realities of a globalized economy are far more constrained than rhetoric about increased freedom of choice or absolute economic freedom imply. Given market distortions in so-called free trade (or the thumbs on the scale disrupting pure equilibria), consumer choices are constrained or coerced from the outset; even prescinding from the morality or prudence of pure free-market economics, the libertarian economic conclusions increasingly clamored for on a domestic front—with dire consequences for the poor and vulnerable, including migrants—remain flawed.[49] Nations' manipulation of their currency, exclusion of other nation's goods from their markets, subsidies for industries, and employment of lax labor standards all mean that when a consumer purchases inexpensive products they are less exercising free choice than they are benefiting from someone else's coercive subsidy. Whereas the price system cannot tell the difference, as indicated in chapter 2, whenever consumers purchase goods that are less expensive due to these practices (whether subsidies and slave labor abroad or the labor practices and costs enabled by undocumented immigration at home), we encourage and sustain these systems that are neither free nor just.[50] These examples reflect the interconnected nature of social sin unpacked in chapter 2, for freedom is a powerful cultural symbol employed in the service of a false consciousness that sustains and is reinforced by global structural injustices.

Globalization's concealing patterns and operative priorities are readily internalized in ways that shape the perceptions and actions of the dominant culture. Orlando Espín describes globalization as a process that occurs within us rather than outside us, influencing our "ways of being, of thinking, of knowing, of acting, and of believing."[51] Whether in fatalistic understandings of the "price of progress" or the "neutrality" of the market system, these more ideological currents of globalization configure our coordinates for what becomes normal or conceivable.[52] Observers have aptly characterized these different tendencies in religious terms. George Soros has famously criticized the widespread slavish adherence to the principles of unfettered free trade as "Market Fundamentalism"—US society's dominant belief system, in his view.[53] The billionaire laments that adrift without an anchor of firm principles, people increasingly rely upon wealth and success as the criteria of value.[54] Economist Dani Rodrik similarly terms blind faith in the Washington consensus ideology of self-interest and deregulation "'faith-based economics.'"[55] The elevation of wealth and influence to absolute status can become an authentic bondage that contributes to scotosis. As the Appalachian bishops have put it, capitalism "wants to teach people that happiness is what you buy . . . and that all of life is one big commodity market. It would be bad enough if the attack only tried to take the land, but it wants the soul, too."[56]

Connected to ideologies of wealth and inequality is the "gospel of consumption" exacerbated by economic globalization—that is, the credo that companies can maximize profits if people habituate themselves to consume at high levels.[57] An idolatrous commitment to growth at all costs and the spread of consumerist values is also tied to globalization's homogenization of culture.[58] Anthropologist Marcelo M. Suárez-Orozco identifies as a "paradox of globalization" the pattern by which global forces (cultural, information technology, goods and services) infiltrate the cultural imaginaries of developing countries, even as they destabilize local economies; in this way "globalization generates structures of desire and consumption fantasies that local economies cannot fulfill."[59] Many have lamented economic idolatries' focus on having over being, and we encountered in chapter 2 ways in which economic idolatries inform migration as much as nationalistic ones: They shape loyalties, frame questions, and inform votes and spending practices. Whether marked by the

Homo consumptor, the technological imperative, or globalization's need for victims, corporate globalization is driven by and sustains a belief system squarely at odds with a Christian relational anthropology, love command, and transcendent telos.

As Gorringe posits, in contrast to the global economy's "pirating of life" in its attempts to patent seeds known by peasant communities for millennia and its habituation to endless consumption ("to destroy, devour"), the Christian ethic is characterized by nurturing and celebrating life.[60] This sense of theft reflects culpable complicity even where masked by resigned fatalism. Ecofeminist activist and scholar Vandana Shiva departs from mainstream neoliberal globalization critics like Jeffrey Sachs, who suggest that capitalism and industrialization are capable of moving everyone out of poverty, and that the remaining challenge simply entails including those bypassed by the process of wealth generation. Shiva disputes this view, insisting rather that "the poor are not those who have been 'left behind,' they are the ones who have been robbed."[61] Reminiscent of our examples of colonial structures of violence in chapter 2, Shiva contends that Sachs and others ignore the forms of dispossession and exploitation inseparable from modern modes of wealth creation.[62]

Without impugning the motives of globalization's proponents and more reformist critics, I suggest that the Catholic tradition's affirmation of the universal destination of created goods and its inclusive conception of human rights support Shiva's critique.[63] The unjust structures and internalized ideologies of neoliberal globalization reveal the scope of modern empire. Even before narrating Jesus's execution at the hand of the Roman empire, the scriptures record the domineering exploits of the Egyptian, Assyrian, Babylonian, Persian, and Greek empires. Yahweh repeatedly warns Israel against seduction by the imperial vices that characterize oppressive regimes. Biblical narratives of mercy for the *anawim* (Heb. "the afflicted," "the poor seeking God's deliverance") and Jesus's radical table fellowship stand in sharp contrast to the slavery and elitism that mark such abuses of power. The above analysis makes clear why much of theological reflection following Christianity's transformation from a nonviolent reform movement into the official religion of the Roman empire in the fourth century has critiqued Constantinian legacies uniting Christianity with empire, from the Crusades and the Spanish Conquests to today's more subtle forms of economic and cultural control, including the reach and impact of global capitalism profiled here.

Pope Benedict XVI has decried passivity in the face of such imperial patterns, denouncing "those who squander the earth's riches, provoking inequalities that cry out to heaven."[64] In his social encyclical *Caritas in veritate* he identifies the financial crisis beginning in the first decade of the twenty-first century as a clear and tragic indication of inadequacy of contractual justice for redressing both the privations of underdevelopment and the excesses of "superdevelopment."[65] In contrast to a capitalistic narrative of the self-made person (human as consumer, climber, *conquistador*), a Christian understanding of our selves as freely gifted can motivate actions that enact gratuity in response. The Christian vision of the human person and human goods presented throughout this book profoundly contest market fundamentalism's truncated anthropology and distorted ends.

NEW ANCHORS FOR THE UNMOORED: POLITICAL JUSTICE IN A GLOBALIZING CONTEXT

As unwilling migrants become dislodged from traditional livelihoods, cultures, and homelands by globalized economic forces, they confront political boundaries in likewise transitional conditions. These shifts, which stateless persons and transnational citizens both encounter and contribute to, entail structural and ideological dimensions. Temptations to enthnonationalisms are pervasive in the face of the upheaval of traditional notions of territory and membership, for example. Yet as David Hollenbach has shown, retreating into safe enclaves is ultimately impossible and constitutes a "destructive response to the psychic, cultural, political and economic weight of interdependence."[66] Just as in the case of market fundamentalism, elevating nation-states (or their laws as presently configured) to ultimate status remains a form of idolatry, attempting to absolutize the lesser good or solidarity of a circumscribed "us," "ours," or "here." As the deepening inequalities profiled above contribute to migration push factors, state security and domestic politics are impacted by migratory patterns.[67] Global corporate networks challenge states' sovereignty by altering public-private sector relationships, encouraging corporations to fuse national markets, and creating an "economic geography that subsumes multiple political geographies."[68] Given the reach of global capitalism and its effects, a reappraisal of existing national and citizenship constructs warrants consideration.

The transition from a bipolar to a multipolar political arrangement post-1989 has led to the diminished importance of territory as a way of mapping reality.[69] Suárez-Orozco characterizes these ambivalent forces as globalization's centrifugal (as the territory of the nation-state) and centripetal dimensions (as supra-national nodes), together resulting in "the deterritorialization of basic economic, social and cultural practices from their traditional moorings in the nation state."[70] Nation-states likewise respond in paradoxical ways: through what he terms "hyper-absence" regarding the flows of capital across national borders, and "hyper-presence" in terms of militarizing borders and regulating membership.[71] As the volume of migrants and number of sending countries rise, migrants' transnational communities increasingly problematize the notion of state membership even as they face barriers to reception.[72]

The right of states to control their borders figures centrally in Westphalian sovereignty. Whereas the state continues play the chief role in immigration policymaking and implementation, the growth of the global economy has affected the state's regulatory role and capacity in these regards. Saskia Sassen argues that "there is more on-the-ground transnationalism than hits the formal eye," naming the shift to supranational institutions, and privatized regimes for the circulation of workers. Realist approaches to international policy are challenged as transnational security, health issues, and environmental threats transgress borders. Further, the evolving international human rights regime—including global, regional, national, and nongovernmental human rights institutions—increasingly challenge state sovereignty by holding nations accountable to norms that transcend their national interests as traditionally understood.[73] These de facto forms of interdependence obscure the autonomy of the peoples of nation-states.[74]

Amid these currents, transnational economies are developing while immigration policy remains stagnant, as evidenced in the centrality of state sovereignty and border control to regulation.[75] Those in liminal or multiple spaces often remain deprived of "the right to have rights," in Hannah Arendt's words, and thus remain subject to "total domination."[76] Historian Mae Ngai has termed them "impossible subjects," arguing they are legal and political subjects without rights, persons who cannot be, and problems that cannot be solved, produced by immigration restrictions.[77] We have encountered myriad examples of how existing systems threaten immigrants' lives, bodily integrity, and family unity. Whereas the basic human rights reflected in international rights regimes and presupposed in Catholic social thought are universal in theory, in contemporary practice their exercise depends upon legally sanctioned membership in a political community.[78] Understanding immigration as "individual actions of emigrants," wherein individuals are the primary site for enforcement and responsibility, has become increasingly incompatible with transnational politics and economies.[79] Sassen rightly questions the "substantive nature of state control over immigration," given both the social and political rights of immigrants recognized in international human rights agreements and the increasing spheres of immigration concern (e.g., agribusiness, manufacturing, humanitarian groups, unions, ethnic organizations, and zero-population growth advocates).[80] Hence existing frameworks for immigration policy remain problematic: On the one hand, the displacement of government functions onto nongovernmental institutions and need to enforce human rights protections indicate a change in the exclusivity and competence of state authority; on the other hand, despite these institutional and philosophical shifts, the state continues to guarantee and distribute rights.[81]

A spectrum of academic and political responses, ranging from fiercely protectionist to advocating open borders, marks the altering landscape. In the European and African unions we encounter examples of pooled sovereignty. Whereas EU citizens of member countries enjoy the privileges of political membership whether or not they reside in their nations of origin, approaching cosmopolitan norms internally, the union continues to act "with outmoded Westphalian conceptions of unbridled sovereignty toward those who are on the outside."[82] Generally speaking, classical liberals urge more open borders than migrants now enjoy on the grounds of the moral weight of freedom of movement whereas social liberals appeal to values of equality and justice to ground migrants' welfare.[83] For those who subscribe to cosmopolitan approaches, national boundaries require moral justification.[84] Kwame Anthony Appiah's "rooted cosmopolitanism" attempts to affirm common humanity without effacing concrete cultural, religious, and gender particularities or rootedness in communities.[85] Differences are celebrated on this model as long as basic human rights are respected. These appeals to a globalization of citizenship—claiming membership in the world community and obtaining rights that derive primarily from one's humanity as such and only secondarily as members of existing nation-states—hold promise for transnational migration by considering human rights independent of community membership, but fall short absent adequate enforcement mechanisms in the present nation-state configuration or an effectively operative global authority.

Beginning from a more narrowly circumscribed understanding of belonging, communitarian arguments regarding border control root defense of membership restrictions in the duties of states to preserve particular cultures or political identities. Michael Walzer's proposal that "the very idea of distributive justice presupposes a bounded world" of members and outsiders, such that membership in such a political community is the "primary good that we distribute to one another," continues to hold relevance.[86] This framework does not provide migrants with any claim for admission in justice.[87] Walzer's argument for communitarian justice elevates the value of democratic sovereignty over that of global justice; given the historical values, traditions, and practices that mark political societies, "admission and exclusion are at the core of communal independence."[88] On this view, justice resides chiefly within and not between states due to the overriding values of a cultural community identified with the nation-state.[89] Related to this set of rationales is a democratic association argument, which appeals to values of democracy, sovereignty, and self-determination, elevating an interest in democratic deliberation such that citizens should have the freedom to decide on matters of common concern, such as admissions restrictions, with their co-citizens.[90]

Critics have pointed out the ways in which any one model falls short of meaningful protections and provisions for the stateless.[91] William O'Neill asserts that in communitarianism, undocumented migrants are at best owed forbearance, lacking "legal title to the primary good of citizenship and its attendant claim-rights."[92] He notes that "even with the partial eclipse of the Westphalian nation-state system," enjoying or enforcing positive claim rights remains bound to citizenship, so that the loss of home and political status is tantamount to "expulsion from humanity altogether.'"[93] On the other hand, he suggests that a global rights regime likewise restricts migrants' claims, for liberal respect for the "generalized other" largely fails to generate substantive obligations of provision for migrants or to protect would-be migrants from the systemic deprivation outlined above.[94] O'Neill forwards a *via media* between these dominant approaches rooted in a rights-based conception of the common good, arguing that Catholic social thought's generalized respect for the concrete other—envisioned as "solidarity with near and distant neighbors"—mediates between the communitarian recognition of concrete members and strangers and liberalism's respect for "abstract citizens."[95] More broadly, "recognition of the 'stranger' or 'alien' as neighbor—and thus as a juridical person and claimant—attests to our common 'faith in fundamental human rights, in the dignity and worth of the human person,' a faith underwritten by, even as it is expressed within, our different comprehensive religious traditions."[96]

As outlined in chapter 1, the range of human rights rooted in human dignity in the tradition of Catholic social thought encompasses civil-political rights and social-economic rights, guaranteeing freedom for participating in the life of the community. In terms of political arrangements that safeguard such rights for the most vulnerable, a Catholic understanding of the state ordered to safeguard basic human rights and promoting the common good transcends border- or culture-specific claims.[97] As the experiences we have encountered make clear, for migrants unable to meet their basic needs in their origin countries the protection of basic rights related to family and work, for example, cannot in practice be "realized without a generous path to citizenship."[98] Rather than conditioning political membership on the particular beliefs, language, ethnicity, or history of an immigrant, the Catholic understanding is rooted in the purpose of states, rights of immigrants, and nature of the common good.[99]

While the Catholic social tradition recognizes the right of sovereign nations to control their borders, as with the right to private property, sovereignty is not an absolute right. Human rights violations can supersede the right to control borders, as "states exist to vindicate rights, but they do not create them."[100] For in contrast to a Hobbesian notion that sovereignty defines legitimacy, "our particular institutional arrangements, including citizenship in a particular polity, are legitimate only if they subserve the global common good, our 'moral citizenship' in a world community. Yet it is just this 'cosmopolitan' citizenship that is mediated in, and across our concrete, particular polities, so that the victims of forced migration, even if 'undocumented,' are never rhetorically effaced, never 'rightless.'"[101] In the case of a political community neglecting to secure basic socioeconomic or political rights for its members, the community has failed in its obligations qua political community.[102]

Amid calls for open or closed borders, the Catholic tradition advocates porous borders. In their pastoral letter "Strangers No Longer: Together on the Journey of Hope," the US and Mexican bishops' conferences emphasize the presumption of migration and reception over sovereignty in light of the contemporary situation of global poverty and persecution.[103] They judge nations like the United States that "have the ability to protect and feed their residents [to] have a stronger obligation to accommodate migration flows."[104] Finally, a Catholic theory of nationality calls for new immigrants (as all community members) to concretely contribute to dignified life in community of all—demonstrating solidarity with their fellow residents and contributing to society. Rather than fearfully navigating in the shadows or hitting the ceiling of high school or the culmination of covert college scholarships, this route would allow immigrants to work, advance in their studies, and to secure basic health services and police protection, thereby furthering the good of all. In the Catholic tradition, rights fundamentally secure participation in the life of the community, and imply correlative responsibilities. As Donald Kerwin puts it, "rights do not just allow, but *require*, immigrants to contribute to their new communities."[105] The implications of this theory of nationality for challenges to civic and cultural integration of new immigrants will be taken up in chapter 5.

Global Solidarities: Reorienting the Immigration Paradigm

Understanding human rights as transcendent of citizenship and immigration dynamics as related to unjust international political and economic divides makes the cultivation of solidarity with "near and distant neighbors" ever urgent. In contrast to focusing on the symptoms of immigration alone, the concept of global solidarity helps reframe migration as an international issue linked to trade and geopolitics. We have encountered patterns that reveal the shadow sides and growing pains of globalization. Solidarity—understood alternately in the Catholic tradition as an attitude, virtue, feeling, principle, or norm—can help convert inadequate structures and distorted visions in the face of our de facto interdependence.[106] Pope John Paul II identifies solidarity as the key virtue demanded in a globalized era, developing the category throughout his social encyclicals. Rooted in the relational anthropology emphasized in chapters 1 and 3, he articulates solidarity as the moral response to the web of interdependence, "the social face of Christian love."[107] As John Paul famously emphasizes, the virtue "is not a feeling of vague compassion or shallow distress at the misfortunes of so many people, both near and far . . . but rather a firm and persevering determination to commit oneself to the common good . . . to the good of all and of each individual."[108] I suggest that several features of solidarity are particularly well suited to addressing the challenges surfaced herein: institutional solidarity, incarnational solidarity, and conflictual solidarity.

INSTITUTIONAL SOLIDARITY

Given the transnational actors noted above and their palpable effects on vulnerable migrants, a commitment to solidarity calls nations to understand themselves as collectively responsible for the international order. This institutional solidarity will require nations to share accountability in the wake of the Westphalian model's partial eclipse and to convert from opportunistic patterns of interdependency now at play.

Hollenbach has written extensively about the forms of solidarity demanded in an era of globalization and displacement. He identifies institutional solidarity, which engenders wider participation and mutual accountability, as a necessary means of moving patterns of global interdependence from ones marked by domination and oppression to ones marked by equality and reciprocity. Institutional solidarity demands the development of structures that offer marginalized persons a genuine voice in the decisions and policies that impact their lives.[109] Whereas many have lamented the restriction of the IMF and WTO to political and economic elites, Hollenbach views transnational non-governmental organizations (NGOs) like Human Rights Watch (and the Roman Catholic Church as an NGO of sorts) well-poised to redress this "democratic deficit."[110] Due to the fact that much of the planet experiences marginalization, or at least "economic development takes place over their heads," a meaningful recovery of the sense that persons who are poor or on the move are agents rather than beneficiaries of forbearance, philanthropy, or pity remains essential.[111] Hence institutional solidarity demands the inclusion of comprehensive sets of stakes at the decision-making table, structures of institutional accountability and transparency, and empowered participation (subsidiarity).[112] In this vein, Hollenbach calls for the democratization of the governance of global institutions via a multilayered approach that combines formal governmental bodies (local, national, regional, and international levels) with intergovernmental regimes in which NGOs play a key role.[113]

Hence institutional solidarity would reorient international relations in terms of a "community of nations."[114] Christopher Steck suggests that such international solidarity demands nations and their peoples develop "jointly cooperative endeavors which help turn them away from narrow national interests and foster in them a sense for the global common good and a deepening commitment to it." Given the structural roots of economic migration considered herein, institutional solidarity moves responses beyond humanitarian efforts or fine tuning judicial discretion to "a prior attitudinal change in which nations see themselves as collectively responsible for the problem because they are collectively responsible for the international order."[115] In his recent encyclical, Benedict XVI similarly calls for more international collaboration between host and sending countries on migration policy, in contrast to present practice.[116] To this end, some have proposed forms of a global social contract to manage international migration. Chilean economist Andrés Solimano contends that a global agreement (and enforcement mechanism) that addresses both economic fundamentals (e.g., development gaps, regional inequalities) and migration governance would help ensure that cross-border movement becomes "an inherent, fundamental feature of a truly global and equitable economic order more than an appendix of the economic interests of recipient countries and of neoliberal globalization."[117]

This collective institutional approach could ameliorate economic and politically coercive factors that drive unwilling migrants. A more just global trading system would enshrine the participation and basic requirements for survival and development of all parties in rules that transcend particular treaty negotiations.[118] In the case of NAFTA, for example, modest but influential first steps might include the following: putting "teeth" in its supplemental environmental and labor side agreements; correcting its nontransparent tribunal system that can override laws; establishing a continental fund to invest in Mexico's economic infrastructure as Europe did with the EU; and, more broadly, furthering efforts at debt reduction.[119] Hence in efforts to support joint political responsibility and just economic order, institutional solidarity would help counter exclusionary and damaging patterns and move toward a more authentic globalization.

INCARNATIONAL SOLIDARITY

Given the depth and lure of sinful resistance to the steep challenge global solidarity imparts, I propose the consideration of two additional dimensions of solidarity: incarnational and conflictual.[120] In the face of the idolatrous temptations outlined above, observers have described the reception of recent Catholic teaching on solidarity (as with social sin) as "inconsistent, superficial or non-existent."[121] Many factors contribute to such "moral torpor," such as the privatization and domestication of sin more generally and the distancing that geography, social circumstance, and informational ambiguity impart.[122] Whereas imperial ambitions conflict with core Christian values beyond global solidarity—such as God's sovereignty, the sacredness of all human life, a presumption against violence, the universal destination of created goods, and care for the vulnerable—Christian defenses of a prosperity gospel or selective use of scripture regarding state submission have sometimes, in fact, served to bolster imperial tendencies.[123] The tendency for Christianity to become blind to the reach of neoliberal globalization or too muted in its response is fueled by the proliferation of myths sustained through powerful imagery and language.

Christine Firer Hinze's evocative metaphors for the reach of consumerism reflect both the idolatrous and blinding features outlined above: She writes of a culture whose "kudzu-like values and practices so crowd the landscape of daily lives that solidarity finds precious little ground in which to take root."[124] She highlights consumerist culture's use of seduction and misdirection (such as the rhetoric of "individual freedom") to "lay a soothing, obfuscating mantle over systemic injustices that solidarity would expose, [as] its participants are fitted with Oz-like lenses, fed a stream of distractions and novelties, and situated in a 24/7 schedule of work-spend-consume that virtually ensures they will 'pay no attention' to the suffering multitudes behind the curtain."[125] Given the interconnection between unjust international structures in need of reform and these pervasive ideologies, an "incarnational" solidarity like Hinze has proposed complements the institutional solidarity advanced above.

Incarnational solidarity departs from valuable intellectual and institutional dimensions of solidarity to immerse our bodies and expend precious energy in practices of presence and service in the real world. Hinze describes the virtue in terms of "cultivating concrete, habitual ways of acknowledging our we-ness by being *with* the neighbor, especially the suffering and needy neighbor." She distinguishes incarnational solidarity from the "cheap, 'virtual,' or sentimental forms of solidarity proffered by a consumerist culture and economy."[126] Such virtual solidarity legitimates the consumer's subjectivity rather than disrupts it, according to Vincent Miller. By contrast, he notes:

> Unlike the symbolic solidarity of consumption, real solidarity requires the effort of departing from the well-worn channels of our lifestyle niches. We must make time in our daily routines, travel to parts of town we do not frequent, struggle with language barriers, wrestle with just what we want from or for these other people who have their own lives and projects. This is both inconvenient and excruciating. It is much easier to have them singing [streaming on our iPhone] as we write a check to a relief organization [or prompting us via a friend's linked status update on Facebook to "like" their cause] and go on living lives largely untroubled by their struggles.[127]

Technology conspires to distance us at least as much as genuinely connect. Constant media exposure to news stories about global suffering not only serves to desensitize but deceive us into equating such awareness of social injustice with actual solidarity with others.[128] Gregory Boyle similarly rejects virtual solidarities, objecting that it is too easy to phone in isolated efforts like participating in an immigration rally or postcard campaign without sustained commitment. Boyle's own life's work and posture, by contrast, model dwelling in the shared joys and sorrows in order to dismantle borders that exclude. In addition to his work at Dolores Mission profiles in chapter 2, Boyle founded and directs Homeboy Industries in Los Angeles. His description of kinship—a term he suggests surpasses conventional understandings of justice and solidarity—reflects well the incarnational sense of solidarity: "At the edges, we join the easily despised and the readily left out. We stand with the demonized so that the demonizing will stop. We situate ourselves right next to the disposable so that the day will come when we stop throwing people away."[129]

Isolated in enclaves, the "have's" can become detached from those who struggle in a globalized economy—connected though they may be by the goods and services the latter provide. Hinze points out that incarnational solidarity entails a kenotic (or self-emptying) posture that helps us traverse power differentials: "To be truly 'for' in a way that avoids paternalism, sentimentality, or a protected and aloof throwing of alms to the poor, whom we want to keep their distance, requires a praxis of humble presence and collaboration. . . . Thus understood, solidarity has a hierarchy-melting, deeply egalitarian thrust."[130] As illustrated in chapter 2, churches may be well poised to overcome differences in this way, particularly in cases of socioeconomically and otherwise diverse congregations. Miller identifies such parish structures as alternative social spaces with the potential to challenge social stratification.[131] As William Cavanaugh puts it, with God, the "Wholly Other" at the center, the pilgrim church can "simultaneously announce and dramatize the full universality of communion with God, a truly global vision of reconciliation of all people, without thereby evacuating difference."[132] Churches are equally vulnerable to distracting forces in various guises, however.

Practices that counter the "kudzu-like" regnant values, from justly compensating caregiving work to "greening" our eating and transportation habits, can transform our imaginations in ways that help us "swim against the broader tide of the commodification."[133] In particular, incarnational solidarity calls us into concrete relationship with the marginalized in ways that better attune us to our connections. I think, for example, of the alliances forged among students and janitorial or food services staff on college campuses that have led to mutual understanding, and in some cases more just labor arrangements. As noted, Dean Brackley has termed opportunities to "act ourselves into new ways of thinking" cognitive hygiene, emphasizing the importance of engagement at the level of practice in order to adequately challenge intellectual and moral commitments.[134] Accompanying homeless families or undocumented immigrants in at-risk neighborhoods can disrupt students' (and faculty's) comfort levels; the opportunities immersive and community-based learning provide to encounter the realities of suffering persons can begin to expand participants' perspective or challenge established myths like that of the even playing field. These modest examples of incarnational solidarity help practitioners resist "the distraction, abstraction, alienation, and apathetic hedonism cultivated by late capitalist consumerism."[135]

Sobrino writes about the encounter with globalization's victims as necessary for conversion, as well:

Placing the suffering of the victims at the centre of the "globe" leads to truth and the universalization of human values. This has nothing to do with "victim culture" but with the need-invitation to respond to the victims with *mercy* and *justice* . . . The victims can convert "a globe" into "a family," "a giant super-market" into "a home." They can also bring in something that, to our great detriment, is virtually absent from present-day civilization: grace. Jesus of Naz-areth shows us that we become human not just by "making" ourselves but by allowing ourselves to be "made" by others: this is the reality and experience of gift.[136]

This praxis of encounter with the "crucified" better captures the mutual dynamics of an incarnational solidarity than do more narrow interpretations of virtuous but unidirectional largesse or theologically rich yet abstract notions of Trinitarian communion. In this vein, Mark Potter draws upon the work of Sobrino to offer an understanding of "solidarity as spiritual exercise." He argues that this praxis grounds efforts in pursuit of justice in an experience of the divine, mediated through those suffering or in need.[137] Potter describes five movements of a "spiritual exercise of solidarity," encounters that culminate in "the courage for the poor and non-poor to continue to live their lives in reference to the truth that their salvation depends upon one another—dignity, justice, and a commitment to the Reign of God depend upon their ongoing relationship and mutual transformation."[138]

CONFLICTUAL SOLIDARITY

Whether in its institutional, intellectual, incarnational, or spiritual dimen-sions, the solidarity demanded amid the chasm wreaked by unjust forms of globalization necessarily entails conflict, an element particularly underplayed in Catholic social thought. In his earlier work, Hollenbach frames the conflic-tual implications of commitment to common good with pointed relevance for macroconsiderations of immigration: "1) The needs of the poor take priority over the wants of the rich; 2) the freedom of the dominated takes priority over the liberty of the powerful; 3) the participation of marginalized groups takes priority over the preservation of an order which excludes them."[139] Whereas John Paul II acknowledges the changes in lifestyle, established power struc-tures, and models of production and consumption solidarity requires, he "qualifies the radical implications of this claim, emphasizing, in line with his predecessors, that justice will be achieved not by overturning all current eco-nomic or social structures, but by re-orienting them to their authentic pur-poses in service of the common good."[140] Even where he draws upon the liberationist preferential option for the poor, John Paul seeks to temper its conflictual implications by emphasizing solidarity entails collaboration among rich and poor, and among the poor themselves.[141]

Yet the path to humanizing globalization by solidarizing institutions and persons cannot bypass conflict and loss. Liberation theologians and social ethicists have likewise noted magisterial Catholicism's tendency to prioritize unity, harmony, and synthesis in ways that circumvent necessary conflict. Some feminist theologians contest the priority given to the preservation of order and top-down social change through the personal conversion.[142] Without confronting issues of economic and political power and engaging grassroots mobilization, work toward and implementation of changes to the status quo will remain stunted; this "demands a tolerance for disagreement, resistance and conflict."[143] Bryan Massingale characterizes John Paul II's development of solidarity as marked by caution at the service of safeguarding social peace. He notes that the African American ethical tradition is severely critical of a "solidarity without social struggle," the dominant approach that summons the powerful to care for the weak or presumes that, "imbued with the virtue of solidarity, social elites voluntarily will undertake practices of social dispossession and divestment of privilege."[144] He offers Frederick Douglass's classic expression of this critique and an alternative approach: "If there is no struggle, there is no progress. Those who profess to favor freedom, yet deprecate agitation, are [people] who want crops without plowing up the ground. They want rain without thunder and lightning. They want the ocean without the awful roar of its mighty waters. This struggle may be a moral one; or it may be a physical one; or it may be both moral and physical; but there must be struggle. Power concedes nothing without a demand. It never did and it never will."[145] For Massingale, as for Malcolm X, amid contexts of injustice and social conflict, "authentic faith-inspired solidarity forbids an attitude of neutrality and demands an unambiguous commitment on behalf of the victims of injustice."[146] His insistence that genuine solidarity cannot evade conflict if it is to serve social transformation is especially relevant to the exploitative injustices of our global economy and its racially charged causes and consequences. By contrast, the tradition of Catholic social thought has expressed optimism that harmful features of neoliberalism can be overcome or significantly mitigated largely by reforms undertaken voluntarily by capitalists.[147]

Given the stakes and the distortions at play in our topic at hand, Massingale's emphasis on the obstacles justice faces and the power struggle required to achieve justice proves valuable for a sanguine approach. He notes that "without an appreciation of what might be called 'conflictual solidarity,' Catholic theology cannot answer the summons to attend to the new subjects in its midst—the poor, the exploited, and those of color—who bear the image of God."[148] As we attune our attention to the insights from those on the underside of globalization, Massingale's warnings that social Catholicism underestimates "both the recalcitrance of the privileged and the potential power of the dispossessed" are well taken. He suggests that such recalcitrance "yields only in the face of sustained demands, determined pressure, ideological struggle, and nonviolent social conflict."[149] Yet whereas inflammatory rhetoric around immigration may attempt to pit classes, races, and ethnicities against one another, persons of all classes are invited to participate in the social struggle that fostering solidarity and justice require, as the end goal is not class victory but reconciliation and the common good.[150] Facile calls for assimilation in the name of unity or overly temperate and timid legislative compromise fail to meet the conflictual solidarity threshold—with human costs. Massingale has described cross-racial solidarity as entailing lament, compassion, and transformative love in order to avoid merely "superficial palliatives that leave the deep roots of justice undisturbed."[151]

Duncan's characterization of existing trade negotiations reflects the absence of incarnational solidarity and potential for conflictual solidarity: "Our wealthy, well-educated trade representatives often get together at international conferences in opulent surroundings, where they work out smooth, efficient trade policies, and then go home without speaking to a single small farmer from Iowa or *campesino* from Guatemala. It's not that they hate poor people or intentionally want to 'crush the face of the poor into their poverty' . . . it's just that the conditions of the poor and struggling seldom come up unless they are standing outside the gates with pitchforks and sabers demanding some small say in the proceedings."[152] In a world where luxury and misery rub shoulders, economic idolatry serves to avert our gaze from Lazarus; further, amid such skewed access to power, genuine solidarity demands conflict.[153] The Australian bishops have noted that righteous anger in the face of injustice is a Christian and necessary response of love. They also promote proactive engagement of the poor and the oppressed as the engine of such change, given that "God has chosen the little and excluded ones to play the key role in the drama of humanity and to act as the central agents of the Kingdom."[154]

In contrast to magisterial hesitations, Niebuhr's realism considered in chapter 1 helps hone a sense of conflictual solidarity.[155] His consideration of group egotism purifies an overly irenic approach to structural and ideological change alike, emphasizing groups' distortion by "the effects of members' inattention and ignorance due to finitude, their culpable flights from understanding and responsibility, and their selfish grasping after power, possessions and profit."[156] An awareness of power dynamics and the entrenched temptations of sin at personal, social, and structural levels prompts Christians to hopeful and shrewd resistance to the economic idolatries and structural injustices neoliberal globalization inflicts. Hinze does not shy away from the conflict and struggle solidarity may invite. She channels saintly combat in the ancients' sense, not of dying, "but suffering, without groveling in the abject misery to which their executioners have reduced them." These steps to humanizing globalization are, she rightly notes, essential for elite bystanders, "entangled in consumer culture, trained to cling fearfully to our comforts and our comfort zones."[157]

Conclusions

An affirmation of human rights that transcend citizenship status and inclusive of substantive claim rights undermines the legitimacy of both reigning global economic policies and exclusionary political practices. The shameful levels of global destitution and inequality increasingly warrant considerably more open borders than is the norm at present on humanitarian grounds, in order to accommodate not only political and religious refugees but also economic and environmental ones.[158] In contrast to focusing on the symptoms of immigration alone, a commitment to global solidarity demands a more integrated relationship with neighboring trade partners than the dominant market-based one, wherein nations understand themselves as collectively responsible for the international order and consequently the challenges posed by migratory patterns.

Calls to institutional, incarnational, and conflictual solidarity demand courage, not timidity. Whereas the Catholic Church has modeled outreach, advocacy, and calls for civil disobedience on behalf of comprehensive immigration reform, even more prophetic and effective strategies are needed to underscore the urgency and stakes of these life issues. Kinship with migrants in a global age entails risking conflictual solidarity on global and domestic economic justice matters. Some theologians and observers have rightly lamented the bishops' "prophetic" style of public engagement on certain life and marriage issues and more muted, prudential mode on socioeconomic or military ones.[159] The impact of neoliberal policies—together with the brutal border experiences and family separation profiled in earlier chapters—suggest that immigration questions are life issues and threaten family values.[160]

Heeding and incorporating the voices of those who suffer from neoliberal structures and ideologies can enhance the effectiveness of Christian engagement on these issues. John Sniegocki points out that while the Catholic social tradition can offer significant contributions to the globalization debate, dialoging with grassroots critics could offer critical insights that push the tradition in needed directions. For example, he posits that from a dialogue with grassroots critics of globalization the tradition could gain "a deeper awareness of the negative impacts of neoliberal policies on women (an underdeveloped theme in Catholic social teaching), and a deepened appreciation of the seriousness of our world's ecological crises."[161] Incorporation of migrant women's experiences, as noted in chapters 1 and 3, would better attune Christian ethics to urgent social realities, such as ways in which SAPs have served to increase women's workloads and harmed their health and education prospects in developing countries.[162] Sniegocki contends that experiences from the grassroots could increase appreciation for the connections between capitalism and inequality and "the erosion of democracy as wealth increasingly comes to dominate political processes."[163] More broadly, he suggests such exchange could offer the Christian tradition "a deeper understanding of the importance of grassroots movements in facilitating social change and the inadequacy of relying primarily on moral appeals to political and economic leaders."[164]

As CELAM noted in its 2003 document on globalization, "we cannot ignore or fail to recognize the value of the efforts by society's marginalized people to unite, demand their rights and acquire greater power by creating groups that defend these rights. . . . As they prophetically question economic and political power structures, churches, especially the Catholic Church, contribute to this emergence of new civil society groups that confront large economic and political power groups in defense of weaker communities of various types."[165] The Asian bishops have similarly called for the church to support grassroots movements for social change, such as those promoting democracy, participation, and human rights, ecological and women's movements, base ecclesial communities, and neighborhood groups.[166] Insights from these grassroots movements can offer us a step forward toward humanizing globalization in a spirit of solidarity.

Notes

The epigraph is reprinted with permission of Martín Espada.

1. Mary DeLorey, "International Migration: Social, Economic, and Humanitarian Considerations," in *And You Welcomed Me*, ed. Donald Kerwin and Jill Marie Gerschutz, 31–54, at 32.

2. See Robert O. Keohane and Joseph S. Nye, "Globalization," 104–19.

3. Robert J. Schreiter, *The New Catholicity*, 7.

4. Ibid.

5. 2008 World Bank Development Indicators, as cited in Uchita de Zoysa, "Emerging Challenges of Consumer Activism: Protecting Consumers and Advocating Sustainable Consumption in Developing Countries," in *Sustainable Production Consumption Systems*, ed. Louis Lebel, Sylvia Lorek, and Rajesh Daniel 66.

6. Keohane and Nye, "Globalization," 116. Thomas Friedman has insisted on globalization's "democratization" by contrast; see *The Lexus and the Olive Tree*.

7. Jon Sobrino, "Redeeming Globalization through Its Victims," 106. Sobrino refers to the title of a book in the Cristianismo y Justíca series here: ¿*Mundialización o conquista?* (Barcelona 1999).

8. Adolfo Nicolás, "Depth, Universality and Learned Ministry: Challenges to Jesuit Higher Education Today," keynote delivered at Networking Jesuit Higher Education for the Globalizing World (April 23, 2010), Mexico City, Mexico.

9. Sobrino, "Redeeming Globalization," 106. Sobrino refers to the title of a book in the *Cristianismo y Justíca* series here: Terrae, ¿*Mundialización o conquista?*

10. See Vandana Shiva, *Biopiracy*. For a discussion of development and economic globalization as continuation of colonial processes of "enclosure," or the privatization and concentration of formerly communally accessible resources, see Shiva, *Staying Alive*.

11. This is due, in part, to the fact that the European Union and the United States protect their own economic interests under the pretense of free market policies, a pattern discussed further below. See Philip Marfleet, *Refugees in a Global Era*, chapter 1.

12. Gloria Albrecht, *Hitting Home*, 13.

13. Mark Weisbrot, Dean Baker, Egor Kraev, and Judy Chen, *The Scorecard on Globalization*, 2–3. In 2007 the poorest 40 percent of the world's population accounted for 5 percent of global income, whereas the richest 20 percent accounted for three-quarters of the world's income. See 2007 Human Development Report, United Nations Development Program (November 27, 2007), 25.

14. The chairman of Telmex, Carlos Slim Helu ("and family") is the wealthiest man in the world as of this writing. His net worth hit $74 billion in 2011, more than the poorest seventeen million of his fellow Mexicans. See the World's Billionaires List, *Forbes* (March 9, 2011), available at http://www.forbes.com/wealth/billionaires/list (accessed July 1, 2011).

15. Luisa Kroll and Allison Fass, "The World's Richest People," *Forbes* (March 8, 2007), available at www.forbes.com/2007/03/06/billionaires-new-richest_07billionaires_cz_lk_af_0308 billieintro.html (accessed June 30, 2011); Eileen Alt Powell, "Some 600,000 Join Millionaire Ranks in 2004," Associate Press (June 9, 2005), available at http://web.worldbank.org/WBSITE/EXTERNAL/TOPICS/EXTDEBTDEPT/o,,contentMDK:20260049~menuPK:528655~pagePK:64166 (accessed June 30, 2011).

16. Timothy Jarvis Gorringe, "Invoking: Globalization and Power," in *The Blackwell Companion to Christian Ethics*, ed. Stanley Hauerwas and Samuel Wells, 346–59, at 349. In 2000, "the sales of each of the world's top five corporations . . . were bigger than the Gross Domestic Product (GDP) or 182 countries." Daniel Groody, *Globalization, Spirituality and Justice*, 14. These statistics are available at the Institute for Policy Studies' site: www.ips-dc.org/reports/top200.htm (accessed February 1, 2010).

17. Sarah Anderson and John Cavanaugh, "Top 200: The Rise of Corporate Global Power," (Washington, DC: Institute for Policy Studies, 2000), 3, as cited in Groody, *Globalization, Spirituality and Justice*, 14.

18. Stan Duncan, *The Greatest Story Oversold*, 19.

19. *Citizens United v. Federal Election Commission*, 558 U.S. 08–205 (2010). Agribusiness contributions to Congress rated second highest after health institutions in the 2004 election. Duncan, *The Greatest Story Oversold*, 29.

20. "Debt—The facts," New Internationalist 312 (May 1999), available at www.newint.org/features/1999/05/01/facts/ (accessed July 1, 2011).

21. Based on World Bank data and statistics, debts of the developing world $2.7 trillion totaled in 2006 and total official development assistance totaled $106 billion in 2006. See http://econ.worldbank.org/WBSITE/EXTERNAL/DATASTATISTICS/0,,contentMDK:20394689~menuPK:1192714~pagePK:64133150~piPK:64133175~theSitePK:239419,00.html and http://econ.worldbank.org/WBSITE/EXTERNAL/DATASTATISTICS/0,,contentMDK:20394658~menuPK:1192714~pagePK:64133150~piPK:64133175~theSitePK:239419,00.html (accessed July 1, 2011).

22. Duncan, *The Greatest Story Oversold*, 54–56.

23. Ibid., 7, 80–82.

24. DeLorey, "International Migration," 38–39. The United States-Dominican Republic-Central American Free Trade Agreement (DR-CAFTA) passed in 2005 has had similar effects.

25. Jeff Faux, "South of the Border—The Impact of Mexico's Economic Woes," *San Francisco Chronicle* (May 18, 2006).

26. NAFTA was signed in 1992 and implemented in 1994. Whereas some tariffs were maintained on maize and beans until 2008, in practice the government of Mexico permitted substaintal above-quota tariff-free corn imports. See Sandra Polaski, "Jobs, Wages and Household Income," in "NAFTA's Promise and Reality: Lessons from Mexico for the Hemisphere," ed. John J. Audley, Demetrios G. Papademetriou, Sandra Polaski, and Scott Vaughan, Carnegie Endowment for Peace (2004), available at www.google.com/search?q=NAFTA+promise+and+reality+polas ki&ie=utf-8 &oe=utf-8&aq=t&rls=org.mozilla:en-US:official&client=fire fox-a (accessed June 17, 2011), 14.

27. Eliseo Pérez-Álvarez, "The Tortilla Curtain," 24.

28. The Catholic encyclical tradition has been slow to recognize the inherent value of nonhuman nature. Its largely instrumental understanding of the goods of nature hinder its critique of neoliberal globalizations' (damaging) ecological and cultural consequences.

29. Duncan, *The Greatest Story Oversold*, 28.

30. From 1994–2004 real wages for Mexicans declined and diverged from US wages, and Mexican income inequality was on the rise. During this period NAFTA had an insignificant net effect on US jobs. See Sandra Polaski, "Jobs, Wages and Household Income," 12–14.

31. Pérez-Álvarez, "The Tortilla Curtain," 24. Total migrant remittances (including personal transfers sent from the United States by foreign-born workers and the compensation of foreign employees who were in the country for less than a year) totaled an estimated $48 billion in 2009. Of that total, $38 billion consisted of personal transfers by foreign-born residents in the United States sent to households abroad, and the remainder, about $11 billion, consisted of the compensation of employees who were in the United States for less than a year. (Because some of that compensation was spent in the United States, however, the measure termed migrants' remittances somewhat overstates the amount of money actually sent from the United States.) The measure describes gross outflows; that is, it does not count funds sent by American workers in other countries to households in the United States. Adjusted for inflation, remittances by migrants in the United States grew at an average rate of 3 percent per year from 2000 to 2009. Congressional Budget Office, "Migrant Remittances and Related Economic Flows" (February 2011), available at www.cbo.gov/doc.cfm?index=12053 (accessed June 22, 2011).

32. Duncan, *The Greatest Story Oversold*, 106.

33. Ibid., 128–30.

34. See Sandra Polaski, "Jobs, Wages and Household Income," 12–14.

35. Duncan, *The Greatest Story Oversold*, 107–9. From 2000–2007 China rose from the seventh largest US trading partner to its second, whereas manufacturing in Mexico declined by 10 percent. By 2002 foreign investment entering Mexico fell rather than rose for the first time since NAFTA's initiation, from $14 billion to $10 billion. Julie Jetter, "NAFTA at Ten: Did It Work?" Harvard Business School: Working Knowledge, Archive (April 12, 2004), available at http://hbswk.hbs.edu/archive/4056.html (accessed June 21, 2011).

36. Polaski, "Jobs, Wages and Household Income," 20.

37. Pérez-Álvarez, "The Tortilla Curtain," 24.

38. Duncan, *The Greatest Story Oversold*, 124, emphasis in original. See also Gonzalo Fanjul and Arabella Fraser, *Dumping without Borders: How U.S. Agricultural Policies Are Destroying Mexican Corn Farmers*, Oxfam Briefing Paper (London: Oxfam UK, 2003), 3.

39. Bread for the World Institute, *Hunger 2007: Healthy Food, Farms and Families* (Washington, DC: Bread for the World, 2007), 3, as cited in Duncan, *The Greatest Story Oversold*, 123.

40. The Asian bishops conference has likewise emphasized the need to analyze unjust structural dynamics, charging that capitalistic free enterprise has commodified the working class: "Clearly, political, economic and agricultural structures have made both urban and rural workers cogs of an anonymous productive machine." Federation of Asian Bishops' Conferences, "The Vocation and Mission of the Laity in the Church and in the World of Asia," in *For All the Peoples of Asia*, ed. Gaudencio Rosales and C. G. Arévalo, 188.

41. Pope Leo XIII, *Rerum novarum*, no. 45. Pope Paul VI applied this principle to contracts made between nations. Pope Paul VI, *Populorum progressio*, no. 59.

42. Michael Walzer, *Spheres of Justice*, 100 (on his "desperate exchanges," see 102). Walzer credits Arthur Okun with the term in *Equality and Efficiency*, 20.

43. Pope Paul VI, *Populorum progressio*, nos. 58–59.

44. John Sniegocki, *Catholic Social Teaching*, 291.

45. Ulrich Duchrow, "Christianity in the Context of Globalized Capitalistic Markets," in *Outside the Market No Salvation?*, ed. Dietmar Mieth and Marciano Vidal, 33–43, at 36–38.

46. Ignacio Ellacuria, "Uncovering a Civilization of Capital, Discovering a Civilization of Work," in *New Visions for the Americas*, ed. David Batstone, 72–82, at 74, 78–80.

47. Gemma Tulud Cruz, "Between Identity and Security," 372.

48. Timothy Jarvis Gorringe, "Invoking: Globalization and Power," in *The Blackwell Companion to Christian Ethics*, ed. Hauerwas and Wells, 346–59, at 349. Similarly, although some claim that the nation-state has become increasingly irrelevant to the market amid globalization, it may be more accurate to acknowledge state intervention on behalf of the freedom of increasingly transnational corporations. In fact, William Cavanaugh identifies government subsidies for corporate pursuits or cases of the government running enormous deficits while cutting taxes on corporations as interventions that are less overtly coercive but consequential nonetheless. William T. Cavanaugh, "Migrant, Tourist, Pilgrim, Monk," 342. Cavanaugh likewise characterizes the "rhetoric of borderlessness" as deceptive: "Transnational corporations are not really transnational, for almost all are based in the West . . . The globalized economy . . . depends upon the maintenance of a center and a periphery . . . the primary boundary, then, that globalization must constantly reinforce is that between the modern and the premodern, the developed and the undeveloped" (348).

49. During 2010–11 the United States witnessed the latest iteration of efforts to enact legislation with libertarian rationales, such as Wisconsin's efforts to severely limit union bargaining rights or the budget and debt ceiling debates that cloaked cuts to social services for the poor and elderly in the philosophy of Ayn Rand.

50. See Ian Fletcher, *Free Trade Doesn't Work.*

51. Orlando O. Espín, "Immigration, Territory and Globalization," 50.

52. Gorringe, "Invoking," 353.

53. Duncan, *The Greatest Story Oversold*, 44.

54. Ibid., 44. Bill Moyers has similarly characterized free market economics as the nation's dominant religion. He elaborates: "Its god is profit. Its heaven is the corporate board room. Its hell is regulation. Its Bible is the *Wall Street Journal.* Its choir of angels is the corporate media." Interview with author and economist Thomas Frank, *Now*, Public Broadcasting System, broadcast February 1, 2002 as cited in Duncan, *The Greatest Story Oversold*, 44.

55. Duncan, *The Greatest Story Oversold*, 47–48.

56. Catholic Bishops of Appalachia, "This Land Is Home to Me: A Pastoral Letter on Powerlessness in Appalachia" (Webster Springs, WV: Catholic Committee of Appalachia, 1975), 493–94 as cited in Sniegocki, *Catholic Social Teaching*, 333.

57. José Ignacio González Faus, "The Utopia of the Human Family," 100. Here González Faus refers to the work of Jeremy Rifkin, *The End of Work*, 42ff. Dean Brackley characterizes the consumer society as one in which everything can be bought and sold and "social relations become more and more market relations" (Brackley, "A Radical Ethos," 21).

58. Gorringe, "Invoking," 354. Orlando Espín argues that the Catholic Church's catholicity and unity can dismantle the barriers globalization imposes, offering diversity in the face of globalization's homogenizing trends and equality and respect in the face of its inequity. Espín, "Immigration, Territory and Globalization," 55.

59. Marcelo M. Suárez-Orozco, "Right Moves? Immigration, Globalization, Utopia and Dystopia?" in Nancy Foner, ed., *American Arrivals*, 45–74, at 46.

60. He calls the entire process "an expression of ingratitude, disrespect and contempt, a claim to domination inherent in the imperial worldview." Gorringe, "Invoking," 354.

61. Vandana Shiva, "New Emperors, Old Clothes," *Ecologist Online*, available at www.the ecologist.org/blogs_and_comments/commentators/other_comments/268520/new_emperors _old_clothes.html (accessed June 23, 2011) as cited in John Sniegocki, "Neoliberal Globalization," 334. Neoconservative critiques of this connection between first-world wealth and the deprivation of those left behind (and of Catholic social thought's critiques of unjust patterns of globalization) are present in the work of Michael Novak, for example. See *The Spirit of Democratic Capitalism.* For an overview of the differences between critiques reflected in the work of Novak (as well as George Weigel and Richard John Neuhas) and that of Pope John Paul II, see John Sniegocki, "The Social Ethics of Pope John Paul II."

62. Sniegocki, "Neoliberal Globalization," 334.

63. Its notion of integral development likewise emphasizes factors such as "just distribution, ecological sustainability, and the impacts of economic policies on community, culture and spiritual well-being." Sniegocki, "Neoliberal Globalization," 338.

64. Pope Benedict XVI, *Sacramentum caritatis*, no. 90 (cf. James 5:4).

65. Benedict's subsequent summons surpasses a merit-based or a legal sense of justice to demand practices and institutions marked by reciprocity, friendship, even mercy. He contends that "without internal forms of solidarity and mutual trust, the market cannot completely fulfill its proper economic function." Pope Benedict XVI, *Caritas in veritate*, no. 35.

66. David Hollenbach, *The Common Good*, 242.

67. Jonathan Seglow, "The Ethics of Immigration," 318. For a comprehensive overview of other contributing push factors, such as human rights infringements, violent conflict, and environmental degradation, see David Hollenbach, *Driven from Home.*

68. Wolfgang Reinicke, "Global Public Policy," 130.

69. Schreiter, *The New Catholicity*, 5–6. Further, nations exercised far less sovereign control over the persons moving across their borders prior to World War I, so irregular migration flows are a relatively recent phenomenon. Christopher Llanos, "Refugees or Economic Migrants: Catholic Thought on the Moral Roots of the Distinction," in Hollenbach, *Driven from Home*, 249–69, at 251.

70. Marcelo M. Suarez-Orozco, "Right Moves? Immigration, Globalization, Utopia and Dystopia?" in Nancy Foner, ed., *American Arrivals*, 45–74, at 50.

71. Ibid., 51.

72. Seglow, "Ethics of Immigration," 318.

73. Seyla Benhabib calls this "one of the most promising aspects of contemporary political globalization processes," noting international human rights developments in areas of crimes against humanity, genocide and war crimes, and humanitarian interventions. Seyla Benhabib, *Another Cosmopolitanism*, 27–29. See also Hollenbach, *The Common Good*, 215.

74. Ibid., 231.

75. Saskia Sassen, *Globalization and Its Discontents*, 6–8. Sassen names The Convention of Hague of 1930, the 1952 Convention of Refugees, GATT, and NAFTA as examples in this regard.

76. See Hannah Arendt, *The Origins of Totalitarianism*, chapter 9. Building on Arendt's sentiment, Supreme Court chief justice Earl Warren insisted, "Citizenship is man's basic right for it is nothing less than the right to have rights. Remove this priceless possession and there remains a stateless person, disgraced and degraded in the eyes of his countrymen. He has no lawful claim to protection from any nation, and no nation may assert rights on his behalf. His very existence is at the sufferance of the state within whose borders he happens to be." Dissent in *Perez v. Brownell* as cited in Mae M. Ngai, *Impossible Subjects*, 229.

77. Ngai, *Impossible Subjects*, 4–5.

78. William O'Neill, "Rights of Passage." Relying on John Rawls, O'Neill argues that "'positive' obligations extend primarily to fellow citizens privy to the social contract underlying the moral legitimacy of the State. In such 'closed social systems,' noncitizens are owed the duty of forebearance; but as 'aliens,' they lack legal title to the primary good of citizenship and its attendant claim-rights" (115–16). See John Rawls, *Political Liberalism*, 41.

79. Sassen, *Globalization and Its Discontents*, 6–8.

80. Ibid., 12–13.

81. Ibid., 24–26. See also Benhabib, *Another Cosmopolitanism*, 175. Benhabib identifies a concomitant development as the "disaggregation of citizenship." She notes that as institutional developments unbundle three constitutive dimensions of citizenship—collective identity, the privileges of political membership, and the entitlements of social rights and benefits—an increasing number of people worldwide "find themselves not sharing in the collective identity of their host countries while enjoying certain rights and benefits as guest workers or permanent residents" (45).

82. Ibid., 46–47.

83. Arash Abizadeh, "Closed Borders, Human Rights, and Democractic Legitimation," in Hollenbach, *Driven from Home*, 147–68, at 150–53. See also Seglow, "Ethics of Immigration," 319. As Benhabib notes, for some this more universalist perspective signifies an enlightened

moral attitude that does not elevate "love of country" above love of humankind (see Martha Nussbaum, "Patriotism and Cosmopolitanism," in *For Love of Country,* ed. Joshua Cohen, 2–20 (the essay originally appeared in *Boston Review* (October/November 1994). For others, she notes, "cosmopolitanism signifies hybridity, fluidity, and recognizing the fractured and internally riven character of human selves and citizens, whose complex aspirations cannot be circumscribed by national fantasies and primordial communities." See Jeremy Waldron, "Minority Cultures and the Cosmopolitical Alternative," in *The Rights of Minority Cultures,* ed. Will Kymlicka, and Benhabib, *Another Cosmopolitanism,* 19.

84. Benhabib advances cosmopolitan norms that frame the morality of law in a global context, governing relations among individuals in a global civil society. Benhabib, *Another Cosmopolitanism,* 20.

85. See Kwame Anthony Appiah, "Cosmopolitan Patriots," in Cohen, ed., *For Love of Country,* 21–29.

86. Walzer, *Spheres of Justice,* 31.

87. Seglow, 320. Walzer concedes a principle of "mutual aid" in cases where strangers "have no other place to go," but he claims citizens have no formal obligations in this regard. See Walzer, *Spheres of Justice,* 45–46.

88. Walzer, *Spheres of Justice,* 62.

89. Seglow, "Ethics of Immigration," 321.

90. Ibid., 323–24, 330.

91. For a critique of liberal egalitarian arguments for open and closed borders, see Arash Abizadeh, "Closed Borders, Human Rights, and Democractic Legitimation," 147–68.

92. O'Neill, "Rights of Passage," 115–16. Claim rights entail substantive responsibilities on the part of other parties toward the right-holder beyond immunities from intrusion or coercion.

93. Ibid., 116. He cites Hannah Arendt, "The Perplexities of the Rights of Man," in *The Origins of Totalitarianism,* 297.

94. William R. O'Neill, "Anamnestic Solidarity: Immigration from the Perspective of Restorative Justice," paper delivered at the 2009 Catholic Theological Society of America (Halifax, Nova Scotia), June 5, 2009.

95. O'Neill, "Rights of Passage," 123. O'Neill alludes to the call in *Gaudium et spes* to "make ourselves the neighbor of every person without exception." Second Vatican Council, *Gaudium et spes,* no. 27.

96. O'Neill, "Rights of Passage," 123. O'Neill quotes here the "Universal Declaration of Human Rights," 310.

97. As O'Neill puts it, in the Catholic tradition the common good "entails neither the collectivist subordination of the individual to a suprapersonal entity such as the State or ethnic group, nor the reductive individualism of modern liberalism. For the common good is conceived distributively, not en masse, as 'the sum total of those conditions of social living' which protect and promote the dignity and rights of every person, including, a fortiori, their rights of effective participation in civil society and the state." O'Neill, "Anamnestic Solidarity."

98. Donald Kerwin, "Toward a Catholic Vision of Nationality," 203. The Church charges the state with the duty of reception of immigrants if consistent with the common good. See Pope John XXIII, *Pacem in terris,* 106.

99. Kerwin, "Toward a Catholic Vision of Nationality," 205.

100. Donald Kerwin, "Rights, the Common Good, and Sovereignty in Service of the Human Person," in *And You Welcomed Me,* ed. Donald Kerwin and Jill Marie Gerschutz, 93–122, at 95. This conception is rooted in a Thomistic sense that humans need the state because we are

social rather than an Augustinian-read-through-Reformers sense of the need for the state to restrain sin. See Michael J. Himes and Kenneth R. Himes, *Fullness of Faith*, 30–32. John Courtney Murray understood the service of the human person as the state's reason as connecting the moral and juridical orders.

101. O'Neill, "Rights of Passage," 123.

102. Llanos, "Refugees or Economic Migrants," 259. Llanos emphasizes that this political failure is the ground of the refugee claim, including economic refugees, rather than the severity of deprivation (258–59).

103. United States Conference of Catholic Bishops and *Conferencia del Episcopado Mexicano*, "Strangers No Longer: Together on the Journey of Hope" (Washington, DC: USCCB, 2003) no. 39. The bishops' conferences assert that the right of a sovereign state to control its borders in order to promote the common good and the human right to migrate in order to realize God-given rights are complementary, for while reasonable limits may be set, the common good is served when basic human rights are not violated.

104. Ibid., no. 36.

105. Kerwin, "Toward a Catholic Vision of Nationality," 205.

106. Kevin Doran argues that the terms express different ways of considering the moral obligation to solidarity and do not necessarily contradict one another. Kevin P. Doran, *Solidarity*, 192–93.

107. John Paul II, *Solicitudo rei socialis*, no. 40.

108. Ibid., no. 39.

109. David Hollenbach, "The Life of the Human Community," 7. Hollenbach develops these distinct forms of solidarity in his book on the *Common Good and Christian Ethics*.

110. Ibid., 7. Joseph S. Nye, Jr. coined the term "globalization's democratic deficit" for the exclusive membership of such international organizations; see Nye, "Globalization's Democratic Deficit."

111. Pope John Paul II, *Centesimus annus*, in *Catholic Social Thought*, ed. David J O'Brien and Thomas A. Shannon, 463.

112. Hollenbach, *Common Good*, 225.

113. Ibid., 224, 237.

114. Institutional solidarity responds to de facto relativized state sovereignty by proactively making it instrumental to not only "the comprehensive good of international cooperation but, ultimately, to the common good of all nations." Christopher Steck, "Solidarity, Citizenship, and Globalization," 165–66.

115. Ibid., 164.

116. Benedict XVI, *Caritas in veritate*, no. 62.

117. Andrés Solimano, *International Migration*, 190–91.

118. James E. Hug, "Economic Justice and Globalization," in *Globalization and Catholic Social Thought*, ed. John A. Coleman and William F. Ryan, 55–71, at 61.

119. Duncan, *The Greatest Story Oversold*, 116. NAFTA's two supplemental agreements include the North American Agreement on Environmental Cooperation (NAAEC) and the North American Agreement on Labor Cooperation (NAALC).

120. Hollenbach counsels the cultivation of social and intellectual solidarity in addition to institutional solidarity. My attention to incarnational and conflictual solidarity here would complement rather than supersede these dimensions. Social solidarity, challenges forms of globalization that reinforce existing patterns of exclusion and intellectual solidarity moves beyond unengaged tolerance to risk genuine conversation across difference and divisions about the good life. See Hollenbach, *The Common Good*, chapters 2 and 8.

121. Christine Firer Hinze, "The Drama of Social Sin," 448.

122. See John Mahoney, *The Making of Moral Theology*. See also Hinze, "The Drama of Social Sin," 448.

123. Since Christians have functioned as occupiers and as the voice for occupied alike, it is unsurprising that modern Christian theological and practical analyses of empire fall on a continuum from resistance and rejection to complicity and reinforcement.

124. Christine Firer Hinze, "Straining toward Solidarity in a Suffering World: *Gaudium et spes* 'After Forty Years,'" in *Vatican II*, ed. William Madges, 165–95, at 180.

125. Ibid., 181–82.

126. Ibid., 174.

127. Vincent Miller, *Consuming Religion*, 137. For an analysis of Internet technology that closely parallels Miller's commodification critique see Jaron Lanier, *You Are Not a Gadget*.

128. Christine D. Pohl, *Making Room*, 91.

129. Gregory Boyle, *Tattoos on the Heart*, 190.

130. Hinze, "Straining toward Solidarity," 175.

131. Miller, *Consuming Religion*, 205.

132. Cavanaugh, "Migrant, Tourist, Pilgrim, Monk," 352.

133. Miller, *Consuming Religion*, 183. For theological reflections on household, community and political strategies in this regard, see Pamela K. Brubaker, Rebecca Todd Peters, and Laura A. Stivers, eds., *Justice in a Global Economy*.

134. Dean Brackley, "Higher Standards for Higher Education: The Christian University and Solidarity," address delivered at Creighton University, Omaha (November 4, 1999), available at http://onlineministries.creighton.edu/CollaborativeMinistry/Martyrs/UCA/brackley.html (accessed May 1, 2011).

135. Hinze, "Straining toward Solidarity," 184.

136. Sobrino, "Redeeming Globalization," 109, 112.

137. Mark W. Potter, "Solidarity as Spiritual Exercise."

138. Ibid., 836–37.

139. David Hollenbach, *Claims in Conflict*, 204.

140. Hinze, "The Drama of Social Sin," 448, drawing upon John Paul II, *Centesimus annus*, no. 58.

141. Hinze, "The Drama of Social Sin," 447.

142. See Mary Hobgood, *Catholic Social Teaching and Economic Theory*, chapter 6.

143. Hinze, "Straining toward Solidarity," 178. See also Sniegocki, *Catholic Social Teaching*, 314, and the critiques posed by Gregory Baum, Donal Dorr, Mary Hobgood, and Larry Rasmussen. Miller, *Consuming Religion*, 178. See also Charles E. Curran, *Catholic Social Teaching*, 85–91.

144. Other observers level similar critiques, as Massingale notes: William K. Tabb, "John Paul II and Fidel Castro: Two Views of Development," and Mary E. Hobgood, "Conflicting Paradigms in Social Analysis," both in *The Logic of Solidarity*, ed. Gregory Baum and Robert Ellsberg. See Massingale, "*Vox Victimarum, Vox Dei*," 81–82. Like Malcolm X, Martin Luther King was convinced that "privileged groups seldom give up their privileges voluntarily." Rev. Martin Luther King, Jr., "Letter from Birmingham Jail" (April 16, 1963). Just after this passage King invokes Reinhold Niebuhr: "Individuals may see the moral light and voluntarily give up their unjust posture; but, as Reinhold Niebuhr has reminded us, groups tend to be more immoral than individuals."

145. Frederick Douglass, "West Indian Emancipation Speech," August 4, 1857. The text of this address can be found in Lerone Bennett, Jr., *Before the Mayflower*, 160–61.

146. Massingale, "*Vox Victimarum, Vox Dei,*" 83.

147. Sniegocki, *Catholic Social Teaching,* 294. Mary Hobgood argues that urging class collaboration is to demand the impossible within present capitalist systems: "Contrary to the view in Catholic social teaching that the problem is distribution rather than the organization of production, radical analysis demonstrates that the process of generating wealth cannot be separated from the process of generating the maldistribution of wealth. Although there may be temporary alliances, genuine, long-term cooperation between capitalists and the rest of the society is ruled out by the very dynamics of the system." Hobgood, *Catholic Social Teaching and Economic Theory,* 239–40.

148. Massingale, "*Vox Victimarum, Vox Dei,*" 84. Sally Scholz similarly characterizes "political solidarity" as oppositional in nature and informed by the influence of strong moral obligations. Scholz, *Political Solidarity,* 36.

149. Bryan Massingale, "The Scandal of Poverty," 61.

150. See Gregory Baum, *Theology and Society* (New York: Paulist Press, 1987), 32–47 as cited in Sniegocki, *Catholic Social Teaching,* 315. The US bishops reflect some of the shortcomings of a nonconflictual solidarity when they caution that the preferential option for the poor should not be interpreted as pitting groups or classes against one another, highlighting the need for cooperation and partnership in a harmonious, consensual mode of social change. Sniegocki, *Catholic Social Teaching,* 320–21. Sniegocki notes that a notable exception to this downplaying of social struggle in US bishops' documents are those by the bishops of the Appalachia region, such as "This Land Is Home to Me: A Pastoral Letter on Powerlessness in Appalachia" (1975) and "At Home in the Web of Life: A Pastoral Message on Sustainable Communities" (1995).

151. Bryan Massingale, *Racial Justice and the Catholic Church,* 120.

152. Duncan, *The Greatest Story Oversold,* 125. Mary Hobgood also uses the term "preferential option for the rich" to describe capitalism. See Hobgood, *Catholic Social Teaching and Economic Theory,* 242.

153. Second Vatican Council, *Gaudium et spes,* no. 63. See also Denis Goulet, *The Cruel Choice,* 170 as cited in Sniegocki, *Catholic Social Teaching,* 314.

154. Australian Catholic Bishops Conference, "A New Beginning: Eradicating Poverty in our World" (1996), 68, as cited in Sniegocki, *Catholic Social Teaching,* 320.

155. See my discussion of John Paul II's circumscription of social sin in chapter 2. In addition, perhaps reflecting his history of engagement with liberation theology, Benedict XVI neglects to include in *Caritas in veritate* any references to social sin or the option for the poor, even within discussions of distributive injustices or dangerous ideologies and sinful effects evident in the economy.

156. Niebuhr's distinct approach better attunes us to the profound challenges facing structural conversion as he "tracks the way sinful self-interest clouds awareness of structural sin, confounds efforts to understand it, and removes the motivation to combat it." See Hinze, "The Drama of Social Sin," 457.

157. Christine Firer Hinze, "Over, Under, Around, and Through." She cites Bruno Chenu Claude Prud'Homme, France Quere, and Jean-Claude Thomas, *The Book of Christian Martyrs,* 28–29.

158. Abizadeh, "Closed Borders, Human Rights," 153, 159. For a discussion of displacement of persons due to economic degradation and climate change, see Mary M. DeLorey, "Economic and Environmental Displacement: Implications for Durable Solutions," in Hollenbach, *Driven from Home,* 231–48.

159. Hinze notes that affluent Catholics' "mediocre reception" is matched by "Catholic leadership's less-than-insistent proclamation of teachings on social sin and solidarity." Hinze, "The Drama of Social Sin," 458.

160. Contrasting the US bishops' treatment of issues related to the church's social doctrine to those related to "human life and marriage," Vince Miller notes that "the bishops are unwilling to directly confront policies and Catholic partisans who dissent on other points of social teaching" and that "absent a serious media strategy" or "high profile ecclesial exchange" on socioeconomic matters, existing efforts "have almost no effect on public life or the faith of Catholics." Miller, "A Memo to the Bishops."

161. He also notes that from globalization's "radical critics" the tradition could gain a deeper analysis of capitalism's inner dynamics rather than focusing on end results of capitalist systems and ideologies. For an overview of policy alternatives advanced by grassroots critics, see Sniegocki, *Catholic Social Teaching,* chapter 6.

162. Ibid., 302.

163. Ibid., 295.

164. Sniegocki, "Neoliberal Globalization," 339.

165. Consejo Episcopal Latinoamericano (CELAM), *Globalization and the New Evangelization in Latin America and the Caribbean,* trans. Walter Blake (Bogota, Colombia: Publications CELAM, 2003), no. 117.

166. Federation of Asian Bishops' Conferences, "Journeying Together toward the Third Millennium," in *For All the Peoples of Asia,* ed. Rosales and Arévalo, 277–78. The Canadian bishops have also called for a broad-based, grassroots movement to redress social and economic injustice. Episcopal Commission for Social Affairs, "Supporting Labour Unions—A Christian Responsibility," in *Do Justice,* ed. E. F. Sheridan, 455. See also Sniegocki, *Catholic Social Teaching,* 317–20.

CHAPTER FIVE

Civic Kinship and Subversive Hospitality

A Christian Immigration Ethic

If the abolition of slave-manacles
began as a vision of hands without manacles,
then this is the year;

—MARTÍN ESPADA, "Imagine the Angels of Bread"

FOLLOWING NAFTA'S FAILURE to deliver returns on Mexican development, the consequent surge in irregular migration was met with an appre-
hensive-to-hostile reception amid an increasingly divisive political landscape.
The events of September 11, 2001, played a role in diverting a binational path
heading toward positive reforms at the time. The George W. Bush administration was attempting to build bipartisan support around guest worker and
earned amnesty program proposals, and Mexican President Vicente Fox
pledged to combat illegal trafficking and migration through and from his
country. Following September 11, these initiatives came to a halt and congressional and administrative efforts turned toward severely restricting entry and
strengthening enforcement mechanisms.[1] As the economic downturn beginning in 2007 hit, rising unemployment rates only heightened anxieties about
immigrant competition with native-born residents for jobs, and concerns
about the deficit cast doubt on the country's ability to absorb additional low-
wage workers.[2] The United States has typically alternated between peaks of
anti-immigrant sentiment (during the 1840s, 1920s, 1970s, and, arguably, the
2000s) and more hospitable stances, typically during periods of economic
growth.[3] The combination of these forces has produced paralysis for comprehensive immigration policy, and state and local governments have enacted
legislation to attempt to redress matters at local levels. Ostensibly to take federal enforcement shortcomings into their own hands, states like Arizona,
South Carolina, Georgia, and Alabama enacted punitive measures that damage

immigrant families as well as community safety, local economies, and constitutional protections.[4]

Amid this shifting milieu marked by new fears along with more timeless temptations to power and security, the immigration debate has been framed in hyperbolic and often misleading terms that distract from actual motives and consequences for migrants and communities. Talking points that highlight scarce resources, scheming lawbreakers, or demographic threats often fail to register the pervasive realities of ruptured family lives and gender-based violence examined herein. One of the contributions Christian theology can offer is to unmask these frames for what they are, and reveal what reigning motives sanctify. In other words, scrutinizing dominant rhetoric sheds light on the interests and values that principally drive immigration practices. Immigration is a sufficiently complex issue without the predominant bait-and-switch techniques. We have encountered throughout the text how both self-legitimating, lofty rhetoric, and blatantly anti-immigrant rhetoric serve to distort reality and scapegoat victims. In extreme cases, the same interests that engineer punitive ordinances under the ruse of community protection have a financial stake in private detention facilities.[5] More diffuse subterfuge occurs as the same constituents who demonize immigrants and pit them against native-born workers support trade agreements and hiring practices that ensure an expendable labor force.

The violence wreaked via this "narrative of the lie," to use Robert Schreiter's term, issues broken lives and indicates the urgency of truth-telling and Christian critique.[6] This chapter considers ways in which dominant factors shaping the immigration debate—such as rule of law and sovereignty defenses or private industry interests—mask realities and become surrogates for other cultural and political concerns. Having elaborated basic Christian commitments as reorienting values—relational agency, family flourishing, solidarity—I conclude with attention to both how such resources ultimately shape an immigration ethic, and how migrant experiences can in turn inform normative frameworks. A Christian ethic of immigration marked by kinship offers signposts for what justice requires in the life of the state and civil society, the family, the economy, and the academy.

Rule of Law?

As the dynamics of social sin and collective egotism profiled have shown, complex factors contribute to the distortions and assumptions that characterize the immigration debate. In some instances, deceitful tendencies are driven by misinformation rather than malice: Contrary to popular belief, whereas undocumented immigrants receive some of the public benefits that citizens do, the Congressional Budget Office reports that in the aggregate and over the long term, the tax benefits immigrants generate exceed the cost of services they use.[7] Between 50 to 75 percent of undocumented immigrants pay federal, state, and local taxes: Those working without a false Social Security number pay sales and property taxes, whether directly or indirectly, and those working with false IDs contribute as much as $9 billion a year to the Social Security fund.[8] Misinformation about immigrant crime rates also abounds, whereas crime rates in US cities with large immigrant populations (as in the nation at large) have, in fact, declined at the same time undocumented immigration surpassed historic highs in recent decades.[9]

In other cases, anxiety fuels hostile reception, whether economically based amid wage stagnation, or cultural and race-based in the face of perceived threats to national identity. Shifts in the tenor of cable news and talk radio discourse fuel and reflect these anxieties.[10] As people fear their dominant language or cultural cohesion under siege, the manner in which they feel threatened influences how they judge others.[11] William O'Neill suggests that "the modern carceral imagination eclipses the common good, and with the criminal or alien, or criminal alien, it is difference as such that we punish, blurring the line between retribution and vengeance."[12] As with an enforcement-centered immigration approach, the punitive regime remains largely unquestioned and the social contract itself an economy of exclusion.[13] One of the scripts dominating the immigration debate is that of willful lawbreaking; as we have seen, the realities of irregular immigration present a more complex story, particularly when we consider the inadequacy and impact of current law and the failure of approaches that begin and end with enforcement.

The bait-and-switch pattern shaping the immigration debate is evident in the widespread reference to the rule of law. At a general level, the debate over immigration tends to assign negative outcomes associated with immigration to irregular immigrants and benign or positive ones to legal immigrants; yet as political scientist Peter Skerry insists, "while this formulation may provide convenient cover to politicians and policymakers, it drastically distorts reality. Certainly the social-order effects of immigration do not easily fit into this neat legal-illegal paradigm."[14] It is understandable that notions of rule of law play a significant role in US immigration discussions, given the prominent role legal values play in the nation's self-conception.[15] How the rule of law functions, however, requires critical analysis.

Whereas the rule of law occupies a privileged place in a country whose membership is based on a commitment to shared ideals rather than nationality or race, it is important to distinguish its limits and how its value is employed. The democratic process legitimizes laws, yet it does not guarantee they are just or nondiscriminatory laws, much less fairly applied to vulnerable persons.[16] As Donald Kerwin distinguishes, "the rule of law means more than 'law and order,'" for a core principle of the UN Declaration of Human Rights holds that "human rights should be protected by the rule of law."[17] At present the immigration system in the United States lacks many attributes of a legal system that we would understand as honoring the rule of law: laws that are written and prospective in form, serve a substantive good such as respect for human rights, and are the project of a credible and legitimate legal system.[18] By contrast, legal reform reports have criticized various aspects of the US immigration laws at odds with this complement of features: their retroactivity, inconsistent application, lack of proportionality, procedural unfairness (in terms of the effects of availability of legal counsel and assignment of particular judges on the strengths of immigrants' claims), and failure to comport with basic due process norms.[19] Hence despite protectionists' charges that undocumented immigration and its supporters undermine respect for the rule of law, when the present system fails to protect fundamental human rights in these ways, it does not itself honor the rule of law.

From his experiences representing immigrants, Thomas Greene laments that their treatment by the judiciary evidences their devaluation by society. He notes that immigration judges may be appointed without prior immigration law experience or demonstrating adequate training.[20] By contrast, a district judge in New Mexico has undergone a change of heart and mind during his years on the federal bench. In six years Robert C. Brack, district judge for the United States District Court of Las Cruces, has averaged 100 felony sentencings per month (most judges average approximately seventy-five felonies per year), 95 percent of them immigration-related.[21] His experiences have convinced the Bush appointee that those who come before him are not criminals, but parents trying to feed their families who are bearing the brunt of broken policies.[22] In response to those who reject amnesty as rewarding lawbreakers, Brack suggests that the current voluntary return policy in which we sometimes apprehend and repatriate people *twice in the same day* in fact encourages people to break the law.[23] His reflections suggest the inadequacy of rule-of-law-oriented condemnations:

> Of course they come across. If they try to cross the border there are three possible outcomes, and only one is bad. They can die trying to cross, which is

bad, but mostly they don't. Mostly they either make it across, which is good, or they get a free ride back to the border where they can try again to cross the border, and they know nothing will happen to them. That's good too, but here's the thing: After letting folks go back and try again to cross fifteen times, on the sixteenth time, we charge them with a felony attempt to reenter, and they end up in my courtroom where I have to sentence them as felons.[24]

If ineffective as a deterrent, the government-funded industry that has evolved is booming financially. In the mid-1970s there were five public defenders, two lifetime-appointed judges, and one magistrate in Tucson, Arizona; today the city boasts five lifetime judges, seven magistrates, 40 public defenders, and 60 assistant US attorneys.[25] Under Operation Streamline, the cost to prosecute defendants averages $10,000 a day and $50,000 per week.[26] The number of detainees who agreed to deportation without appearing before a judge increased fivefold from 2004 to 2007, and approximately 95 percent of those who consented to fast-track deportations since 1999 were not represented by lawyers.[27]

Whereas the maxim was originally introduced to protect against arbitrary governance, the rule of law has been elevated in immigration debates as a fundamental litmus test of US identity—and hence inviolable. Otherwise law-abiding immigrants who enter or remain in the United States without proper documents are cast as criminals. Unauthorized immigrants do not commit a felony by crossing the border; entering the country illegally is classified as a federal misdemeanor, whereas simply lacking legal immigration status is a civil violation. A rhetorical criminal frame facilitates condemning immigrants as lawbreakers who threaten law and order rather than evoking skepticism about the faulty structures and outdated policies examined herein. Evoking rule of law has offered some who support local anti-immigrant measures a platform for legislating a certain quality of life and excluding those who do not fit their conception of what it means to be American.[28]

Daniel Kanstroom has written about the related evolution of deportation's function: Since its expansion from border control to postentry social control laws in the early twentieth century, deportation has come to serve not only as part of the US immigration control system but also as a "key feature of the national security state, and a most tangible component of the recurrent episodes of xenophobia that have bedeviled our nation of immigrants." He characterizes deportation as a mechanism of scapegoating, family and community separation, and banishment. Echoing the patterns outlined in chapter 1, he suggests this function "lives in a peculiar equipoise with our society's openness to legal immigration, our legal system's general protections for the rights of noncitizens, and our grant of birthright citizenship to virtually all persons born on U.S. soil."[29]

Beyond using rule of law and its procedural defenses in counterproductive or ideologically harmful ways, different senses of the law get conflated in immigration discourse. Much of the discussion focusing on irregular immigrants as lawbreakers fails to distinguish between different types of law or levels of binding force, whereas given the stakes explored herein, distinct types of law are at work: "laws of nations that control borders; laws of human nature that lead people to seek opportunities for more dignified lives; natural law that deals with ethical dimensions of responding to those in need; and divine law that expresses the Creator's will for all people."[30] Human laws are valid only according to the extent they reflect God's eternal law, according to Thomas Aquinas. The impact of present laws we have reviewed throughout indicates a disconnect between certain civil laws and the natural law. Hence the affirmation of laws for their own sake—particularly given the suffering some inflict—suggests "that international borders are more deserving of protection than are the humans who cross them. Such an approach renders to Caesar what belongs to God."[31] Bishop Thomas Wenski puts the fallacy plainly: "The so-called 'illegals' are so not because they wish to defy the law, but because the law does not provide them with any channels to regularize their status in our country—which needs their labor; they are not breaking the law, the law is breaking them."[32] The transcendent *telos* of the common good cautions Christians against elevating law to an idolatrous status.

Just as the Catholic tradition rejects sovereignty as an expression of absolute power, so it cautions against absolutizing security as an idol.[33] Elevating narrow visions of sovereignty or rule of law divorced from the protection of human rights of the vulnerable continues to harm migrants under the guise of fundamental American values. Mae Ngai details the consequences of sovereignty's central place in immigration policy: "It has allowed Congress to create, as even the Supreme Court described, 'rules that would be unacceptable if applied to citizens.' Second, it has marginalized or erased other issues from consideration in policy formation, such as human rights and the global distribution of wealth"[34] Despite diversionary rhetoric to the contrary, the human rights violations of irregular immigrants—before, during, and after their stay—undermine the rule of law and its legitimacy.

Immigration-Industrial Complex

In contrast to the trumpeted support for rule of law, the pervasive commodification of migrants is rarely recognized as such. Whether in the treatment of family farmers by trade policy architects, unaccompanied women by traffickers, contingent workers by managers, or future offspring by lawmakers and pundits, we repeatedly encounter not only a latent economic idolatry at play but also an instrumentalization of migrants at odds with persons' intrinsic value. The increasing tolerance for reductive epithets has not been limited to fringe militant organizations or extremist media portrayals. Steve King (R-Iowa) "stood in the House chamber assembling a mock-up of a border fence, with concrete wall panels and coiled wire on top, to show how simple immigration reform could be. We could electrify the wire, he said: 'We do that with livestock all the time.'"[35] In a House Appropriations Committee discussion about the problem of feral swine in Kansas, Rep. Virgil Peck (R-Tyro) suggested "if shooting these immigrating feral hogs works, maybe we have found a (solution) to our illegal immigration problem."[36] In sharp contrast to assumptions that migrants are themselves illegal or far worse, Christians should recall that "persons can engage in illegal movements but their Creator does not do illegal things."[37]

Commodification practices extend to a privatized prison industry that profits from the prevailing enforcement-heavy approach that defers comprehensive reform. In 2009 the US government detained over 383,000 people in immigration custody in 350 facilities, and its immigrant detention system is expected to cost tax payers $2.75 billion in 2012.[38] The cost of detaining an immigrant averages $122 per person per day.[39] Over 67 percent of these facilities include the space the Department of Homeland Security purchases from over 312 county and city prisons nationwide, and 17 percent in contract detention facilities.[40] Immigrants detained in local jails are combined with local prison populations serving time for criminal offenses.[41] The steady shift to privatized detention results in lower wages and benefits for personnel and diminished public oversight and accountability. Privatization is defended as more efficient and cost-effective (with roots of accelerated privatization in all sectors during the 1980s), yet the billion-dollar industries of detention and deportation have inflicted human costs.

As companies and local governments vie to profit off of detainees, immigrants and their attorneys report abuses and egregious conditions.[42] The level of opacity concomitant with detention contracting has made the tracking of detainees and defense of their rights difficult; some ICE facilities confine people in unmarked commercial or office park settings.[43] With expansion and lack of regulation, detention conditions have worsened, with reports of overcrowding and inadequate ventilation, food, health care, telephone access, and functioning showers, together with pervasive physical and verbal abuse.[44] The private prison corporations have seen revenues and stock prices soar, and they regularly lobby for more detention facilities and funding. As Ohio Congressman Ted Strickland, a former correctional officer, testified in 2000: "For-profit prisons have created a multibillion dollar industry and are as likely to be traded on Wall Street as be listed as defendants in litigation."[45] Corrections Corporation of America has enjoyed record profits annually since 2003, earning $1.67 billion in revenue with a net income of $155 million in 2009.[46] Thus the burgeoning immigration-industrial complex conflates not only national security with immigration law enforcement, but also public and private sector interests with the criminalization of undocumented migration.[47]

These reigning methods privilege violence and profiteering alike. Despite its ineffectiveness as a deterrent, the United States proceeds with militarizing the border—the Border Patrol remains the largest arms-bearing branch of the US government outside of the military itself.[48] Through its immigrant detention system, as it does with other native-born populations, the nation continues to incarcerate its "social problems."[49] This raises troubling questions about the justification for the use of force and coercion to protect a certain way of life at a cost to the vulnerable.[50] In a 2005 survey of 603 returned migrants and first-time migrants conducted by the Center for Comparative Immigration Studies at the University of San Diego, nearly two-thirds indicated they knew someone personally who had died trying to enter the United States clandestinely.[51] Following enhanced Border Patrol operations since 1993 (with Hold the Line in Texas, Gatekeeper in California, Safeguard in Arizona, and Rio Grande in southern Texas), eight out of ten interviewed stated that crossing the border undetected had become more dangerous than in previous years. Yet even when migrants had suffered physical harm in their most recent crossing or knew someone who died crossing the border, they were "significantly *more* likely to risk a crossing themselves, indicating that even awareness of the risk of death does not deter entry."[52] Hence militarized borders and punitive measures have not delivered the desired effect of stemming irregular flows, even as they are championed and funded in the name of protecting the cherished rule of law.

Christian Ethics: Reorienting Immigration Rhetoric and Realities

The immigration-industrial complex and militarized borders indicate how patterns of dehumanization explored throughout the book rely on a narrow view of justice and reductive view of migrants as threats. These violent and instrumentalizing undercurrents are not only masked by legitimizing rhetoric, but also, as signaled in chapter 2, themselves conceal the face of God insofar as they impede our grasp of authentic values.[53] The retributivist outlook revealed in rule of law rhetoric and detention industry practices engenders a calcification of divisions rather than a restoration of right relationships. An approach committed to truth-telling regarding the nation's historical confrontations with immigrant waves and repentance regarding its complicity in generating push and pull factors can move the debate beyond amnesic scapegoating. I have suggested throughout how attentiveness to actual migrants' experiences and motives together with Christian understandings of the nature of the human person, sin, family, and solidarity significantly reorient reigning paradigms and practices. The tradition's historic commitments to neighbor love and hospitality likewise shape its counternarrative of our common humanity, our kinship, with implications for a just immigration ethic.

The story of the Jewish and Christian pilgrim communities is one of migration, diaspora, and the call to live accordingly. The formative liberation of Israel by God from enslavement by the Egyptians led to commandments regarding hospitality to strangers (Ex 23:9; Lv 19:33–35; 24:22; Deut 14:28–29; 16:14; Num 15:15–16; 35:15). Indeed, after the commandment to worship one God, no moral imperative is repeated more frequently in the Old Testament than the command to care for the stranger.[54] Moreover, the people of Israel are repeatedly commanded not to exploit the oppressed and the vulnerable, also relevant categories for our consideration of migrant workers.[55] When Joseph, Mary, and Jesus flee to Egypt, the émigré Holy Family becomes the archetype for every refugee family.[56]

In Jesus's parables such as the Good Samaritan (Lk 10:25–37) and the Last Judgment (Mt 25:31–46), he identifies neighbor love and just living with care for the vulnerable stranger among us. Hence, the Christian disciple "must become a neighbor to the despised stranger if she or he is to follow Jesus on 'the way.' In Jesus's reading of the law, 'the world with its sure arrangement of insiders and outsiders' is subverted by God's reign."[57] In *Deus caritas est*, Pope Benedict XVI notes that neighbor love enjoined by the Good Samaritan parable can no longer be limited to "the closely knit community of a single country or people." Rather, "Anyone who needs me, and whom I can help, is my neighbor . . . Love of God and love of neighbor have become one: In the least of the brethren we find Jesus himself, and in Jesus we find God."[58] Thus who constitute our neighbors does not depend on birthplace or possession of documents.[59]

This centrality of neighbor love does not reduce the immigration paradigm to charity or largesse, or move it out of the inclusive civic conversation, but enjoins justice. This summons does not circumvent basic fairness, which is already in short supply; as we have seen, the United States accepts their labor, taxes, and purchasing power, yet does not offer undocumented migrants the protection of its laws.[60] We have encountered legion examples of distributive, commutative, structural, and even legal injustice throughout, which Christian ethics bids citizens to resist and redress. The standard treatment of day laborers violates fundamental fairness in exchange (commutative justice). The regional juxtaposition of relative luxury and misery while basic needs go unmet challenges basic notions of distributive justice. The asymmetry and impact of free-trade agreements and utterly outmoded visa policies impede rather than empower persons' active participation in societal life (social justice).

At a basic level, then, what are receiving nations' responsibilities in justice? Justice requires, negatively, that countries refrain from creating or substantially contributing to situations that compel people to emigrate and that host countries refrain from exploiting or extorting undocumented laborers. Positively, receiving immigrants fleeing situations of dire economic need, offering citizenship protections to those they do employ, and developing policies that reflect actual labor needs and hiring practices and the protect family unity are obligations in justice.[61] David Hollenbach invokes the Kew Gardens Principle as a means to determine nations' positive ethical duties: Where "(a) there is a critical *need*; (b) the agent has *proximity* to the need; (c) the agent has the *capability* to respond; and (d) the agent is likely the *last resort* from whom help can be expected."[62] He argues existing special relationships (historical, political, economic, cultural or geographical) generate particular responsibilities to outsiders, particularly if the nation from which the displaced seek protection has contributed to migration factors or benefitted from the country of origin.[63] As the role the United States has played in shaping conditions that directly contribute to irregular migration has come into view throughout the book, this relational understanding of a host country's duties to undocumented immigrants in terms of restorative justice holds particular relevance.[64] A Christian outlook also calls forth more robust senses of justice as radical inclusion and as leavened by mercy, to which I now turn.[65]

Rather than restricting our moral understanding to adequately identifying my neighbor—strictly parsing out what we owe to whom, when, and under what circumstances, with what papers—Christians are invited to focus on "being the neighbor, selving as neighbor."[66] With a recollection of biblical narratives that recount humans' experience of God's hospitality, of our own being as gift (and ancestry as immigrant), Christians are called to restore the covenant in turn. As O'Neill elaborates this "anamnestic solidarity"—that is, recalling experiences and models of compassion that issue the Christian call to "go and do likewise" (Lk 10:37), as the Good Samaritan—the disciple "must enter the world of the *anawîm*, of the half-dead stranger," taking the victim's side as her own.[67] The radical hospitality that tutors our vision exceeds supererogatory pity or minimal justice. As James Keenan characterizes the richness of scriptural hospitality, "the host must understand the perspective of the alien."[68]

Jesus repeatedly serves as both host and guest in gospel narratives. He "preaches a radical hospitality to those in need, and . . . commands the same of anyone hoping to sit down at the messianic banquet."[69] Gospel hospitality is unqualified in nature, and its issuance converts lives—a despised tax collector, an estranged Samaritan woman, the exiled blind—even as it provokes animosity and criticism.[70] Far from narrowly circumscribed or withholding, in the image of the eschatological feast, "hospitality is offered not only to kin and kind, but also to those whose only claim is vulnerability and need."[71] Hence as a central biblical motif, "hospitality (*philoxenia*: love of the stranger) is constitutive of discipleship" just as "rights rhetoric is constitutive of, and not merely incidental to citizenship."[72]

Christine Pohl forwards a "radical subversive hospitality" that has been central to the Christian tradition historically as a "way of being the sacrament of God's love in the world."[73] She connects the recognition of Jesus in the stranger—celebrated in the example of *Las Posadas*—to a subversive hospitality that welcomes the "least."[74] This countercultural virtue entails action on behalf of those whom society excludes and discards. Given the power differentials between those whose citizenship or other status is marked by security and those who continue to live in fearful shadows, subversive hospitality demands the incarnational solidarity profiled in chapter 4. The complicity of would-be hosts in the dynamics of injustice also entails the lament and atonement signaled in chapter 2.

In light of the myriad ways US society excludes undocumented migrants, Miroslav Volf's movements from exclusion to embrace are particularly fruitful for a radical hospitality demanded in the present context: repentance, forgiveness, making space for the other, and the healing of memory.[75] The gospel narrative of hospitality as a road toward martyrdom suggests a "revolutionary displacement of the center."[76] Taking the victim's side as our own then enjoins not only compassion but also liberation. Just as the Good Samaritan promises additional recompense to the innkeeper, Christians are called to enter the world of the neighbor and "leave it in such a way that the neighbor is given freedom along with the very help that is offered."[77] The unfreedom of present and would-be migrants detailed herein pointedly illustrates the urgency of this responsibility.

Conceiving of our duties to one another not in terms of relative strangers but near and distant neighbors suggests significant shifts in the reigning paradigms observed: Gratuity is called for, not indebtedness; neighborliness over xenophobia; and solidarity instead of exclusion.[78] A stance of subversive hospitality penetrates ideologies that oppress and conceal, refusing to equate "law-abiding" with "just," worship at an altar of market fundamentalism, or abstract from concrete persons' suffering into theoretical debates alone. This chapter's final section suggests shifts in dominant emphases in Christian ethics that a posture of attentive hospitality also invites.

A subversive hospitality that "passes to the victim's side" shapes institutional obligations to protect human rights in more widely shared terms, as well.[79] As chapters 1 and 4 indicate, an expansive understanding of human rights and the nature of the political community grounds a defense of twin rights to emigration and immigration that generally privileges reception over exclusion. It is the tradition's affirmation of social and economic rights that establishes persons' rights *not to migrate* (fulfill those rights in their homeland) and *to migrate* (if they cannot support themselves or their families in their country of origin).[80] The state's purpose is to protect the common good of its citizens, and when the common good remains so distant from attainment that a population is deprived basic human rights, people may seek a new home elsewhere. Furthermore, the right to emigrate is empty without a corresponding right to immigrate, a point on which Catholic social thought remains unambiguous.[81]

Additional Christian foundations for the right to migrate remain consonant with some cosmopolitan political theories: an understanding of the universal destination of created goods and a social mortgage on private property.[82] A person's citizenship in a particular state, then, does not deprive her of membership in that human family nor "citizenship in that universal society."[83] This sense of cosmopolitan citizenship (just as thicker notions of kinship) challenges absolute understandings of sovereignty, as we have seen. For in contrast to the dominant political discourse absolutizing sovereignty claims, sovereignty and hospitality are mutually implicating in Catholic social thought, with legitimate exercises of sovereignty dependent upon prior demands of human rights protections and basic conditions of social justice.[84]

Given the kudzu-like operative values and exclusive, exploitative practices evident throughout, the demands of justice and subversive hospitality require bold and creative rather than reformist macro-solutions to avoid replicating unjust patterns and tendencies. The impact of neoliberal globalization and cultural commodification commend proposals that orient economics toward integral human development and total family well-being by utilizing inclusive democratic processes to determine the sharing of social benefits and burdens.[85] Given reigning models and gendered experiences of migration and globalization, strategies that reposition persons rather than capital at the center can only be achieved with women's coequal and meaningful participation.[86]

Even as subversive hospitality and anamnestic solidarity demand more fundamental changes, constraints of the present context invite simultaneous efforts at collaboration open to compromise. Approximating justice between the times will always fall short, but the well-being of the vulnerable amid legitimate pluralism requires pursuing imperfect efforts, even if a piecemeal legislative approach risks dirty hands, tests patience, or tempts despair. Despite the changes in the global economy outlined in chapter 4, the United States has not significantly changed its legal immigration system for over twenty years and has not overhauled it since 1965.[87] Whereas a Christian immigration ethic requires more than a policy response, it necessarily entails attention to the politically possible in light of the stakes of ongoing suffering.

POLICY CONTOURS

Immigration regulation retains a significant purpose for a people to exert some influence over the shape of their present and future, yet the impact of policies and practices detailed herein makes clear the moral limits to such regulation require reconsideration.[88] Given the demands of justice sketched above, the United States has obligations to redress its role in abetting irregular migration and to offer those who live and work within its borders a viable path to earned legalization. Often dismissed as an amnesty that rewards lawbreakers, earned legalization proposals typically yoke lawful permanent residence to conditions such as continuous employment, payment of a fine, rigorous criminal background and security screenings, and English proficiency.[89] Earned legalization programs should safeguard against imposing disproportionately burdensome requirements; for example, undocumented women and children may be adversely impacted by employment-based, language competency or continuous residency requirements. Just as through community involvement (long-term residence and good conduct) undocumented residents can work toward citizenship in other countries, migrant workers in the United States likewise embedded in and contributing to their host society should be afforded permanent residency with the possibility of US citizenship.[90] Given that nearly two-thirds of undocumented immigrants living in the United States have resided in the country for at least ten years, mass deportation is impractical and unjust. At a minimum, a path to legal residency for minors brought to the United States like the one offered by the decade-long attempted DREAM Act is overdue.

In view of the outdated visa allocations detailed in chapter 3, a new worker visa program responsive to actual employment needs (for both agricultural and nonagricultural low wage workers) is also urgently needed. Whereas temporary or guest worker programs have historically proven vulnerable to abuses, many migrants continue to express the desire for legal avenues for seasonal (agricultural or construction) work in the United States. Approaches in this vein would improve upon the present de facto guest worker program of undocumented labor, but should include labor protections with adequate enforcement, job portability, and personal mobility.

Reform of family visa backlogs and inadequate country quotas to allot more Western Hemisphere visas will help expedite family reunification; at present the United States allocates the same number of visas to neighboring Mexico as to Botswana and Nepal.[91] Unjust costs to migrants and to communities necessitate reforming border security and enforcement regimes that respect core principles of due process and reflect the nature of civil violations as well as mitigating the local costs of accommodation (e.g., federal revenue sharing should disperse funds to states with large immigrant populations by having populations used in the revenue formula reflect foreign-born residents). Establishing a standing commission on immigration to advise Congress regularly on warranted adjustments on an ongoing basis would provide flexibility and help ensure the United States does not reinvent the immigration reform wheel every few decades.[92] Mechanisms that offer enforcement authorities more flexibility in exercising discretion in immigration cases are also warranted, in light of the complex factors and relationships that pressures to fill detention beds or fast-track deportations override.

Reorienting the immigration paradigm in terms of transnational human rights also suggests that reform efforts need to take a more holistic approach appropriate to the interconnected dimensions investigated herein. Initiatives will need to better integrate trade, development, labor, border security, detention, and family unification policies to approach the intersecting considerations from a comprehensive if not fully transnational perspective. Whereas US policymakers have indicated an awareness of connections between the conditions in origin or sending countries and migration patterns since the early twentieth century, the relationship between migration and development policy has remain unsettled. Immigration policies are shaped primarily by domestic concerns (often in isolation), whereas international development policies respond to different administrative concerns.[93] We have noted that economic liberalization has opened capital but not labor flows, and, in the words of economist Gordon Hanson, there has never developed a "Washington consensus" on international migration.[94]

Most immigrants to the United States hail from middle-income countries, whereas most development aid is targeted toward low-income countries (each of which faces a distinct set of issues). Given the inability of those in greatest need to migrate, pursuing trade equity and longer-term development and investment that do not replicate the destructive patterns of the recent past would align reform efforts toward more future-oriented solutions with a wider reach. In the service of protecting human rights, wealthy states' substantial duties to admit outsiders in need coexist with their duty to collaborate toward a more just global order.[95]

At home, care must be taken that reform efforts not accomplish greater justice for new immigrants at the expense of native-born low-wage workers. Legislative efforts should carefully consider the interplay between US obligations to those in need beyond its borders and to its own citizens. Earnings inequalities within the US labor market have increased dramatically in recent decades. The economic downturn beginning in 2007 has further exacerbated such effects, "as the rates of job destruction outpaced those of job creation for more than two years, leading to the net loss of several million jobs."[96] Additionally, globalization trends have reduced the availability of well-paid jobs in the goods-producing sectors, such as durable manufacturing, which have traditionally paid good wages to workers with a high school level education or less.[97] Whereas economists differ on whether undocumented immigration suppresses wages, fills needed gaps, or stimulates economies (and complex variables alter the dynamics in various locales), it is essential that duties to lower-wage citizens be considered alongside the impact of proposed reforms. Regularizing workers presently laboring in the informal sector, with such care taken, can potentially prevent native-born, low-wage workers from being undersold by unscrupulous employers looking to exploit the vulnerability of those without documents. To this end, reforms should incorporate an extension of core federal labor protections to unauthorized workers and strengthen penalties for violations to promote compliance.[98] Solutions that thus raise the floor for all workers must be sought.

Immigration policies will invariably need to achieve compromise in piecemeal fashion at first, given the challenge of achieving legislative consensus. Pitting constituents against one another—whether native-born vs. immigrant workers, or children vs. parents in the case of DREAM Act proposals—does violence to the common good and fails to consider pieces of the immigration puzzle in light of its whole. In some cases recognizing the moral priority of relative need (gravity and imminence of harm) will be necessary in elaborating policy guidelines, given particular vulnerabilities and complicities.[99] Ultimately an approach rooted in Christian commitments must both reduce the need to migrate and protect those who find themselves compelled to do so as a last resort. Taken together, such comprehensive measures not only serve justice and approximate hospitality, they better reflect the nation's own founding principles. The impact of inaction on immigration reform in the United States prompts reflection on who the nation has become: What does it honor by awarding personhood to corporations and excluding its tax-paying workers from labor protections, for example? Immigration debates compel national communities to confront deep questions of identity. Hence beyond needed legislative reform, a Christian immigration ethic must also address questions of how newcomers reshape national identity and a receiving community integrates newcomers.

INTEGRATION: CIVIC KINSHIP

While political debates typically focus upon immigration policies determining entry or employment, the United States lacks a coherent mechanism for addressing the integration of its foreign-born population—to the detriment of newcomers and shared civic life alike.[100] The cultural retrenchment outlined in chapter 1 violates an ethic of hospitality and presumes an American homogeneity that has never existed.[101] Those who distinguish their immigrant forebears from those today who "break the law to get ahead" conveniently overlook the generous immigration policies prior to World War I and the prejudices against "degraded races of Europe."[102] As I noted in chapter 4, the shifting nature of boundaries has provoked anxiety not only from senses of cultural loss or economic threat, but as part of a larger disorientation. The duties of new immigrants to contribute to host societies must be carried out against this backdrop dominated by dueling understandings of nationalism and integration.

In the first decade of the twenty-first century, debates over immigration have ensued amid a fragile sense of public commitment to the common good and diminished institutional capacities for incorporating newcomers. Noah Pickus attributes this not only to the dislocation caused by global markets, but also to the rise of a rights-oriented culture and the weakening of local government and traditional civic associations.[103] Within this setting, three basic theories of nationality continue to compete for primacy: the nativist, conservative civic nationalist, and liberal civic nationalist.[104] Represented in the historical waves referenced in chapter 1, a nativist view understands race, religion, ethnicity, culture, and blood as binding nations and therefore determining membership. On this view, immigrants possess inherited characteristics (like ethnicity) or must alter immutable characteristics (like religion) to belong.[105] This perspective (also identified as "ethnocultural nationalism") aims to exclude newcomers who lack the attributes of the people they wish to perpetuate.[106]

For civic nationalists, shared commitment to civic ideals—such as freedom, equality, rights, liberty, opportunity, and democracy—defines membership. In its conservative form, as represented in the ideas of Samuel Huntington alluded to earlier, ideology and culture are central to national identity; these typically include Anglo-Protestant values, the English language, a European artistic heritage, and the liberal democratic creed.[107] Conservative civic nationalism emphasizes the need for linguistic, civic, and patriotic assimilation into what they perceive to be a relatively fixed cultural identity, stressing exclusive loyalty to the American democracy (which causes many to oppose dual and birthright citizenship) and way of life, and fearing that high rates of immigration threaten to dilute national culture.[108]

Whereas liberal civic nationalists share a commitment to such democratic ideals, they hold that immigrants are able to embody and even renew such core values.[109] On their view most immigrants residing within US borders already share such commitments, and find themselves here without documents not due to a disavowal of the rule of law, but to an immigration system out of sync with labor needs that sets family unity in opposition to lawful obedience.[110] As a result, liberal civic nationalists typically favor systemic reform and an intentional commitment to foster immigrant integration. The groups differ on what binds the country's citizens—whether inherited attributes like ethnicity and race (nativism), a broader array of cultural beliefs and practices (conservative civic nationalism), or more "universal" values that overlap with the American creed (liberal civic nationalism).[111] Kerwin contends that whereas Catholic teaching does not align with a single theory of nationality, it supports some elements of each form of civic nationalism and strongly challenges exclusive understandings of political membership rooted in blood and history alone.[112]

I argue in chapter 1 that collective egotism is operative in ethnocultural nationalisms with destructive effects. Means of incorporating newcomers and inviting their contributions to the life of a common project, without diluting their particular histories and identities, are essential to effective and respectful integration. Given the landscape described, Pickus's centrist civic nationalism offers promise for both strengthening civic resources and fostering common aims. It falls to civil society, including NGOs and religious communities, to help cultivate a new civic nationalism that revalues shared identity and articulates community membership in a manner that forges the broadest possible political communities.[113] His approach resists more exclusionary forms of nationalism while fostering a meaningful, democratic form of citizenship that incorporates immigrants into a shared sense of belonging more robust than one based on principles alone.[114] Mediating institutions that support immigrants' agency and provide them with experience in the practice of civic values enable them "to participate in the core democratic endeavor of renewing their nation."[115] *Familismo* carriers can serve as forms of social capital vital to the integration of migrant families into mainstream society.

Both conceptually and practically incorporating immigrants—avoiding pitfalls of assimilation, Americanization, enculturation—are a fraught and daunting tasks. It is far easier for sedentary populations to decry the other's difference than take responsibility for encounter amid pluralism. Without dismissing the depth of competing visions of the good life, a commitment to civic nationalism (and democracy) bids diverse residents to coexist.[116] Seyla Benhabib reminds us that the geography of the outsider in fact remains fluid, "as many citizens are of migrant origin, and many nationals themselves are foreign-born." As a result, "practices of immigration and multiculturalism in contemporary democracies flow into one another."[117] In the US context, whereas Hispanics surpassed African Americans in 2003 to become the most populous pan-ethnic minority in the United States, there remains a tendency to uncritically lump them together as an undifferentiated racialized category.[118]

Mae Ngai argues that race and illegal status have historically remained closely connected throughout US history, and that "restrictive immigration laws produced new categories of racial difference."[119] She points out that whereas nationalism's ultimate defense is sovereignty, cultural pluralism is largely an immigrant invention born of newcomers' efforts to simultaneously retain their ethnic identity and be American. In 1915 philosopher Horace Kallen contested the idea that nationality groups be coercively Americanized and stripped of their cultural identities. Rather, he envisioned the United States as a "federation" or "democracy of nationalities," rejecting the image of a melting pot in favor of an orchestra, in which "every type of instrument has its specific timbre and tonality . . . as every type has its appropriate theme and melody, and the harmony and dissonances and discords of them all make the symphony of civilization."[120] The stories of courage and resilience signaled throughout offer narratives of how immigrants chime in and shape US identity, rather than defining identity in contractual terms or only over and against an evolving other.

US history offers cautionary tales for a nation of immigrants' ongoing integration project. Drawing upon Frederick Jackson Turner's frontier thesis that US social development experiences continual rebirth at the frontier, Roberto Goizueta interprets contemporary nativism as rooted in an understanding of the border as the new frontier:

> The modern frontier myth, or ideology, still underlying U.S. culture impedes our society's ability to promote "life, liberty, and the pursuit of happiness" at a time when the frontier has been replaced by the "border" as the central symbol of U.S. identity ad extra. In other words, late modernity is a world of borders; but, given our history, the profound fear of immigrants reflected in recent legislation suggests that U.S. society continues to view these borders through the lenses of a frontier myth, open to economic expansion but closed to human immigration . . . If the United States of the 1890s perceived national identity as linked to the western frontier, and thus feared a future with closed frontiers, contemporary political, military, and legislative attacks against immigrants suggest that the United States of the early twenty-first century perceives national identity as linked not to the frontier but to the "border," and fears a future with open borders.[121]

Identifying with Jesus (of Galilean borderlands), by contrast, entails kinship: an embrace of human difference and of the border as a place of encounter rather than a frontier of conquest.[122]

The mutual dynamics of solidarity outlined in chapter 4 remind participants that integration is an endeavor in which all parties have something to offer; thanks to ongoing encounter and new immigrants' contributions, the story of the United States (and the Americas) is not one that is static and therefore threatened but one marked by dynamic vitality. Raúl Fornet-Betancourt insists that the subjectivity of strangers must help constitute the new reality.[123] He calls not for a politics of integration or reestablishment of disrupted unity but a "politics of public recognition" that acknowledges strangers as subjects who have the right to live their culture.[124] Fornet-Betancourt's proposed "intercultural *convivencia*," which advocates the intercultural transformation of a culture and its members, diverges from static versions of culture that risk "collective narcissism" on the part of those who manipulate tradition at the service of social control rather than cultural development.[125] In the interim, he insists, as long as xenophobia is normalized we should practice a civil courage that welcomes strangers as citizens requiring protection.[126] Pursuing two-way integration that empowers migrants' participation requires substantive protection for such cultural rights (antiracism policies beyond benign neglect, for example) and processes of "exculturation" or attempts to extricate dehumanizing aspects of a receiving country's culture.[127]

The relational anthropology animating my critiques of dehumanizing practices across workplace, family, geopolitical, and detention venues throughout likewise informs a migration *integration* ethic. As Shawn Copeland has written, "if personhood is now understood to flow from formative living in community rather than individualism, from the embrace of difference and interdependence rather than their exclusion, then we can realize our personhood only in solidarity with the exploited, despised poor 'other.' In this praxis of solidarity, the 'other' retains all her (and his) 'otherness.'" Against tendencies to project fears onto reductive caricatures of migrants or demand unidirectional assimilation, Copeland's conclusion that "a new and authentic human 'we' emerges in this encounter" realized only in "the gift of grace" beckons us toward a new spirit of integrative, civic kinship.[128] Our irreducibly distinct yet irrevocably common humanity grounds a Christian immigration ethic that profoundly challenges present practices and conceptualizations alike. Subversive hospitality calls us to resist such dehumanization without taking flight from civic contexts of the shared task.

Migrants' Experiences: Reorienting Christian Ethics

As J. Kameron Carter posits, "whites are joining browns and blacks in diaspora, but what if the truth of our existence is sojourn, and therefore those who have lived in diaspora are our north star?"[129] The mutual dynamics necessary for integration in the spirit of *convivencia* and kinship prompts consideration of how Christian ethics' own commitments and methodologies must continually be informed and reformed by new voices. Goizueta's allusion to Jesus of the borderlands evokes God's identification with the marginalized and rejected, in particular. This peripheral focus does not simply compel social justice and charity, or yield principles for application.

Rather, as Goizueta writes, "if Juan Diego is to be evangelized, it will be through a dark-skinned Lady on Tepeyac, the sacred place of the Nahuas, not through a Spanish bishop in his palace. Indeed, through Guadalupe, the very relationship between evangelizer and evangelized is reversed: The indigenous man, Juan Diego, is sent to evangelize the bishop."[130] Heeding migrant experiences in settled lives and ethics safeguards against the frontier myth that erects fences at the border, that views the border as "the meeting point between savagery and civilization."[131] Migrant experiences throughout poignantly cast immigration as a life issue that demands prophetic and costly advocacy. Migrants' agency has also suggested the complexity of their subjectivity and inadequacy of idealized family norms. I turn now to ways in which migrant women's agency, in particular, challenges a focus on autonomy in dominant forms of Christian ethics. Let us not, like Bishop Juan de Zumárraga five centuries ago, "turn away Juan Diego as he approaches us bearing in his *tilma* the precious gift of God's great love for all of us."[132]

Letting migrants' experiences speak to the immigration debate interrogates a secular law and order ethic—yet attending to such voices also challenges narrow normative frameworks, as well. Even when Christian ethics is nourished by feminist theory, the latter risks focusing on the concerns of white, middle-class women leading to faulty assumptions that "relative economic security exists for mothers and families," and that "all women enjoy the racial privilege that allows them to see themselves primarily as individuals in search of personal autonomy, instead of as members of racial ethnic groups struggling for power."[133] *Mujerista* theologians have contributed enormously to the ongoing task of animating Christian praxis and epistemology with the distinctive experiences of US Latinas.

Womanist theologian Katie Canon's critique of the dominant moral tradition in light of African American experience is also instructive in considering the impact migrants' experiences have on Christian ethics.[134] Prevailing ethical frameworks tend to equate responsible action with conceiving of and executing actions with clear and predictable results, reflecting free self-determination.[135] In Canon's words, "the cherished ethical ideas predicated upon the existence of freedom and a wide range of choices prove null and void in situations of oppression. . . . Racism, gender discrimination, and economic exploitation, as inherited, age-long complexes, require the Black community to create and cultivate values and virtues in their own terms so that they prevail against the odds with moral integrity."[136] Building upon Canon's work on the impact of social power on moral agency, Sharon Welch distinguishes between an "ethic of control," which equates responsible action with control on the assumption one is free to "guarantee the efficacy of one's actions," and an "ethic of risk," which understands moral agency in terms of "responsible actions within the limits of bounded power" entailing "persistent defiance and resistance in the face of repeated defeats."[137] Insofar as the latter attends to strategic risk-taking and rootedness in community, it resonates with the fullness of migrant women's experience and the survival strategies struggling migrant families adopt.[138]

The experiences Canon recounts are not dissimilar from those of migrant women of color; her analysis also reflects the role of ideology and structural injustice examined in chapter 2. Considering the difference social and economic power make for the conception and execution of moral agency, the alternate ethic of risk acknowledges that actions may only lead to partial results but, amid a long-term struggle with oppressive situations, the goal of moral action is "the creation of new conditions of possibility for the future."[139] An ethic of risk thus entails redefining responsible action, in terms of "the creation of a matrix in which further actions are possible, the creation of the conditions of possibility for desired changes."[140] Whereas an ethic of control reflects but does not exhaust the tendencies of a secular protectionist ethic or idealized Christian family ethics, these distinctions help draw attention to consequences of constrained agency—damaging consequences that get diminished in frameworks that privilege autonomous control. An ethic of risk likewise seems more adequate to the task of accounting for the resourcefulness and courage migrant women exhibit than paradigms that privilege autonomy or efficacy.

Cynthia Crysdale rightly cautions that whereas the exercise of control *can* reflect misuse of power, insofar as it means claiming the power to act with probable consequences, it "can be instrumental in establishing resources of empowerment for those on the margins of society."[141] Our considerations of human rights in chapter 1 and structural and ideological factors in chapter 2 suggest we envision moral agency as integrating both control and risk, such that we seek to engender "conditions of possibility for agents to have more control over their lives and the systems that affect them," while attending to both structural and ideological injustice and the responsibilities of migrant women and those whose choices impact them. Crysdale's own hybrid of risk and control forwards a worthwhile end for this purpose: "The goal of one's actions may be to enhance *control* for those who lack it, but this goal will be undertaken in a stance of *risk*"—that is, a stance marked by redefinition of responsible action, grounding in community, and strategic resourcefulness over the long haul.[142]

Experiences from the underside of history, including those of migrant women profiled here, indicate that "to the degree that women have found themselves, proportionately, in social, economic and political roles that deny them moral agency, they are more aware of the fact that moral choice includes ambiguity, vulnerability and risk." This is not to suggest that vulnerability is the goal or that women are essentially different moral reasoners; rather, those who "suffer from the powerlessness of social class, race or sexual orientation are able to be more honest about the risk inherent in all moral choice."[143] These distinctions may help enlarge narrow normative frameworks with significance for our understanding of migrant women's agency and integrity.[144]

The impact of these daunting constraints also contextualizes moral judgments that too often focus upon individual acts in isolation. Bishop Kevin Dowling has testified to his accompaniment of women and their young children dying of AIDS in rusted zinc shacks near platinum mines in South Africa. He laments the structural injustices that conspire to force such undocumented economic refugees into what he terms "survival sex," alongside Church declarations that give the impression that HIV contraction results from free, sinful choices alone. "Where does one find in Church pronouncements a holistic awareness and systematic focus on the structural issues (economic, cultural and social) which affect the very possibility of making a free, moral choice or decision by the poor and vulnerable?" he recently pleaded.[145] As Paul Farmer similarly laments, "there is something unfair about using personal agency as a basis for assigning blame while simultaneously denying those blamed the opportunity to exert agency in their lives."[146]

The US criminal justice system and Christian churches alike too seldom focus on enduring structures and ideologies that abet crime and sin. The experiences of migrant women can help alert both spheres to these inadequate notions of agency. A migrant woman's decisions to have sexual relations with another male migrant (or inject contraceptives) to ensure safe passage, to abandon her children for better long-term prospects for them, or to work without documents or reside without authorization occur within constrained social contexts. These means are not morally or otherwise desirable, but understanding the realities shaping these choices highlights the shortcomings of individualistic paradigms and absolutist categories, and approaches that privilege autonomy or sexual purity. An ethic of risk resonates with the ways in which immigrants' initiatives establish conditions for the possibility of change, shifting probabilities toward meaningful survival, including even their willingness to repeatedly undertake perilous border crossing journeys.[147]

Insights from migrant women further inform a responsive and responsible Christian ethic for those in positions of power and vulnerability alike. We have seen how scapegoating and subterfuge via false narratives conceal; it is important to bear in mind ways in which dominant ethical frameworks likewise mask complex realities and genuine values when they overlook the experiences of seemingly vulnerable agents. This oversight risks sinful complicity, for ideals founded on privileged social locations "sustain the cruel innocence of the privileged and the harmful economic arrangements that create 'others.'"[148] The limits of an ethic of control highlight the shortcomings of dominant modes of Christian ethics for penetrating the full moral experience of marginalized subjects. Rather than contending with patriarchal power in general or particular familial situations, "women of color are concerned with their power and powerlessness within an array of social institutions that frame their lives."[149] These social structures facilitate pervasive rights violations that threaten bodily integrity, dignified labor, and family unity. In response, as Ivone Gebara and María Pilar Aquino urge, Christians are called to make an option for the impoverished woman.[150]

Conclusions and Strategies for Change

Hence, even as fundamental Christian categories expose and squarely condemn pervasive threats to migrants' well-being, they remain inadequate to the fullness of their experience. Keeping the three-dimensionality of the immigrant in our range of vision—at once constrained and courageous, compromised and competent—remains essential for the work of ethics and the work of social change alike. Justice demands the protection and empowerment of immigrants amid the thicket of barriers they confront. Whereas economic and policy reforms offer important routes forward, a Christian immigration ethic invites concrete practices in other realms of our lives—personal, ecclesial, even financial—that reflect commitments to kinship and justice.

As the discussion of incarnational solidarity in chapter 4 reveals, seemingly micro-level steps such as investigating where your food comes from or how those who clean your office are compensated directly connect to immigration issues. One of the more creative practices of incarnational solidarity I have encountered occurred at an event planned by my university's Labor Action Committee, which convened campus food services workers and undergraduates with the invited Day Laborer theater troupe for karaoke: The shared risk of making a fool out of oneself by singing off-key was a small but significant step toward dismantling power differentials and forging mutual understanding. One need not become a full-fledged urban homesteader to cease supporting major agribusiness offenders or reaping the benefits of laborers' underpayment. Patronizing "fair trade plus" farmer-owned cooperatives—such as Café Justo, which provides a living wage and benefits to Chiapans—helps stem reluctant migration.[151] Alternative channels of news and communication offer information from the perspective of the marginalized and about the work of grassroots organizations.[152] Habituating subversive hospitality thus extends across varied aspects of our daily lives.

As evident in the parish profiled in chapter 2, churches have served and accompanied immigrants through pastoral and charitable outreach, political advocacy campaigns, and community organizing efforts (for example, an interreligious PICO affiliate in San Jose has successfully improved relationships between law enforcement and immigrant communities in the face of new federal and local strategies). The Catholic, binational Kino Border Initiative in Ambos Nogales (Nogales, Arizona and Nogales, Sonora, Mexico) combines humanitarian assistance, formation, research, and advocacy modeling partnership and mutual "evangelization."[153] In their efforts moving forward, Christian churches should guard against defenses of immigrants motivated by waning members; if migrants' rights are human rights, their basic defense should not differ for Muslim refugees in Europe or for Protestant border-crossers from Mexico. As Bartolomé de las Casa cautioned, authentic evangelization "is utterly incompatible with conquest and destruction. Indeed it is the very opposite."[154]

Given that many churches and individuals heavily invest in the stock of multinational corporations, transferring significant portions of funds to socially and ecologically constructive alternatives can help foster just economic alternatives.[155] In terms of more direct shareholder advocacy, after six years of incremental dialogue, a Jesuit-led coalition's shareholder resolution on human rights was adopted by Chevron Corporation in 2010. Whereas the policy still leaves room for improvement, especially in terms of implementation and monitoring, its adoption affirms not only the need to promote human rights in the extractive sector, but more broadly Chevron's growing awareness of its "social footprint" and "potential as a force for integral human development."[156] Private sector engagement thus provides opportunities to educate transnational corporations about core principles that can help serve companies' ethical and fiduciary interests alike.[157]

The multidimensionality of immigration issues emphasized herein suggests the urgent need to convert attitudes and imaginations as well as change institutions and practices. Some argue that ethos must predate structural change, while others insist that as with the civil rights movement, the law will have to lead. Whereas fear of the other is easily mass-marketed, mutual understanding across difference can be more challenging to come by and engender. For those whose experiences remain far from border realities, second-hand encounters with the undocumented may provide a first step in shaping their imagination. José Arreola, recent college graduate, publicly broadcast his own example:

> We had to decide whether we were going north or south to get into California. My friend decided it was best to go south, to avoid a big snowstorm up north. But south would take us through Arizona. I really, really didn't want to go through Arizona.
>
> I got more and more nervous. I felt paralyzed. My friend kept asking me what my problem was. Finally, I told him: I'm undocumented. I came to the United States when I was three with my family. And Arizona had just passed a law that gave police officers the authority to check peoples' immigration status. If we got stopped in Arizona, I could be detained and deported.
>
> My friend is white. He comes from a really privileged, upper-class background. He attended a private high school, then Santa Clara University, with me. I went on scholarship. Politically, he sees things a little differently than I do. We've had our disagreements.
>
> He was quiet for a while.
>
> Then, he barraged me with questions. I answered the best that I could. Silence again.
>
> Then he told me about his grandfather, how he hadn't been able to find work in Ireland, so he decided to hop on a fishing boat, and get off in New York. He worked as a janitor, without citizenship. Now his son, my friend's father, is a high-ranking bank executive.

The whole time, through Arizona, my friend drove, like, 50 miles an hour. He didn't even wanna change lanes. He told me he wasn't gonna lose his best friend. He wasn't gonna let that happen.

The immigration debate became real to my friend in the car that day. We had a very different conversation than the one politicians are having right now. The minute actual undocumented immigrants are included, the conversation changes.

Now, I'm completely open about my status. I'm still afraid. Conversations don't always go well. And it's always a risk. But as long as I remain in the shadows, I will never really get to know you, and you will never really know me.[158]

José's courage, together with the resilience of so many others, witnesses to enduring hope. Christians are called to live in anticipation of a new heaven and a new earth (Is 65:17–25, Rev 21:1–4), cooperate with the abundance of life already inaugurated (Jn 10:10), and participate in the unfolding of God's kin-dom. May a praxis of subversive hospitality and kinship among all of earth's sojourners offer us "eschatological glimpses" toward its liberating reality.[159]

Martín Espada's poetry urges throughout the book to actively imagine beyond slavery and deprivation, with the hope that "this is the year." Let every mouth "fill with the angels of bread."[160]

Notes

The epigraph is reprinted with permission of Martín Espada.

1. For an overview of the legislative and structural changes impacting immigration apprehension and detention following the events of September 11, 2001, see Charles Hill and Donald Kerwin, "Immigration and Nationality Law." For further historical context on immigration law and policy in the US context, see Aristide R. Zolberg, *A Nation by Design*; Mary C. Waters and Reed Ueta, eds., *The New Americans*; and Alexandra Delano, *The Mexican Diaspora*.

2. Kate Brick, A. E. Challinor, and Marc R. Rosenblum, *Mexican and Central American Immigrants*, 16.

3. Aaron Terrazas, *Migration and Development*, 10. Noah Pickus cautions that whereas "economic interests have played a significant role in regulating the admission and incorporation of immigrants," they do not fully account for the treatment of newcomers in the United States: "Waves of restriction have not followed the turns of the economy. Neither the Naturalization Act of 1790 nor the National Origins Act of 1924 was passed in a period of extensive economic turmoil." Pickus, *True Faith and Allegiance*, 11.

4. On April 23, 2010, Governor Jan Brewer of Arizona signed into law an especially broad and stringent immigration bill (S.B. 1070), criminalizing the failure to carry immigration papers and granting police wide latitude to detain anyone suspected of being in the country

outside of legal channels. See Randal C. Archibold, "Arizona Enacts Stringent Law on Immigration," *New York Times* (April 24, 2010) A1. The 287(g) programs described in chapter 3 and the state measures like SB1070 and imitative measures raise concerns about the potential for racial profiling, dismantling community members' trust in local law enforcement officials, and diversion of resources.

5. For a discussion of close links between Arizona Senator Russel Pearce, the American Legislative Exchange Council (ALEC), and donations from prison lobbyists and prison companies such as ALEC-member Corrections Corporation of America and The Geo Group to thirty of thirty-six cosponsors of SB 1070, see Laura Sullivan, "Prison Economics Help Drive Arizona Immigration Law," *National Public Radio* (October 28, 2010) available at www.npr.org/tem plates/story/story.php?storyId = 130833741 (accessed June 1, 2011).

6. For a meditation on theological vocation as truth-telling see M. Shawn Copeland, "Racism and the Vocation of the Christian Theologian."

7. CATO Institute, CATO Handbook for Congress: Policy Recommendations for the 108th Congress, www.cato.org/pubs/handbook/hb108/hb108–63.pdf; Executive Office of the President: Council of Economic Advisors, "Immigration's Economic Impact," June 20, 2007, www.whitehouse.gov/cea/cea_immigration_062007.html; Congressional Budget Office, "The Impact of Unauthorized Immigrants on the Budgets of State and Local Governments" (December, 2007), accessed July 13, 2011.

8. Congressional Budget Office "The Impact of Unauthorized Immigrants," (Dec. 2007), 6; Immigration Policy Center, "Undocumented Immigrants as Taxpayers" (November 2007), www.ailf.org/ipc/factchecks/UndocumentedasTaxpayer.pdf (accessed July 13, 2011). A 2006 poll conducted by ABC News and *The Washington Post* found that one-third of US citizens cited irregular immigrants' use of more public services than they pay for in taxes as their chief objection to their presence in the country.

9. From 1994 to 2005 the violent crime rate declined by 34.2 percent overall. See Rubén G. Rumbaut and Walter A. Ewing, "The Myth of Immigrant Criminality and the Paradox of Assimilation: Incarceration Rates among Native and Foreign-Born Men" (Washington, DC: American Immigration Law Foundation), 2007.

10. Nationalistic inhospitality is not unique to the (post–September 11) US context; anti-immigration parties have burgeoned in Western Europe, as well: Vlams Bloc in Belgium, Freedom Party in Austria, People's Party in Denmark, and Front National in France. See Marcelo M. Suarez-Orozco, "Right Moves? Immigration, Globalizaiton, Utopia and Dystopia?" in Nancy Foner, ed., *American Arrivals*, 45–74, at 47.

11. I am indebted to Stephen J. Pope for this insight.

12. William O'Neill, "Response to 'The Last Judgment: Christian Ethics in a Legal Culture,'" Catholic Theological Society of America annual convention (June 11, 2011).

13. Ibid.

14. Peter Skerry, "Immigration and Social Disorder," in (eds.), *Uniting America*, ed. N. Garfinkle and D. Yankelovich, 124–38, at 126.

15. Mary Ann Glendon, "Principled Immigration," *First Things* (June/July 2006), available at www.firstthings.com/article/2007/12/principled-immigration (accessed July 1, 2011).

16. Donald Kerwin, "Rights, the Common Good, and Sovereignty in Service of the Human Person," in *And You Welcomed Me*, ed. Donald Kerwin and Jill Marie Gerschutz, 93–122, at 111.

17. Ibid.

18. Ibid., 111. Here Kerwin draws on the work of Brian Tamanaha, *On the Rule of Law*, 110.

19. Kerwin, "Rights, the Common Good and Sovereignty," 111. For an excellent analysis of the US deportation system on this score, see Daniel Kanstroom, *Deportation Nation*, chapter 6.

20. Thomas Greene, "Families and Social Order" panel presentation, annual meeting of the Society of Christian Ethics (January 4, 2008), Atlanta, GA.

21. A Catholic, Brack reflects, "I don't find that faith is something I can compartmentalize, and faith has tenderized my heart toward everyone I meet." See Ben Daniel, *Neighbor*, 75–77 (Daniel interviewed Judge Brack for his book).

22. Operation Streamline was introduced in 2005, routing border crossers (whether first-time or repeat, with or without criminal records) through the federal criminal justice system rather than civil deportation proceedings. The fast-track program facilitates the resolution of federal criminal cases (with prison and deportation consequences) in two days or less.

23. Daniel, *Neighbor*, 80. Emphasis added.

24. Ibid. 77.

25. Tom Roberts, "A 'Maddening' System, from Courtrooms to Shelters," *National Catholic Reporter* (July 1, 2011), available at http://ncronline.org/news/immigration-and-church/maddening-system-courtrooms-shelters (accessed July 1, 2011).

26. Ibid.

27. Anna Gorman, "Concerns Arise over Fast-Track Deportation Program," *Los Angeles Times* (March 2, 2009).

28. Caroline B. Brettell and Faith G. Nibbs, "Immigrant Suburban Settlement," 17.

29. Kanstroom argues that the Supreme Court's incremental and uncritical acceptance of such laws "has rendered tenuous any claims by noncitizens to concrete, substantive, constitutional rights against, for example, retroactive deportation or deportation for espousing unpopular ideas." Kanstroom, *Deportation Nation*, 5.

30. Daniel Groody, "Crossing the Divide," 638–67.

31. Daniel, *Neighbor*, 52.

32. Most Reverend Thomas Wenski, "U.S. Immigration Policy Outdated and Unjust toward Working Immigrants," Diocese of Orlando, FL, website (May 13, 2005), available at www.orlandodiocese.org/en/btw-columns/item/228-us-immigration-policy-outdated-and-unjust-toward-working-immigrants-%E2%80%93-may-13-2005 (accessed June 21, 2011). Bishop Wenski chairs the US bishops' migration committee.

33. Donald Kerwin, "The Natural Rights of Migrants and Newcomers: A Challenge to U.S. Law and Policy," Daniel Groody and Gioacchino Campese, eds., *A Promised Land*, 192–209, at 204.

34. Mae M. Ngai, *Impossible Subjects*, 12.

35. Editorial, "Immigration Hardball," *New York Times* (November 14, 2010).

36. Representative Peck later issued an apology. Todd Fertig, "Rep. Apologizes for Remark about Shooting Illegal Immigrants," *The Wichita Eagle* (March 16, 2011), available at www.kansas.com/2011/03/16/1764580/rep-apologizes-for-remark.html; nsixzz1GmNOnv iR (accessed June 28, 2011).

37. Rev. Fr. Michael A. Blume, S.V.D., Pontifical Council for the Pastoral Care of Migrants and Itinerant People, *Migration and the Social Doctrine of the Church*, Part 1(e) (2002), available at www.vatican.va/roman_curia/pontifical_councils/migrants/pom2002_88_90/rc_pc_migrants_pom88-89_blume.htm (accessed June 22, 2011).

38. According to the *Washington Post*, "with roughly 1.6 million immigrants in some stage of immigration proceedings, the government holds more detainees a night than Clarion Hotels have guests, operates nearly as many vehicles as Greyhound has buses and flies more people

each day than do many small U.S. airlines." Spencer S. Hsu and Sylvia Moreno, "Border Policy's Success Strains Resources," *Washington Post* (February 2, 2007), available at www.wash ingtonpost.com/wp-dyn/content/article/2007/02/01/AR2007020102238.html (accessed July 12, 2011). See also Migration Policy Institute, "Immigrant Detention under Scrutiny in Australia, United Kingdom, and the United States" (December 1, 2011), available at www.migrationin formation.org/Feature/display.cfm?id = 868.

39. The Detention Watch Network indicates that "Alternatives to detention, which gener- ally include a combination of reporting and electronic monitoring, are effective and signifi- cantly cheaper, with some programs costing as little as $12 per day. These alternatives to detention still yield an estimated 93% appearance rate before the immigration courts." Further, the "delegation of detention management reduces ICE's incentive to utilize more humane alternatives to detention, even though alternatives may be more cost-effective." Detention Watch Network, "About the Deportation and Detention System" available at http://www .detentionwatchnetwork.org/aboutdetention (accessed July 1, 2011); Detention Watch Net- work, "The Money Trail," available at http://detentionwatchnetwork.org/node/2393 (accessed July 1, 2011).

40. The remaining13 percent are detained in ICE-owned facilities with 3 percent in other facilities such as those run by the Bureau of Prisons. Detention Watch Network, "The Impact of Enforcement," available at www.detentionwatchnetwork.org/node/2382 (accessed July 1, 2011). In 2006, DHS ended "catch and release," a practice wherein the Border Patrol released apprehended non-Mexican migrants into the United States, where they awaited removal hear- ings. Catch and release was a way of coping with overcrowded immigrant detention facilities. As part of the Secure Border Initiative DHS increased detention bed space and shortened stays in detention facilities by expanding the use of expedited removal. Expedited removals accounted for more than 25 percent of all removals in 2009. See Jeanne Batalova and Kristen McCabe, "Immigration Enforcement in the United States," *Migration Information Source* (Washington, DC: Migration Policy Institute, 2010) available at www.migrationinformation .org/USFocus/display.cfm?ID = 806#23 (accessed July 1, 2010). The Obama administration created the Office of Detention Policy and Planning in August 2009 to make the system more closely resemble a civil detention system. The Office of Detention Oversight was created to improve federal monitoring of ICE's detention facilities.

41. Roughly half of all immigrants detained have no criminal record; the remainder may have committed a crime in their past but have paid their societal debt. Detention Watch Net- work, "About the Deportation and Detention System."

42. For a discussion of the treatment of detainees by the Immigration and Naturalization Service and then Department of Homeland Security, see Mark Dow, *American Gulag*.

43. Detention Watch Network, "The Money Trail."

44. Anil Kalhan, "Rethinking Immigration Detention," 47. Based on a 2009 report by a then–senior Department of Homeland Security official (Dora Schriro), the government pledged to overhaul a detention regime acknowledged by the Schriro Report to be inappropri- ate to immigrants' noncriminal status. While the impact of the Obama Administration's pro- posed reforms remain to be seen, Kalhan warns that the proposals leave intact a range of practices that threaten detained noncitizens (e.g., the government is disinclined to implement stronger oversight mechanisms, enforceable detention standards, or stronger rules limiting transfers) 51–55.

45. Dow, *American Gulag*, 87.

46. Detention Watch Network reports that Corrections Corporation of America (CCA) "boasts being the sixth largest corrections system in the U.S., behind only 4 states and the

federal government. CCA operates 65 facilities in 19 states and the District of Columbia with more than 75,000 beds and nearly 17,000 employees. 12 of CCA's facilities are used to hold immigration detainees. CCA has been able to charge up to $200/day per bed in the Don T. Hutto family detention facility in Texas." Detention Watch Network, "The Money Trail."

47. Tanya Golash-Boza, "The Immigration Industrial Complex," 295. For an analysis of how the theories and methods of criminal law enforcement have been incorporated into immigration proceedings without criminal adjudication's procedural protections, see Stephen H. Legomsky, "The New Path of Immigration Law."

48. The vast majority of migrants apprehended in fortified corridors attempt to reenter within a couple of days. There is also "growing evidence that tighter border enforcement in the post-1993 period has lengthened the U.S. sojourns of unauthorized migrants and increased their probability of settling permanently in the United States." See Wayne A. Cornelius, "Introduction: Does Border Enforcement Deter Unauthorized Immigration?" in *Impacts of Border Enforcement on Mexican Migration* ed. Wayne A. Cornelius and Jessa M. Lewis, 1–15, at 5.

49. I am indebted to Maureen O'Connell's work in this regard.

50. Joseph H. Carens, "Aliens and Citizens: The Case for Open Borders."

51. The migrants interviewed were from Jalisco and Zacatecas, leading Mexican sending communities. Cornelius, "Introduction," 8–11. Nonetheless, given a more than 11:1 wage differential between minimum-wage jobs in the United States and in Mexico many opt to undertake the journey anyway. Seidy Gaytan, Evelyn Lucio, Fawad Shaiq, and Anjanette Urdanivia, "The Contemporary Migration Process" in Cornelius and Lewis, *Impacts of Border Enforcement*, 33–51, at 41.

52. Jezmin Fuentes, Henry L'Esperance, Raul Perez, and Caitlin White, "Impacts of U.S. Immigration Policies on Migration Behavior," in Cornelius and Lewis, *Impacts of Border Enforcement*, 53–73, at 54, 57, 59.

53. Mark O'Keefe, "Social Sin and Fundamental Option," in *Christian Freedom*, ed. Clayton N. Jefford, 131–43, at 141.

54. William O'Neill, "Rights of Passage." O'Neill cites W. Gunther Plaut, "Jewish Ethics and International Migrations," *International Migration Review: Ethics, Migration and Global Stewardship* 30 (Spring 1996), 18–36, at 20–21. For a comprehensive discussion of New Testament themes related to migration, see Donald Senior, " 'Beloved Aliens and Exiles: New Testament Perspectives on Migration," in Daniel G. Groody and Gioacchino Campese, *A Promised Land*, 20–34.

55. See Proverbs 31:8–9; Ecclesiastes 4:8–9; Jeremiah 22:3–4; Zechariah 7:8–11.

56. Pope Pius XII, *Exsul Familia* (On the Spiritual Care to Migrants), (September 30, 1952), in *The Church's Magna Charta for Migrants*, ed. Rev. Giulivo Tessarolo, PSSC (Staten Island, N.Y.: St. Charles Seminary, 1962), introduction.

57. William R. O'Neill and William C. Spohn, "Rights of Passage" at 103, citing Bernard Brandon Scott, *Hear Then the Parable: A Commentary on the Parables of Jesus* (Minneapolis: Fortress, 1989), 202.

58. Pope Benedict XVI, *Deus caritas est* (December 25, 2005), no. 15, available at www.vatican.va/holy_father/benedict_xvi/encyclicals/documents/hf_ben-xvi_enc_20051225_deus-caritas-est_en.html.

59. Bishop Nicholas DiMarzio, Chair, US Bishops' Committee on Domestic Policy, "Labor Day Statement 2006," *Origins* vol. 36, no. 13 (September 7, 2006), 201–4, at 204.

60. Cardinal Roger Mahony, "For Goodness Sake: Why America Needs Immigration Reform," *The Tidings Online* (February 11, 2011).

61. David Hollenbach forwarded similar priorities at the Woodstock Center's meeting on migration in Fairfield, CT (July 19, 2007).

62. David Hollenbach, "Internally Displaced People, Sovereignty, and the Responsibility to Protect," in Hollenbach, ed., *Refugee Rights*, 188 (emphasis in original).

63. Ibid., 7.

64. Hoeffner and Pistone, "But the Laborers Are . . . Many?" 74. For an excellent discussion of such connections see William R. O'Neill, "Anamnestic Solidarity: Immigration from the Perspective of Restorative Justice," paper delivered at the 2009 Catholic Theological Society of America Halifax, Nova Scotia (June 5, 2009). See also Kristin Heyer, "A Response to 'Restorative Justice as a Prophetic Path to Peace?'"

65. James Keenan suggests that mercy thickens notions of justice in Christian communities. See Daniel Harrington and James F. Keenan, *Jesus and Virtue Ethics*, 126.

66. William R. O'Neill, "Anamnestic Solidarity."

67. Ibid.

68. James Keenan, "Jesuit Hosptiality?" in Martin Tripole, ed., *Promises Renewed*, 234. For a discussion of the spirituality of hospitality in Jewish and Christian scriptures, see Gloria L. Schaab, "Which of These Was Neighbour?"

69. Patrick T. McCormick, *A Banqueter's Guide*, 47.

70. Schaab, "Which of These Was Neighbour?" 192–93.

71. William O'Neill, " 'No Longer Strangers,' " 230. O'Neill cites Amos 9:13–15; Joel 3:18; Isa 25:6–8; Matt 8:11; 22:1–14; Luke 14:12–24.

72. O'Neill, "Anamnestic Solidarity."

73. Christine D. Pohl, *Making Room*, 34.

74. *Las Posadas* entails the reenactment of Mary and Joseph's journey from Nazareth to Bethlehem in search of shelter (*posadas*) at the time of Jesus' birth. For nine days pilgrim participants go to homes seeking shelter, but are met with rejection; then at the last home they are welcomed and a celebration ensues. Celebrated in Mexico and Guatemala (and elsewhere in various forms) for centuries, in recent years *Las Posada Sin Fronteras* have been celebrated along stretches of the US–Mexico border fence, drawing attention to the plight of immigrants as illuminated by that of the Holy Family.

75. Mirsolav Volf, *Exclusion and Embrace*, 100; Volf, "From Exclusion to Embrace," in Felix Wilfred and Oscar Beozzo, eds., *Frontier Violations*, 95–103, at 95.

76. Ilsup Ahn, "Economy of 'Invisible Debt,' " 262. Ahn cites Kosuke Koyama, "Extended Hospitality to Strangers: A Missiology of Theologia Crucis," *Currents in Theology and Mission* 20.3, 165–76.

77. John R. Donahue, *The Gospel in Parable*, 133. I am indebted to Christopher Vogt's work for this reference.

78. Robert Schreiter, CSSP, "Theology's Contribution to (Im)migration," in Giacchino Campese and Pietro Ciallella, *Migration, Religious Experience and Globalization*, 170–81.

79. Behabib calls hospitality "a right that belongs to all human beings insofar as we view them as potential participants in a world republic." See Benhabib, *Another Cosmopolitanism*, 22. O'Neill uses "passes to the victim's side" in "Anamnestic Solidarity."

80. See Pope John XXIII, *Pacem in terris* (April 11, 1963), no. 106. All encyclical citations are taken from David J. O'Brien and Thomas A. Shannon, *Catholic Social Thought*, unless otherwise indicated. See also the United States Conference of Catholic Bishops, "Strangers No Longer," no. 34–35.

81. Christiansen adds, "The reasons that justify emigration equally justify immigration, and only 'grave requirements of the common good, considered objectively' permit making

exceptions to this rule." Christiansen, "Sacrament of Unity,"87–89, citing Sacred Congregation of Bishops, *Instruction on Pastoral Care of People Who Migrate* (Washington: USCC, 1969) no. 10. In *Pacem in Terris* John XXIII notes that a person has a right "to enter a political community where he hopes he can more fittingly provide a future for himself and his dependents," and the common good requires the host country fulfill its duty "to accept such immigrants and to help to integrate them into itself as new members" (no. 106).

82. Second Vatican Council, *Gaudium et spes*, 69, 71 see also *Catechism of the Catholic Church*, 2402. Pope John Paul II, *Sollicitudo rei socialis*, no. 42.

83. Pope John XXIII, *Pacem in terris*, no. 25.

84. See Anna Rowlands, "On the Temptations of Sovereignty," 860. See also Pope Pius XII, *Exsul Familia (On the Spiritual Care of Migrants)*, (September 30, 1952), in *The Church's Magna Charta for Migrants*, ed. Rev. Giulivo Tessarolo, PSCC (Staten Island, NY: St. Charles Seminary, 1962), 51, citing 1948 Vatican Letter to US Bishops and *Pacem in terris;* Pope Benedict XVI *Caritas in Veritate* no. 62. Since the time of Pius XII, official Catholic social teaching has "so thoroughly contested the right of sovereign powers of states to unqualified control of their borders that any assertion of sovereign rights in this area must be judged, from the point of view of Catholic social ethics, a secondary or residual right, not one of primary importance." The presumption in favor of state control of borders and regulation of the movement of peoples across its borders holds only "in exceptionally grave circumstances." Christiansen, "Sacrament of Unity," 88–89.

85. Albrecht alludes to versions of participatory economics or economic democracy in this vein, for example. Gloria H. Albrecht, *Hitting Home*, 151.

86. María Arcelia González Butron, "The Effects of Free-Market Globalization on Women's Lives," trans. Paul Burns, in *Globalization and Its Victims*, ed. Jon Sobrino and Felix Wilfred, 43–49, at 48.

87. Donald Kerwin and James Ziglar, "Fixing Immigration: Start by Making Legal Immigration Benefit Everyone," *America* (December 12, 2011).

88. Peter C. Meilaender, *Toward a Theory of Immigration*, 172.

89. Five major proposals for earned legalization were introduced in Congress from 2006–2011.

90. Saskia Sassen, *Territory, Authority, Rights*, 295.

91. Congress' imposition in 1976 (on the logic of formal equality) of country quotas of 20,000 on the Western Hemisphere and closure of a loophole in the law that had permitted undocumented Mexican immigrants with US-born children to legalize their status effectively recast Mexican immigration as illegal. Mae M. Ngai notes that the transfer of Mexican migration from legal to illegal form should have been expected, given that in the early 1960s annual "legal" Mexican migration "comprised some 200,000 *braceros* and 35,000 regular admissions for permanent residency." Deportations of undocumented Mexicans rose by 40 percent in 1968, to 151,000; then in 1976, when the 20,000 per country quota was imposed, it rose to 781,000, whereas the combined total number of apprehensions for all others in the world remained below 100,000 annually. Ngai, *Impossible Subjects*, 261. See also Douglass S. Massey, "Forum" (response to Carens) in Joseph Carens, *Immigrants and the Right to Stay*, 73–80, at 78.

92. This recommendation is made in the Brookings-Duke Immigration Policy Roundtable; its use here does not signify concurrence with all recommendations from that report. See William Galston, Noah Pickus and Peter Skerry, *Breaking the Immigration Stalemate: From Deep Disagreements to Constructive Proposals* (Washington, DC: The Brookings Institution and

Durham, NC: The Kenan Institute for Ethics), 2009, available at http://kenan.ethics.duke.edu/breaking-the-immigration-stalemate/ (accessed July 13, 2011).

93. Since the mid-1970s presidential commissions have identified development as the sole long-term solution to the challenge of irregular immigration from Latin America and the Caribbean; President Barack Obama reiterated this understanding during a visit to El Salvador in March 2011. Terrazas, *Migration and Development*, 11, 3, 20.

94. Gordon Hanson, "International Migration and Development," in *Equity and Growth in a Globalizing World*, eds. Ravi Kanbur and Michael Spence, 229–62 as cited in Terrazas, *Migration and Development*, 19. Whereas immigrants contributed to development in their countries of origin prior to the 1970s without an explicit policy link, during the mid-1970s and 1980s growing immigration led policymakers to seek a "development solution" to irregular immigration's challenges. From the mid-1980s to mid-1990s, as we saw in chapter 4, policymakers embraced openness to economic globalization, and in the subsequent years the increased immigration from the developing world has prompted US development agencies to begin to think beyond remittances and promote partnerships with diasporas as an element of their strategies. See Terrazas, *Migration and Development*, 10–18

95. Jonathan Seglow, "The Ethics of Immigration," 329. The comprehensive claim rights recognized by Catholic social thought and some cosmopolitan approaches far exceed the principles of human rights law regarding migrants.

96. Harry J. Holzer, Julia I. Lane, David B. Rosenblum, and Fredrik Andersson, *Where Are All the Good Jobs Going?*, 3.

97. In fact, the share of US workers employed in durable manufacturing has fallen from about 12 percent in 1970 to 6 percent in 2008 as both technology and globalization reduced the demand for domestic labor in these jobs." Holzer, Lane, Rosenblum, and Andersson, *Where Are All the Good Jobs Going?*, 7.

98. See Donald Kerwin, *Labor Standards Enforcement and Low-Wage Immigrants: Creating an Effective Enforcement System* (Washington, DC: Migration Policy Institute, 2011), available at: www.migrationpolicy.org/pubs/laborstandards-2011.pdf (accessed July 14, 2011).

99. O'Neill, "Anamnestic Solidarity."

100. Donald Kerwin, "The Natural Rights of Migrants and Newcomers: A Challenge to U.S. Law and Policy," in Groody and Campese, *A Promised Land*, 192–209, at 197.

101. Schaab, "Which of These Was Neighbour?" 198.

102. Prior to World War I the US government excluded only 1 percent of the 25 million immigrants who arrived at Ellis Island (largely for health reasons with the exception of Chinese immigrants excluded on the grounds of "racial unassimilability"). Statutes of limitations of one to five years also ensured those living in the country unlawfully did not live long-term under the threat of deportation. The quotas imposed by Congress after World War I "created illegal immigration as a mass phenomenon." Mae Ngai, "How Grandma Got Legal," *Los Angeles Times* (May 16, 2006).

103. Pickus, *True Faith and Allegiance*, 1.

104. Pickus designates four prominent conceptions of citizenship—immigrant rights, minority representation, cultural nationalism, and universal nationalism—that mark the contemporary US landscape: "The rights position stresses fundamentally human (rather than civic or national) basis to freedom and equality. It especially dismisses feelings of belonging at the national level. The minority representation perspective is also wary of claims about national attachment; it prizes ethnic coalition building and multicultural policies that advance the standing of immigrants. The cultural position values abstract civic ideals, especially notions of negative freedom, but regards them as realizable only in a thick cultural or racial context. In

contrast, universal nationalists believe that citizenship is a matter of political artifice and who constitutes 'we the people' is more a matter of consent than culture." Pickus, *True Faith and Allegiance*, 146.

105. Donald M. Kerwin, Jr., "Role of Government–NGO Partnerships," 312.

106. Kerwin, "Toward a Catholic Vision of Nationality," 198.

107. Kerwin, "Role of Government–NGO Partnerships," 312.

108. Kerwin, "Toward a Catholic Vision of Nationality," 200. Kerwin notes that many who are undocumented today may readily allay the concerns of this group by their commitment to their communities and core US values, their hard work, and by their good character or law-abiding nature (201).

109. Kerwin, "Role of Government–NGO Parternships," 312.

110. Kerwin, "Toward a Catholic Vision of Nationality," 202.

111. Ibid., 203.

112. Ibid., 204–7.

113. Pickus, *True Faith and Allegiance*, 10. Kerwin argues that a constitutional democracy relies on civil society in this way, as it "does not grant the government exclusive authority to define the nation's identity or its core values." See Kerwin, "Role of Government–NGO Partnerships," 311.

114. Pickus, *True Faith and Allegiance*, 6.

115. Kerwin, "Role of Government–NGO Partnerships," 311, 315. In its "A More Perfect Union: A National Citizenship Plan," CLINIC identifies several barriers to successful integration that such efforts could target: lack of English language proficiency, ignorance of legal citizenship requirements, and the need for financial and personnel assistance in application. See http://cliniclegal.org/resources/more-perfect-union (accessed July 13, 2011), as cited in Jill Marie Gerschutz with Lois Ann Lorentzen, "Integration Yesterday and Today," in Kerwin and Gerschutz, *And You Welcomed Me*, 143.

116. See for example Michael Walzer, "Liberalism and the Art of Separation."

117. Benhabib, *Another Cosmopolitanism*, 68.

118. See Rubén Rumbaut, "Pigments of Our Imagination: On the Racialization and Racial Identities of 'Hispanics' and 'Latinos,'" in *How the U.S. Racializes Latinos*, ed. José A. Cobas, Jorge Duany and Joe R. Feagin. As Rumbaut puts it, "Race is a pigment of our imagination. It is a social status, not a biological one; a product of history, not of nature; a contextual variable, not a given."

119. See Ngai, *Impossible Subjects*, 2, 7, parts I and II.

120. Ibid., 231. See Horace M. Kallen, "Democracy versus the Melting Pot," *The Nation* (February 25, 1915).

121. Roberto S. Goizueta, "Beyond the Frontier Myth," in *Hispanic Christian Thought at the Dawn of the 21st Century*, ed. Alvin Padilla, Roberto Goizueta, and Eldin Villafane, 150–58, at 151, 154.

122. Roberto S. Goizueta, *Christ Our Companion*, 146.

123. He writes, "fundamentally the strangeness of strangers can only be translated by human beings who are aware that one cannot understand the strangers without their cooperation as subjects and that, consequently, to really understand them, one must learn to understand *together with* them . . . insofar as [the collective task of translation of the strangeness of strangers] is an exercise of understanding achieved through the accompaniment of strangers, it represents also a process of learning about our own reality—[it] is a work that implies important consequences as much for our own self-interpretation as for the positioning of our own culture in relation to that of the stranger." Raúl Fornet-Betancourt, "Hermeneutics and

Politics of Strangers: A Philosophical Contribution on the Challenge of *Convivencia* in Multi-cultural Societies," in Groody and Campese, *A Promised Land*, 210–24, at 216.

124. Ibid., 220.

125. Ibid., 221–22.

126. Ibid., 222. O'Neill characterizes the virtue of hospitality in somewhat similar terms, as it "looks not to the assimilation but rather the integration of migrants . . . hospitality re-weaves our common narrative of citizenship," always "attentive to the 'stranger' in his or her concrete moral truth." O'Neill, "Anamnestic Solidarity."

127. Agnes M. Brazal, "Cultural Rights of Migrants: A Philosophical and Theological Exploration," in *Faith on the Move*, ed. Fabio Baggio and Agnes M. Brazal, 73–74. Anthony Rogers, "Globalizing Solidarity through Faith Encounters in Asia," in Baggio and Brazal, *Faith on the Move*, 203–18, at 215. Jean-Pierre Ruiz cautions that an ethic of hospitality must interrogate power dynamics shaping the construal of the "host" and "stranger" and account for migrants' contributions. See Jean-Pierre Ruiz, *Readings from the Edges*.

128. M. Shawn Copeland, *Enfleshing Freedom*, 89–90.

129. J. Kameron Carter, discussion following his panel presentation "Racism: A Theological Analysis," annual meeting of the Society of Christian Ethics (January 9, 2011), New Orleans, LA.

130. Goizueta, *Christ Our Companion*, 144.

131. Ibid., 152.

132. Ibid., 145.

133. Patricia Hill Collins, "Shifting the Center: Race, Class and Feminist Theorizing about Motherhood," in *American Families*, ed. Stephanie Coontz et al., 173–87, at 175.

134. I am indebted to Ellen Ott Marshall for the suggestion that I incorporate the work of Canon and Welch in this regard.

135. Cynthia S. W. Crysdale, "Making a Way by Walking," 40.

136. Katie Canon, *Katie's Canon*, 58–59.

137. Sharon Welch, *A Feminist Ethic of Risk*, 23, 45.

138. Ibid., 46. Albrecht's research on US working families reflects the experience of many transnational families with a foothold in the United States, as well: "Families adopt survival strategies as society loses its covenantal commitment to family well-being. They work more hours; the average US worker works more hours a year than workers in any other rich industrial nation . . . Due to racial disparities in wages and benefits, black and Hispanic families put in many more hours of work to achieve the same income level as white families." Albrecht, "For Families," in Rebecca Todd Peters and Elizabeth Hinson-Hasty, eds., *To Do Justice*, 12–20, at 17. Womanist ethicists depict mothers' time spent "mothering and other-mothering as time spent in teaching skills of both survival and resistance in a society that never intended the survival of these mothers' children." See Patricia Hill Collins, *Black Feminist Thought*, 122 as cited in Albrecht, *Hitting Home*, 152.

139. Crysdale, "Making a Way by Walking," 40, 41.

140. Welch, *A Feminist Ethic of Risk*, 46.

141. "In the extreme, the ethics of control is the assumption that one has the power to eradicate evil. In the mean . . . one can make decisive choices with the expectation that the goods available to others will and should be garnered for those whose interests one advocates." Crysdale goes on to propose a Lonerganian ethic of emergent probability to help us understand our position as human actors within both an ethic of risk and and ethic of control. Crysdale, "Making a Way by Walking," 45. She writes, "Regularities are themselves conditioned . . . We do not have ultimate control (God is God and we are not!) so that, at times, all we can do is

try and shift probabilities, to set up new conditions of possibility, out of which transformation can arise" (43, 48). Taken together these approaches also allow us to bridge the roles of social sin and individual agency: "Rather than being merely 'conditioned by' our environments, humans are 'conditioners of' our environments and, hence, ourselves." Drawing upon Lonergan's emergent probability, Crysdale continues, "The schemes of recurrence that make our lives possible have to do with habits of meaning, regular choices of value, an antecedent willingness to opt for value when value and satisfaction conflict. 'Survival' is about the survival of meaning, of purpose in life, of self-esteem and dignity, of communities of cooperative interaction" (53–54).

142. Ibid., 57. Responsible action gets redefined in terms of creating conditions of possibility for desired change and maintaining resistance in the face of overwhelming odds. Welch, *A Feminist Ethic of Risk*, 46.

143. Crysdale, "Making a Way by Walking," 54.

144. Canon describes the dynamic in this way: "In the Black community the aggregate of the qualities that determine desirable ethical values, uprightness of character, and soundness of moral conduct must always take into account the circumstances, the paradoxes, and the dilemmas that constrict Blacks to the lowest rungs of the social, political and economic hierarchy . . . To prevail against the odds with integrity, Black women must assess their moral agency within the social conditions of the community. Locked out of the real dynamics of human freedom in America, they implicitly pass on moral formulas for survival that allow them to stand over against the perversions of ethics and morality imposed on them by Whites and males who support racial imperialism in a patriarchal social order." Canon, *Katie's Canon*, 58–59, 61.

145. Bishop Kevin Dowling, "Silence and Horror: HIV/AIDS," Second Conference of Catholic Theological Ethics in the World Church, In the Currents of History: From Trent to the Future, Trento, Italy (July 25, 2010).

146. Paul Farmer, "Women, Poverty and AIDS," in *Women, Poverty and AIDS*, ed. Paul Farmer, Margaret Connors, and Janie Simmons, 28–29.

147. Crysdale, "Making a Way by Walking," 56.

148. Albrecht, *Hitting Home*, 147.

149. Patricia Hill Collins, "Shifting the Center," in *American Families*, ed. Stephanie Coontz et al. 173–87, at 178.

150. See Ivone Gebara, *Out of the Depths*, and María Pilar Aquino, *Nuestro clamor por la vida: Teología latinoamericana desde la perspectiva de la mujer* (San José: Editorial DEI), 194, as cited in Elina Vuola, *Limits of Liberation*, 147.

151. Margaret Regan, "Could Just Coffee, a Small Mexican Co-op, Offer a Solution to the Immigration Problem?" *Tucson Weekly* (February 8, 2007), available at www.tucsonweekly .com/gyrobase/roasting-revolution/Content?oid = 1086797&mode = print (accessed September 4, 2010). For more information on Café Justo see www.justcoffee.org/.

152. See John Sniegocki, *Catholic Social Teaching*, 326 for periodical suggestions in this regard.

153. The Kino Border Initiative serves as "a point of contact and mutual transformation not only for the migrants, staff, and community members who encounter one another in the context of [its] programs, but also for the Provinces of California and Mexico, the Missionary Sisters of the Eucharist, and Jesuit Refugee Services." Reflects cofounder and board member Mark Potter, "We need each other to be present to the broken immigration system and to allow this truth to transform us, and we need to allow the reality of the broken border policies to transform the ways we advocate for justice locally and internationally." See Potter, "Good

Neighbors: Cultivating Ignatian Solidarity at the US/Mexico Border," Catholic Theology Ethics in the World Church conference, Trento, Italy (July 26, 2010).

154. Goizueta, *Christ Our Companion,* 135–36.

155. For a discussion of alternative investment options (such as community development funds and microlending initiatives) see Susan Meeker Lowry, *Invested in the Common Good.*

156. See press release, "Jesuits Respond to New Chevron Human Rights Policy," available at www.jesuitswisprov.org/news.php?content = news&view = 124 (accessed July 13, 2011). For a summary of Chevron's Policy 520 see www.chevron.com/globalissues/humanrights/. Over their six years of engagement, the Jesuit-led coalition filed 5 shareholder resolutions with 140 total cofilers (including seven Jesuit universities, one high school, one parish, and the China province of the Jesuits). In addition to the work with Chevron, the National Jesuit Committee on Investment Responsibility served as the lead shareholder proponents in the processes that eventually led to corporate human rights policies by Occidental Petroleum and Monsanto.

157. In the case of Chevron and its host communities, these principles included "public/private security contractors, the rights of indigenous people, evolving understanding of complicity, new discoveries increasingly found in conflict zones, revenue transparency, and community engagement." Personal correspondence with John Sealey, Provincial Assistant for Social and International Ministries, Wisconsin Province of the Society of Jesus (July 13, 2011).

158. José Arreola, "Get to Know Me," National Public Radio /KQED Radio (July 8, 2011). Audio version in Arreola's voice available at www.kqed.org/a/perspectives/R201107080735 (accessed July 8, 2011). See also José Antonio Vargas, "My Life as an Undocumented Immigrant," *New York Times* (June 22, 2011), available at www.nytimes.com/2011/06/26/magazine/my-life-as-an-undocumented-immigrant.html?pagewanted = all (accessed June 22, 2011), for the Pulitzer Prize winner's revealing narrative about his own life in the United States without legal documents.

159. Ada María Isasi-Díaz, "Solidarity: Love of Neighbor in the 21st Century," in Susan Brooks Thistlethwaite and Mary Potter Engle, eds., *Lift Every Voice,* 30–40, 303–05, at 32.

160. Martín Espada, "Imagine the Angels of Bread," in *Imagine the Angels of Bread,* 18.

BIBLIOGRAPHY

Ahn, Ilsup. "Economy of 'Invisible Debt' and Ethics of 'Radical Hospitality': Toward a Paradigm Change of Hospitality from 'Gift' to 'Forgiveness.'" *Journal of Religious Ethics* 38, no. 2 (2010): 243–67.

Albrecht, Gloria H. *Hitting Home: Feminist Ethics, Women's Work and the Betrayal of "Family Values."* New York: Continuum, 2002.

Amnesty International. "Invisible Victims: Migrants on the Move in Mexico." London: Amnesty International Publications, 2010.

Anzaldúa, Gloria. *Borderlands La Frontera: The New Mestiza* (Third Edition). San Francisco: Aunt Lute Books, 2007.

Aquino, María Pilar. *Our Cry for Life: Feminist Theology from Latin America.* Maryknoll, NY: Orbis, 1993.

Arendt, Hannah. *The Origins of Totalitarianism.* New York: Harcourt, Brace & World, 1966.

Atkinson, Joseph C. "Family as Domestic Church: Developmental Trajectory, Legitimacy and Problems of Appropriation." *Theological Studies* 66, no. 3 (2005): 592–604.

Bacon, David. "Justice Deported: The Swift Plant Raids of 2006." *Peacework* 372 (February 2007): 5–6.

———. *Illegal People: How Globalization Creates Migration and Criminalizes Immigrants.* Boston: Beacon Press, 2008.

Baggio, Fabio, and Agnes M. Brazal. *Faith on the Move: Toward a Theology of Migration in Asia.* Quezon City: Ateneo de Manila University Press, 2008.

Batstone, David, ed. *New Visions for the Americas: Religious Engagement and Social Transformation.* Minneapolis: Fortress Press, 1993.

Baum, Gregory. *Religion and Alienation: A Theological Reading of Sociology.* New York: Paulist, 1975.

———. *Essays in Critical Theology.* Kansas City, MO: Sheed & Ward, 1994.

———, and Robert Ellsberg, eds. *The Logic of Solidarity: Commentaries on Pope John Paul II's Encyclical* On Social Concern. Maryknoll, NY: Orbis, 1989.

Beckley, Harlan, ed. *The Annual of the Society of Christian Ethics.* Washington, DC: Georgetown University Press, 1991.

Behdad, Ali. *A Forgetful Nation: On Immigration and Cultural Identity in the United States.* Durham, NC: Duke University Press, 2005.

Benhabib, Seyla. *Another Cosmopolitanism.* Edited and introduced by Robert Post. New York: Oxford University Press, 2008.

———, and Judith Resnik, eds. *Migration and Mobilities: Citizenship, Borders and Gender.* New York: New York University Press, 2009.

Bennett, Lerone, Jr. *Before the Mayflower: A History of Black America, Fifth Edition.* New York: Penguin Books, 1982.

Berger, Peter L., and Thomas Luckmann. *The Social Construction of Reality: A Treatise in the Sociology of Knowledge.* New York: Anchor, 1966.

Bhahba, Jacqueline. "The 'Mere Fortuity of Birth'? Children, Mothers, Borders, and the Meaning of Citizenship." In *Migrations and Mobilities: Citizenship, Borders, and Gender,* ed. Seyla Benhabib and Judith Resnik. New York: New York University Press, 2009.

Bourg, Florence Caffrey. "Domestic Church: A New Frontier in Ecclesiology." *Horizons* 29, no. 1 (2002): 42–63.

Boyle, Gregory. *Tattoos on the Heart: The Power of Boundless Compassion.* New York: Free Press, 2010.

Brackley, Dean, "A Radical Ethos." *Horizons* 24, no. 1 (1997): 7–36.

———. "Higher Standards for Higher Education: The Christian University and Solidarity." *Listening: Journal of Religion and Culture* 37, no. 1 (2002): 6–24.

Brettell, Caroline B., and Faith G. Nibbs. "Immigrant Suburban Settlement and the 'Threat' to Middle Class Status and Identity: The Case of Farmer's Branch, Texas." *International Migration* 49, no. 1 (2011): 1–30.

Brick, Kate, A.E. Challinor, and Marc R. Rosenblum. *Mexican and Central American Immigrants in the United States.* Washington, DC: Migration Policy Institute, 2011.

Browning, Don S., Bonnie J. Miller-McLemore, Pamela D. Couture, K. Brynolf Lyon, and Robert M. Franklin. *From Culture Wars to Common Ground: Religion and the American Family Debate.* Louisville, KY: Westminster/John Knox Press, 1997.

Brubaker, Pamela K., Rebecca Todd Peters, and Laura A. Stivers, eds. *Justice in a Global Economy: Strategies for Home, Community and World.* Louisville, KY: Westminster/John Knox Press, 2006.

Cahill, Lisa Sowle. *Family: A Christian Social Perspective.* Minneapolis: Fortress Press, 2000.

———, and Dietmar Mieth, eds. *The Family, Concilium.* Maryknoll, NY: Orbis, 1995.

Campese, Giacchino, and Pietro Ciallella. *Migration, Religious Experience and Globalization*. Staten Island, NY: Center for Migration Studies of New York, 2003.

Campese, Gioacchino. "*¿Cuantos Más?* The Crucified Peoples at the U.S.–Mexico Border." In *A Promised Land, a Perilous Journey: Theological Perspectives on Migration*, ed. Daniel Groody and Gioacchino Campese. Notre Dame, IN: University of Notre Dame Press, 2008, 271–98.

Canon, Katie. *Katie's Canon: Womanism and the Soul of the Black Community*. New York: Continuum, 1996.

Capps, Randy, Rosa Maria Castaneda, Ajay Chaudry and Robert Santos. "Paying the Price: The Impact of Immigration Raids on America's Children." The Urban Institute for the National Council of La Raza, 2007.

Capps, Randy, Marc C. Rosenblum, Cristina Rodríguez, and Muzaffar Chishti. "Delegation and Divergence: A Study of 287(g) State and Local Immigration Enforcement." Washington, DC: Migration Policy Institute, 2011.

Carens, Joseph H. "Aliens and Citizens: The Case for Open Borders." *The Review of Politics* 49, no. 2 (1987): 251–73.

———. *Immigrants and the Right to Stay*. Cambridge, MA: The MIT Press, 2010.

Catholic Bishops of Appalachia. "This Land Is Home to Me: A Pastoral Letter on Powerlessness in Appalachia." Webster Springs, WV: Catholic Committee of Appalachia, 1975, 493–94.

Cavanaugh, William T. "Migrant, Tourist, Pilgrim, Monk: Mobility and Identity in a Global Age." *Theological Studies* 69, no. 2 (2008): 340–56.

Chenu, Bruno, Claude Prud'Homme, France Quere, and Jean-Claude Thomas. *The Book of Christian Martyrs*. New York: Crossroad, 1990.

Christiansen, Drew. "Sacrament of Unity: Ethical Issues in the Pastoral Care of Migrants and Refugees." In *Today's Immigrants and Refugees: A Christian Understanding* (Washington, DC: United States Catholic Conference, 1988), 81–114.

Citrin, Jack, Amy Lerman, Michael Murakami, and Kathyn Pearson. "Testing Huntington: Is Hispanic Immigration a Threat to American Identity?" *Perspectives on Politics* 5, no. 1 (March 2007): 31–48 at 31–32.

Clarke, Kevin. "These American Lives: Undocumented Stories." *U.S. Catholic* 71, no. 8 (August 2006): 12–17.

Cobas, José A., Jorge Duany, and Joe R. Feagin. *How the U.S. Racializes Latinos: White Hegemony and Its Consequences*. Boulder, CO: Paradigm Publishers, 2009.

Cohen, Joshua, ed. *For Love of Country: Debating Patriotism and Its Limits.* Boston: Beacon Press, 1996.

Coleman, John A., and William F. Ryan, eds. *Globalization and Catholic Social Thought.* Maryknoll, NY: Orbis, 2005.

Collinge, William J., ed. *Faith in Public Life.* Maryknoll, NY: Orbis, 2008.

Collins, Patricia Hill. *Black Feminist Thought: Knowledge, Consciousness and the Politics of Empowerment.* New York: Routledge, 1990.

Congregation for the Doctrine of the Faith. "Instruction on Certain Aspects of the Theology of Liberation." *Origins* 14, no. 13 (September 13,1984): 194–204.

Conn, Walter E., ed. *Conversion: Perspectives on Personal and Social Transformation.* New York: Alba House, 1978.

Consejo Episcopal Latinoamericano (CELAM). "The Church in the Present-Day Transformation of Latin America in Light of the Council." Washington, DC: U.S. Catholic Conference, 1973.

———. "Evangelization at Present and in the Future of Latin America." Washington, DC: National Conference of Catholic Bishops, 1979.

———. *Globalization and the New Evangelization in Latin America and the Caribbean,* trans. Walter Blake (Bogota, Colombia: Publications CELAM, 2003), no. 117.

Coontz, Stephanie, Maya Parson, and Gabrielle Raley, eds. *American Families: A Multicultural Reader,* 2nd edition. New York: Routledge, 2008.

Copeland, M. Shawn "Racism and the Vocation of the Christian Theologian." *Spiritus* 2, no. 1 (2002): 15–29.

———. *Enfleshing Freedom: Body, Race, and Being.* Minneapolis, MN: Fortress Press, 2009.

Cornelius, Wayne A., and Jessa M. Lewis, eds. *Impacts of Border Enforcement on Mexican Migration: The View from Sending Communities.* San Diego: The Center for Comparative Immigration Studies at the University of California, 2007.

Cruz, Gemma Tulud. "Between Identity and Security: Theological Implications of Migration in the Context of Globalization." *Theological Studies* 69, no. 2 (June 2008): 357–75.

———. "Singing the Lord's Song in a Strange Land: Religious Identity in the Context of Migration." *Forum Mission Yearbook* 4 (2008): 60–87.

Crysdale, Cynthia S.W. "Making a Way by Walking: Risk, Control and Emergent Probability." *Theoforum* 39, no. 2 (2008): 39–58.

Curran, Charles E. *Catholic Social Teaching: A Historical and Ethical Analysis.* Washington, DC: Georgetown University Press, 2002.

————, ed. *Conscience, Readings in Moral Theology No. 14*. New York: Paulist, 2004.

————. *The Moral Theology of Pope John Paul II*. Washington, DC: Georgetown University Press, 2005.

————, Margaret Farley, and Richard McCormick, eds. *Feminist Ethics and the Catholic Moral Tradition*. Mahwah, NJ: Paulist Press, 1996.

Daniel, Ben. *Neighbor: Christian Encounters with Illegal Immigration*. Louisville, KY: Westminster/John Knox Press, 2010.

De La Torre, Miguel A. *Trails of Hope and Terror: Testimonies on Immigration*. Maryknoll, NY: Orbis, 2009.

Delano, Alexandra. *The Mexican Diaspora in the United States: Policies of Emigration since 1848*. Cambridge: Cambridge University Press, 2011.

DeLorey, Mary. "International Migration: Social, Economic, and Humanitarian Considerations." In *And You Welcomed Me: Migration and Catholic Social Teaching*, ed. Donald Kerwin and Jill Marie Gerschutz. Lanham, MD: Lexington Books/Rowman & Littlefield, 2009), 31–54.

Deville, Adam A. J. "The Development of the Doctrine of 'Structural Sin' and a 'Culture of Death' in the Thought of Pope John Paul II." *Église et Théologie* 30 (1999): 307–25.

DiMarzio, Bishop Nicholas. "Labor Day Statement 2006." *Origins* vol. 36, no. 13 (September 7, 2006): 201–4.

————. "John Paul II: Migrant Pope Teaches on the Unwritten Laws of Migration." *Notre Dame Journal of Law, Ethics and Public Policy* 21, no. 191 (2007): 191–214.

Donahue, John R. *The Gospel in Parable*. Philadelphia: Fortress Press, 1988.

Doran, Kevin P. *Solidarity: A Synthesis of Personalism and Communalism in the Thought of Karol Wojtyla/John Paul II*. New York, NY: Peter Lang, 1996.

Dow, Mark. *American Gulag: Inside U.S. Immigration Prisons*. Berkeley: University of California Press, 2004.

Dowling, Bishop Kevin. "Silence and Horror: HIV/AIDS," Second Conference of Catholic Theological Ethics in the World Church, In the Currents of History: From Trent to the Future, Trento, Italy (July 25, 2011).

Downey, Michael, ed. *The New Dictionary of Catholic Spirituality*. Collegeville, MN: Liturgical Press, 1993.

Duffy, Stephen J. "Sin." In *The New Dictionary of Catholic Spirituality*, ed. Michael Downey. Collegeville, MN: Liturgical Press, 1993.

Duncan, Stan. *The Greatest Story Oversold: Understanding Economic Globalization*. Maryknoll, NY: Orbis, 2010.

Durand, Jorge, and Douglas S. Massey, eds. *Crossing the Border: Research from the Mexican Migration Project.* New York: Russell Sage Foundation, 2004.

Dussel, Enrique. *Ethics and Community.* Maryknoll, NY: Orbis, 1988.

Dwyer, Augusta. *On the Line.* New York: Monthly Review Press, 1994.

Dwyer, Judith A., ed. *The New Dictionary of Catholic Social Thought.* Collegeville, MN: The Liturgical Press, 1994.

Ehrenreich, Barbara, and Arlie Russell Hochschild, eds. *Global Woman: Nannies, Maids and Sex Workers in the New Economy.* New York: Metropolitan Books, 2002.

Eigo, Francis A., ed. *Rethinking the Spiritual Works of Mercy.* Villanova, PA: Villanova University, 1993.

Ellacuría, Ignacio, and Jon Sobrino, eds. *Mysterium Liberationis: Fundamental Concepts of Liberation Theology.* Maryknoll, NY: Orbis, 1993.

Espada, Martín. *Imagine the Angels of Bread.* New York: W.W. Norton & Company, 1996.

Espín, Orlando O. "Immigration, Territory and Globalization: Theological Reflections." *Journal of Hispanic/Latino Theology* 7, no. 3 (February 2000): 46–59.

Farley, Margaret A. "A Feminist Version of Respect for Persons." *Journal of Feminist Studies in Religion* 9, no. 1 (Spring/Fall 1993): 183–98.

———. *Just Love: A Framework for Christian Sexual Ethics.* New York: Continuum, 2006.

Farmer, Paul, Margaret Connors, and Janie Simmons, eds. *Women, Poverty and AIDS: Sex, Drugs and Structural Violence.* Monroe, ME: Common Courage Press, 1996.

Fiorenza, Elisabeth Schüssler, ed. *The Power of Naming: A Concilium Reader in Feminist Liberation Theology.* Maryknoll, NY: Orbis, 1996.

Fletcher, Ian. *Free Trade Doesn't Work: What Should Replace It and Why.* Washington, DC: US Business and Industry Council, 2010.

Foner, Nancy, ed. *American Arrivals: Anthropology Engages the New Immigration.* Santa Fe, NM: School of American Research Press, 2003.

———, Ruben G. Rumbaut, and Steven J. Gold, eds. *Immigration Research for a New Century: Multidisciplinary Perspectives.* New York: Russell Sage Foundation, 2000.

Freire, Paulo. *Pedagogy of the Oppressed.* New York: Continuum, 1970.

Friedman Thomas. *The Lexus and the Olive Tree: Understanding Globalization.* New York: Anchor Books, 1999.

Garfinkle, N. and D. Yankelovich, eds. *Uniting America: Restoring the Vital Center to American Democracy.* New Haven: Yale University Press, 2006.

Gebara, Ivone. *Out of the Depths: Women's Experience of Evil and Salvation,* trans. Ann Patrick Ware. Minneapolis: Augsburg Fortress, 2002.

Gilson, Etienne, ed. *The Church Speaks to the Modern World: The Social Teachings of Leo XIII.* New York: Doubleday, 1954.

Glaser, John W. "Health Care Reform as Public Conscience Work: U.S. Health Care as Chronic Social Sin." *A Matter of Spirit (AMOS)* 79 (Summer 2008): 1–2.

Goizueta, Roberto S. "Beyond the Frontier Myth." In *Hispanic Christian Thought at the Dawn of the 21st Century,* ed. Alvin Padilla, Roberto Goizueta, and Eldin Villafane. Nashville: Abingdon Press, 2005, 150–58.

———. *Christ Our Companion: Toward a Theological Aesthetics of Liberation.* Maryknoll, NY: Orbis, 2009.

Golash-Boza, Tanya. "The Immigration Industrial Complex: Why We Enforce Immigration Policies Destined to Fail." *Sociology Compass* 3, no. 2 (Feb 2009): 295–309.

González, Justo. *Santa Biblia: The Bible through Hispanic Eyes.* Nashville: Abingdon, 1994.

González Faus, José Ignacio. "The Utopia of the Human Family." In *Globalization and Its Victims,* ed. Sobrino and Wilfred. London: SCM Press, 2001, 97–104.

Goulet, Denis. *The Cruel Choice: A New Concept in the Theory of Development.* New York: Atheneum, 1971.

Greene, Thomas, "Families and Social Order" panel presentation. Atlanta, GA: Annual Meeting of the Society of Christian Ethics, January 4, 2008.

Groody, Daniel. *Globalization, Spirituality and Justice.* Maryknoll, NY: Orbis, 2007.

———, ed. *The Option for the Poor in Christian Theology.* Notre Dame, IN: University of Notre Dame Press, 2007.

———. "Crossing the Divide: Foundations for a Theology of Migration and Refugees." *Theological Studies* 70, no. 3 (September 2009): 638–67.

———, and Gioacchino Campese, eds. *A Promised Land, a Perilous Journey: Theological Perspectives on Migration.* Notre Dame, IN: University of Notre Dame Press, 2008.

Gútierrez, Gustavo. *On Job: God-Talk and the Suffering of the Innocent,* trans. Matthew J. O'Connell. Maryknoll, NY: Orbis, 1987.

———. *Essential Writings,* ed. James B. Nickoloff. Minneapolis: Fortress, 1996.

Häring, Bernard. *What Does Christ Want?* Staten Island, NY: Alba House 1968.

Harries, Richard, ed. *Reinhold Niebuhr and the Issues of Our Time.* Grand Rapids, MI: Eerdmans, 1986.

Harrington, Daniel, and James F. Keenan. *Jesus and Virtue Ethics: Building Bridges between New Testament Studies and Moral Theology.* Lanham, MD: Sheed & Ward, 2002.

Hauerwas, Stanley, and Samuel Wells, eds. *The Blackwell Companion to Christian Ethics.* Malden, MA: Blackwell Publishing Ltd, 2004.

Haug, Frigga. *Beyond Female Masochism: Memory-work and Politics,* trans. Rodney Livingstone. London: Verso, 1992.

Heyer, Kristin. "Bridging the Divide in Contemporary U.S. Catholic Social Ethics." *Theological Studies* 66, no. 2 (2005): 401–40.

———. "Strangers in Our Midst: Day Laborers and Just Immigration Reform." *Political Theology* 9, no. 4 (2008): 425–53.

———. "A Response to 'Restorative Justice as a Prophetic Path to Peace?' Plenary Address by Stephen J. Pope." *Catholic Theological Society of America Journal Proceedings* 65 (2010): 35–42.

———. "Social Sin and Immigration: Good Fences Make Bad Neighbors." *Theological Studies* 71, no. 2 (June 2010): 410–36.

———, Mark Rozell, and Michael Genovese, eds. *Catholics and Politics: Dynamic Tensions between Faith and Power.* Washington, DC: Georgetown University, 2008.

Hill, Charles, and Donald Kerwin. "Immigration and Nationality Law." *International Law* 36 (2002): 527–47.

Himes, Kenneth R. "Social Sin and the Role of the Individual." *Annual of the Society of Christian Ethics,* ed. Harlan Beckley. Washington, DC: Georgetown University Press, 1986, 183–218.

Himes, Michael J., and Kenneth R. Himes. *Fullness of Faith: The Public Significance of Theology.* New York: Paulist Press, 1993.

Hing, Bill Ong. *Deporting Our Souls: Values, Morality and Immigration Policy.* New York: Cambridge University Press, 2006.

Hinze, Christine Firer. "Bridge Discourse on Wage Justice: Roman Catholic and Feminist Perspectives on the Family Living Wage." In *Feminist Ethics and the Catholic Moral Tradition,* ed. Charles E. Curran, Margaret Farley, and Richard A. McCormick. Mahwah, NJ: Paulist Press, 1996, 511–40.

———. "U.S. Catholic Social Thought, Gender, and Economic Livelihood." *Theological Studies* 66, no. 3 (2005): 568–91.

———. "The Drama of Social Sin and the (Im)possibility of Solidarity: Reinhold Niebuhr and Modern Cathoilic Social Teaching." *Studies in Christian Ethics* 22, no. 4 (2009): 442–60.

———. "Over, Under, Around, and Through: Ethics, Solidarity, and the Saints." *CTSA Proceedings* 66 (San Jose, CA: 2011), 33–60.

Hobgood, Mary. *Catholic Social Teaching and Economic Theory: Paradigms in Conflict*. Philadelphia: Temple University Press, 1991.

Hochschild, Arlie Russell. *The Second Shift*. New York: Penguin, 1989.

———. *The Time Bind: When Work Becomes Home and Home Becomes Work*. New York: Henry Holt, 1997.

Hoeffner, John J., and Michele R. Pistone. "But the Laborers Are . . . Many? Catholic Social Teaching on Business, Labor, and Economic Migration," in *And You Welcomed Me*, 55–92.

Hoeffer, Michael, Nancy Rytina, and Bryan C. Baker. "Estimates of the Unauthorized Immigrant Population Residing in the United States: January 2010." *Population Estimates*, Washington, DC: US Department of Homeland Security, Office of Immigration Statistics, February 2011, 1, 4, 5. www .dhs.gov/xlibrary/assets/statistics/publications/ois_ill_pe_2010.pdf (accessed July 1, 2011).

Hogan, Linda, ed. *Applied Ethics in a World Church: The Padua Conference*. Maryknoll, NY: Orbis, 2008.

Hollenbach, David. *Claims in Conflict: Retrieving the Catholic Human Rights Tradition*. New York: Paulist, 1979.

———. *The Common Good & Christian Ethics*. Cambridge: Cambridge University Press, 2002.

———. "The Life of the Human Community." *America* 187, no. 14 (November 4, 2002): 6–9.

———, ed. *Refugee Rights: Advocacy, and Africa*. Washington, DC: Georgetown University Press, 2008.

———. *Driven from Home: Protecting the Rights of Forced Migrants*. Washington, DC: Georgetown University Press, 2010.

Holzer, Harry J., Julia I. Lane, David B. Rosenblum, and Fredrik Andersson. *Where Are All the Good Jobs Going? What National and Local Job Quality and Dynamics Mean for U.S. Workers*. New York: Russell Sage Foundation, 2011.

Hondagneu-Sotelo, Pierrette, ed. *Religion and Social Justice for Immigrants*. New Brunswick, NJ: Rutgers University Press, 2007.

Huntington, Samuel. *Who Are We? The Challenges to America's National Identity*. New York, NY: Simon & Schuster, 2004.

Isasi-Díaz, Ada Maria. *La Lucha Continues: Mujerista Theology*. Maryknoll, NY: Orbis, 2004.

Jefford, Clayton N., ed. *Christian Freedom: Essays by the Faculty of the Saint Meinrad School of Theology.* New York: Peter Lang, 1993.

John Paul II. *Familiaris consortio (Apostolic Exhortation on the Family).* November 22, 1981.

———. "The Value of This Collegial Body." *Synod of Bishops: Penance and Reconciliation in the Mission of the Church.* Washington, DC: U.S. Catholic Conference, 1984.

———. *Mulieris dignitatem (On the Dignity and Vocation of Women).* August 15, 1988.

Kalhan, Anil. "Rethinking Immigration Detention." *Columbia Law Review* 110, sidebar 42 (July 21, 2010): 42–58.

Kanbur, Ravi, and Michael Spence. *Equity and Growth in a Globalizing World.* Washington, DC: World Bank and the Commission on Growth and Development, 2010.

Kanstroom, Daniel. *Deportation Nation: Outsiders in American History.* Cambridge, MA: Harvard University Press, 2007.

Kaskade, Satya Grace. "Mothers without Borders: Undocumented Immigrant Mothers Facing Deportation and the Best Interests of Their U.S. Citizen Children." *William and Mary Journal of Women and the Law* 15, no. 2 (2009): 447–67.

Kaveny, Cathleen. "Defining Feminism: Can the Church and World Agree on the Role of Women?" *America* 204, no. 6 (February 28, 2011).

Keating, James, ed. *Moral Theology: New Directions and Fundamental Issues; Festschrift for James P. Hanigan.* New York: Paulist, 2004.

Keenan, James F., ed. *Catholic Theological Ethics in the World Church: The Plenary Papers from the First Cross-Cultural Conference on Catholic Theological Ethics.* New York: Continuum, 2007.

———. *History of Catholic Moral Theology in the Twentieth Century: From Confessing Sins to Liberating Consciences.* New York: Continuum, 2010.

Keohane, Robert O., and Joseph S. Nye. "Globalization: What's New? What's Not? (And So What?)." *Foreign Policy* 118 (Spring 2000): 104–19.

Kerans, Patrick. *Sinful Social Structures.* New York: Paulist, 1974.

Kerwin, Donald. "America's Children: Protecting the Rights of Those Born on U.S. Soil." *America* 197, no. 8 (September 24, 2007): 10–13.

———. "Role of Government–NGO Partnerships in Immigrant Integration: A Response to Howard Duncan from the Perspective of US Civil Society." *Studies in Ethnicity and Nationalism* 9, no. 2 (September 2009): 310–15.

———. "Toward a Catholic Vision of Nationality." *Notre Dame Journal of Law, Ethics & Public Policy* 23, no. 197 (2009): 197–207.

————. *Labor Standards Enforcement and Low-Wage Immigrants: Creating an Effective Enforcement System*. Washington, DC: Migration Policy Institute, 2011.

————, and Jill Marie Gerschutz, eds. *And You Welcomed Me: Migration and Catholic Social Teaching*. Lanham, MD: Rowman & Littlefield, 2009.

Knieps-Port le Roi, Thomas. "Innovation or Impasse? The Contribution of *Familiaris consortio* to a Contemporary Theology of Marriage." *Bijdragen, International Journal in Philosophy and Theology* 70, no. 1 (2009): 67–86.

Korgen, Jeffrey Odel. *Solidarity Will Transform the World: Stories of Hope from Catholic Relief Services*. Maryknoll, NY: Orbis, 2007.

Kymlicka, Will, ed. *The Rights of Minority Cultures*. Oxford: Oxford University Press, 1995.

Lanier, Jaron. *You Are Not a Gadget: A Manifesto*. New York: Knopf, 2010.

Lawler, Michael. *Family, American and Christian*. Chicago: Loyola University Press, 1998.

Lazarus, Emma. *The Poems of Emma Lazarus*, vol.1. Boston: Houghton Mifflin, 1889.

Lebel, Louis, Sylvia Lorek, and Rajesh Daniel, eds. *Sustainable Production Consumption Systems: Knowledge, Engagement and Practice*. New York: Springer, 2010.

Legomsky, Stephen H. "The New Path of Immigration Law: Asymmetric Incorporation of Criminal Justice Norms." *Washington & Lee Law Review* 64, no. 469 (2007): 469–528.

Lowry, Susan Meeker. *Invested in the Common Good*. Philadelphia: New Society Publishers, 1995.

Madges, William, ed. *Vatican II: Forty Years Later, College Theology Society Annual Volume* 51 (2005): 165–95.

Mahoney, John. *The Making of Moral Theology: A Study of the Roman Catholic Tradition*. Oxford: Oxford University Press, 1987.

Mahony, Cardinal Roger. "For Goodness Sake: Why America Needs Immigration Reform." *The Tidings*, February 11, 2011.

Marfleet, Philip. *Refugees in a Global Era*. New York: Palgrave Macmillan, 2006.

Massaro, Thomas. *United States Welfare Policy: A Catholic Response*. Washington, DC: Georgetown University Press, 2007.

Massingale, Bryan N. "The Scandal of Poverty: 'Cultured Indifference' and the Option for the Poor Post-Katrina." *Journal of Religion and Society* Supplement Series 4 ed. Dennis Hamm and Gail S. Risch. Omaha: The Kripke Center (2008): 55–72.

———. *Racial Justice and the Catholic Church.* Maryknoll, NY: Orbis, 2010.

———. "*Vox Victimarum, Vox Dei*: Macolm X as a Neglected 'Classic' for Catholic Theological Reflection." *Proceedings of The Catholic Theological Society of America* 65 (2010): 63–88.

McCormick, Patrick T. *A Banqueter's Guide to the All-Night Soup Kitchen of the Kingdom of God.* Collegeville: Liturgical Press, 2004.

Meilaender, Peter C. *Toward a Theory of Immigration.* New York: Palgrave, 2001.

Messori, Vitorio, ed. *Crossing the Threshold of Hope.* New York: Knopf, 1994.

Mieth, Dietmar, and Lisa Sowle Cahill, eds. *Migrants and Refugees.* Maryknoll: SCM Press Ltd and Orbis, 1993.

Mieth, Dietmar, and Marciano Vidal, eds. *Outside the Market No Salvation? Concilium* 97, no. 2 (April 1997): 33–43.

Miller, Vincent. *Consuming Religion: Christian Faith and Practice in a Consumer Culture.* New York: Continuum, 2005.

———. "A Memo to the Bishops: A Call to Preach the Fullness of Catholic Doctrine." *America* 203, no. 15 (November 22, 2010).

Nanko-Fernández, Carmen. "Beyond Hospitality: Implications of Im/migration for Teología y Pastoral de Conjunto." *Perspectivas: Hispanic Theological Initiative Occasional Paper Series* 10 (Fall 2006): 51–62.

National Conference of Catholic Bishops. "Economic Justice for All: Pastoral Letter on Catholic Social Teaching and the U.S. Economy." Washington, DC: United States Conference of Catholic Bishops, 1986.

Ngai, Mae M. *Impossible Subjects: Illegal Aliens and the Making of Modern America.* Princeton: Princeton University Press, 2004.

Niebuhr, Reinhold. *Irony of American History.* New York: Charles Scribner's Sons, 1952.

———. *The Nature and Destiny of Man: Vol.1: Human Nature.* Louisville, KY: Westminster/John Knox Press, 1996.

Novak, Michael. *The Spirit of Democratic Capitalism.* New York: American Enterprise Institute, 1982.

Nussbaum, Martha Craven. *Women and Human Development: The Capabilities Approach.* Cambridge: Cambridge University Press, 2000.

Nye, Joseph S., Jr. "Globalization's Democratic Deficit: How to Make International Institutions More Accountable." *Foreign Affairs* 80, no. 4 (July/August 2001): 2–6.

O'Brien, David J., and Thomas A. Shannon. *Catholic Social Thought: The Documentary Heritage.* Maryknoll, NY: Orbis, 1992.

O'Keefe, Mark. *What Are They Saying about Social Sin?* New York: Paulist, 1990.

Okin, Susan Moller. *Gender, Justice and the Family.* New York: Basic Books, 1989.

Okun, Arthur. *Equality and Efficiency: The Big Tradeoff.* Washington, DC: Brookings Institution Press, 1975.

O'Neill, William. "Rights of Passage: Ethics of Forced Displacement." *The Journal of the Society of Christian Ethics* 27, no. 1 (Summer 2007): 113–36.

———. "A Little Common Sense: The Ethics of Immigration in Catholic Social Teaching." *Explore: An Examination of the Catholic Identity and Ignatian Character in Jesuit Higher Education* 11, no. 2 (2008): 10–4.

———. "Anamnestic Solidarity: Immigration from the Perspective of Restorative Justice." Paper delivered at the 2009 Catholic Theological Society of America (Halifax, Nova Scotia), June 5, 2009.

———. "'No Longer Strangers' (Ephesians 2:19): The Ethics of Migration." *Word & World* 29, no. 3 (Summer 2009): 227–33.

———. "Response to 'The Last Judgment: Christian Ethics in a Legal Culture.'" Catholic Theological Society of America annual convention (June 11, 2011).

O'Neill, William R., and William C. Spohn. "Rights of Passage: The Ethics of Immigration and Refugee Policy." *Theological Studies* 59, no. 1 (1998): 84–106.

Padilla, Alvin, Roberto Goizueta, and Eldin Villafane, eds. *Hispanic Christian Thought at the Dawn of the 21st Century.* Nashville: Abingdon Press, 2005.

Padilla, Mark B., Jennifer S. Hirsch, Miguel Muñoz-Laboy, Robert E. Sember, and Richard G. Parker, eds. *Love and Globalization: Transformations of Intimacy in the Contemporary World.* Nashville: Vanderbilt University Press, 2007.

Pérez-Álvarez, Eliseo. "The Tortilla Curtain: War on the Table of the Poor." *Dialog: A Journal of Theology* 49, no. 1 (Spring 2010): 19–25.

Peters, Rebecca Todd, and Elizabeth Hinson-Hasty, eds. *To Do Justice: A Guide for Progressive Christians.* Louisville, KY: Westminster John Knox Press, 2008.

Pfeil, Margaret. "Doctrinal Implications of Magisterial Use of the Language of Social Sin." *Louvain Studies* 27, no. 2 (2002): 132–52.

Philpott, Dan. "Sovereignty." In *The Stanford Encyclopedia of Philosophy (Summer 2010 Edition)*, ed. Edward N. Zalta. Stanford, CA: Center for the Study of Language and Information, 2010. http://plato.stanford.edu/archives/sum2010/entries/sovereignty.

Pickus, Noah. *True Faith and Allegiance: Immigration and American Civic Nationalism.* Princeton: Princeton University Press, 2005.

Pohl, Christine D. *Making Room: Recovering Hospitality as a Christian Tradition.* Grand Rapids, MI: Wm. B. Eerdmans, 1999.

Pontifical Council for Justice and Peace. *Compendium of the Social Doctrine of the Church.* Washington, DC: United States Conference of Catholic Bishops, 2004.

Pope, Stephen J., ed. *Hope and Solidarity: Jon Sobrino's Challenge to Christian Theology.* Maryknoll, NY: Orbis, 2008.

Potter, Mark W. "Good Neighbors: Cultivating Ignatian Solidarity at the US/Mexico Border." Catholic Theology Ethics in the World Church conference, Trento, Italy (July 26, 2010).

———. "Solidarity as Spiritual Exercise: Accompanying Migrants at the US/Mexico Border." *Political Theology* 12, no. 6 (2011): 830–42.

Powers, Karen Vieira. "Andeans and Spaniards in the Contact Zone: A Gendered Collision." *The American Indian Quarterly* 24, no. 4 (2000): 511–36.

Rasmussen, Larry L. *Moral Fragments and Moral Community.* Minneapolis: Fortress Press, 1993.

Rauschenbusch, Walter. *A Theology for the Social Gospel.* Louisville, KY: Westminster John Knox Press, [1917] 1997.

Rawls, John. *Political Liberalism*, rev. ed. New York: Columbia University Press, 1996.

Reinicke, Wolfgang. "Global Public Policy." *Foreign Affairs* 76, no. 6 (November/December 1997): 127–38.

Rifkin, Jeremy. *The End of Work.* New York: Tarcher/Putnam, 1995.

Rigali, Norbert. "Human Solidarity and Sin in the Apostolic Exhortation *Reconciliation and Penance.*" *Living Light* 21 (1985): 337–43.

Rodriguez, Nestor, and Jacqueline Maria Hagan. "Fractured Families and Communities: Effects of Immigration Reform in Texas, Mexico and El Salvador." *Latino Studies* 2, no. 3 (2004): 328–51.

Romero, Oscar. *The Violence of Love.* Trans. and compiled by James R. Brockman, Maryknoll, NY: Orbis, 2004.

Rosales, Gaudencio, and C.G. Arévalo, eds. *For All the Peoples of Asia: Federation of Asian Bishops' Conferences Documents from 1970–1991.* Maryknoll, NY: Orbis, 1992.

Rowlands, Anna. "On the Temptations of Sovereignty: The Task of Catholic Social Teaching and the Challenge of UK Asylum Seeking." *Political Theology* 12, no. 6 (2011): 843–69.

Rubio, Julio Hanlon. *Family Ethics: Practices for Christians*. Washington, DC: Georgetown University Press, 2010.

Ruiz, Jean-Pierre. *Readings from the Edges: The Bible and People on the Move*. Maryknoll, N.Y.: Orbis, 2011.

Runzo, Joseph, ed. *Ethics, Religion and the Good Society: New Directions in a Pluralistic World*. Louisville: Westminster John Knox, 1992.

Ryan, Maura, and Todd David Whitmore, eds. *The Challenge of Global Stewardship: Roman Catholic Responses*. Notre Dame, IN: University of Notre Dame Press, 1997.

Sacred Congregation of Bishops. *Instruction on Pastoral Care of People Who Migrate*. Washington, DC: USCC, 1969.

Sanchez, Melissa, George F. Lemp, Carlos Magis-Rodriguez, Enrique Bravo-Garcia, Susan Carter, and Juan D. Ruiz. "The Epidemiology of HIV among Mexican Migrants and Recent Immigrants in California and Mexico." *Journal of Acquired Immune Deficiency Syndrome* 37 (2004): 204–14.

Sanchez, Robert Fortune. "Migration and the Family." *Catholic Mind* 79 (February 1981): 19–24.

Santa Ana, Otto. *Brown Tide Rising: Metaphors of Latinos in Contemporary American Public Discourse*. Austin: University of Texas Press, 2002.

Sassen, Saskia. *Globalization and Its Discontents*. New York, NY: The New Press, 1999.

———. *Territory, Authority, Rights: From Medieval to Global Assemblages*. Princeton, NJ: Princeton University Press, 2008.

Schaab, Gloria L. "Which of These Was Neighbour? Spiritual Dimensions of the U.S. Immigration Question." *International Journal of Public Theology* 2, no. 2 (2008): 182–202.

Scholz, Sally J. *Political Solidarity*. University Park: Pennsylvania State University, 2008.

Schoonenberg, Piet. *Man and Sin: A Theological View*, trans. Joseph Donceel. Notre Dame, IN: University of Notre Dame, 1965.

Schreiter, Robert J. *The New Catholicity: Theology between the Global and the Local*. Maryknoll, NY: Orbis, 1997.

Seglow, Jonathan. "The Ethics of Immigration." *Political Studies Review* 3, no. 3 (2005): 317–34.

Segundo, Juan Luis. *Faith and Ideologies*. Maryknoll, NY: Orbis, 1984.

Segura, Denise A., and Patricia Zavella, eds. *Women and Migration in the U.S.–Mexico Borderlands: A Reader*. Durham: Duke University Press, 2007.

Sheridan, E. F., ed. *Do Justice: The Social Teaching of the Canadian Catholic Bishops*. Toronto: Jesuit Centre for Social Faith and Justice, 1987.

Shiva, Vandana. *Staying Alive: Women, Ecology and Development*. Atlantic Highlands, NJ: Zed Books, 1989.

———. *Biopiracy: The Plunder of Nature and Knowledge*. Totnes, Devon: Green Books, 1998.

Slack, Jeremy, and Scott Whiteford. "Violence and Migration on the Arizona–Sonora Border." *Human Organization* 70, no.1 (2011): 11–21.

Slevin, Porter. "Deportation of Illegal Immigrants Increases under Obama Administration." *The Washington Post*, July 26, 2010. www.washingtonpost.com/wp-dyn/content/article/2010/07/25/AR2010072501790.html.

Sniegocki, John. "The Social Ethics of Pope John Paul II: A Critique of Neo-conservative Interpretations." *Horizons* 33, no. 1 (Spring 2006): 7–32.

———. "Neoliberal Globalization: Critiques and Alternatives." *Theological Studies* 69, no. 2 (2008): 321–39.

———. *Catholic Social Teaching and Economic Globalization: The Quest for Alternatives*. Milwaukee, WI: Marquette University Press, 2009.

Sobrino, Jon. *The True Church and the Poor*, trans. Matthew J. O'Connell. Maryknoll, N.Y.: Orbis, 1984.

———. "Sanctuary: A Theological Analysis," trans. Walter Petry Jr. *Cross Currents* 38, no. 2 (Summer 1988): 164–72.

———. *The Principle of Mercy: Taking the Crucified People from the Cross*. Maryknoll, NY: Orbis, 1994.

———. "Redeeming Globalization through Its Victims." In *Globalization and Its Victims*, ed. Sobrino and Felix Wilfred. London: SCM Press, 2001, 105–14.

———. *Where Is God? Earthquake, Terrorism, Barbarity and Hope*. Maryknoll, NY: Orbis, 2004.

———, and Ignacio Ellacuria, eds. *Mysterium Liberationis: Fundamental Concepts of Liberation Theology*. Maryknoll, NY: Orbis, 1993.

———, and Felix Wilfred, eds. *Globalization and Its Victims*, trans. Paul Burns. London: SCM Press, 2001.

Solimano, Andrés. *International Migration in the Age of Crisis and Globalization: Historical and Recent Experiences*. New York: Cambridge University Press, 2010.

Steck, Christopher, "Solidarity, Citizenship, and Globalization: Developing a New Framework for Theological Reflection on U.S.–Mexico Immigration." *Journal for Peace and Justice Studies* 14, no. 2 (2004): 153–78.

Steinfels, Margaret O'Brien, ed. *American Catholics and Civic Engagement: A Distinctive Voice*. Lanham, MD: Rowman & Littlefield, 2004.

Stoll, David. "Which American Dream Do You Mean?" *Society* 46, no. 5 (2009): 398–402.

Supiot, Alain. *Homo Juridicus.* Verso Publications, 2007.

Tamanaha, Brian. *On the Rule of Law, History, Politics, Theory.* Cambridge: Cambridge University Press, 2004.

Terrae, Sal, ed. *¿Mundialización o conquista?* Barcelona: Santander, 1999.

Terrazas, Aaron. *Migration and Development: Policy Perspectives from the United States.* Washington, DC: Migration Policy Institute, 2011.

Tessarolo, Giulivo, ed. *The Church's Magna Charta for Migrants.* Staten Island, NY: St. Charles Seminary, 1962.

Thapan, Meenakshi. "Series Introduction." In *Poverty, Gender and Migration,* ed. Sadhna Arya and Anupama Roy. London: Sage, 2006, 14–15.

Thistlethwaite, Susan Brooks, and Mary Potter Engle, eds. *Lift Every Voice: Constructing Christian Theologies from the Underside.* Maryknoll, NY: Orbis, 1998.

Thorne, Barrie, and Marilyn Yalom, eds. *Rethinking the Family: Some Feminist Questions,* revised edition. Boston: Northeastern University Press, 1992.

Tienda, Marta, and Faith Mitchell, eds. *Multiple Origins, Uncertain Destinies.* Washington, DC: National Academies Press, 2006.

Tracy, David. "The Christian Option for the Poor." In *The Option for the Poor in Christian Theology,* ed. Daniel Groody Notre Dame, IN: University of Notre Dame Press, 2007,

Tripole, Martin, ed. *Promises Renewed: Jesuit Higher Education for a New Millennium.* Chicago: Loyola Press, 1999.

United States Conference of Catholic Bishops. *All Come Bearing Gifts.* Proceedings of the National Migration Conference. Washington, DC: United States Conference of Catholic Bishops, 2003.

———— and *Conferencia del Episcopado Mexicano.* "Strangers No Longer: Together on the Journey of Hope." Washington, DC: United States Conference of Catholic Bishops Inc., 2003.

Valentín, Benjamín, ed. *In Our Own Voices: Latino/a Renditions of Theology.* Maryknoll, NY: Orbis, 2010.

Vogt, Christopher. "Fostering a Catholic Commitment to the Common Good: An Approach Rooted in Virtue Ethics." *Theological Studies* 68, no. 2 (2007): 394–417.

Volf, Mirsolav. *Exclusion and Embrace: A Theological Exploration of Identity, Otherness, and Reconciliation.* Nashville, TN: Abingdon Press, 1996.

Vuola, Elina. *Limits of Liberation: Feminist Theology and the Ethics of Poverty and Reproduction.* New York, Sheffield Academic Press/Continuum, 2002.

Walter, James. J., Timothy E. O'Connell, and Thomas A. Shannon, eds. *A Call to Fidelity: On the Moral Theology of Charles E. Curran.* Washington, DC: Georgetown University Press, 2002.

Walzer, Michael. *Spheres of Justice: A Defense of Pluralism and Equality.* New York, NY: Basic Books, 1983.

———. "Liberalism and the Art of Separation," *Political Theory* 12, no. 3 (1984): 315–30.

Waters, Mary C., and Reeds Ueda, eds. *The New Americans: A Guide to Immigration since 1965.* Cambridge, MA: Harvard University Press, 2007.

Weisbrot, Mark, Dean Baker, Egor Kraev, and Judy Chen. *The Scorecard on Globalization 1980–2000: Twenty Years of Diminished Progress.* Washington, DC: Center for Economic and Policy Research, 2000.

Welch, Sharon. *A Feminist Ethic of Risk* (revised 2nd edition). Minneapolis, MN: Fortress Press, 2000.

Whitehead, James D., and Evelyn Easton Whitehead, eds. *Method in Ministry: Theological Reflection and Christian Ministry.* New York: Seabury, 1980.

Wilfred, Felix, and Oscar Beozzo, eds. *Frontier Violations: The Beginnings of New Identities.* London: SCM Press, 1992.

Zambrana, Ruth E. *Understanding Latino Families: Scholarship, Policy, and Practice.* Thousand Oaks, CA: SAGE Publications, 1995.

Zinn, Maxine Baca. "Political Familism: Toward Sex Role Equality in Chicano Families." *Aztlán: A Journal of Chicano Studies* 6, no. 1 (1975): 13–26.

Zolberg, Aristide R. *A Nation by Design: Immigration Policy in the Fashioning of America.* Cambridge, MA: Harvard University Press, 2008.

INDEX

Adams, John, 32n72
Africa, 111
African American ethics
  and ambiguity, 154–55, 170n144
  and conflict, 120–21
agency
  of immigrants, 20–25
  John Paul II on, 40–41
  moral, 154–55, 170n144
  and solidarity, 123
agriculture, 10–11, 102
  Niebuhr on, 16
  trade policies and, 103–5
AIDS, 68, 156
Albrecht, Gloria, 72, 85, 87, 93n76, 98n167,
  169n138
Alien and Sedition Act, 32n72
ambiguity, and ethics, 154–57, 170n144
American bishops, 49, 113, 130n103, 133n160
  and transmission of values, 36, 50, 132n159
American exceptionalism, 53
  Niebuhr on, 19–20
amnesty, 137, 146–47
Amnesty International, 9, 28n11
anamnestic solidarity, 144
anthropology, Christian, 8–34, 43
Anzaldúa, Gloria, 8
Appalachian bishops, 107, 132n150
Appiah, Kwame Anthony, 111
Aquino, María Pilar, 25, 157
Arendt, Hannah, 110
Arizona, 1–2, 159–60, 160n4
Arreola, José, 159–60
Asian bishops, 123, 126n40, 133n166
assimilation, 19–20, 82, 151
asylum categories, and women, 62–63
Australian bishops, 121
autonomy, Farley on, 21

Bail Romero, Encarnación, 93n61
base communities, 52–53
Baum, Gregory, 42, 46–47, 53–54, 56n35
Beharry v. Reno, 91n48
Behdad, Ali, 18–19, 31n69

Benedict XVI
  on economic issues, 11, 13, 71
  on families, 74
  on imperialism, 108–9
  on migration, 115
  on neighbor love, 142–43
  on solidarity, 127n65
Benhabib, Seyla, 128n73, 128n81, 128n83, 151,
  165n79
Bible
  and base communities, 52–53
  and Christian immigration ethic, 142–43, 160
  and hospitality, 144
birthright citizenship, 75
blindness, 48
  liberation theology on, 42–45
  recommendations for, 50
border(s)
  Catholic tradition on, 113
  characteristics of, 8–9
  frontier thesis and, 152
  as meeting place, 25
  rhetoric on, 126n48
Border Patrol, 9, 27n2, 141
Boyle, Gregory, 51, 116
Brack, Robert C., 137–38
Brackley, Dean, 50, 118, 127n57
Bush, George W., 69, 92n54, 134

Café Justo, 158
Cahill, Lisa Sowle, 41, 77, 86, 98n168
Campese, Gioacchino, 9, 36
campesinos. See agriculture
Canadian bishops, 133n166
Canon, Katie, 154–55, 170n144
capital, relationship to labor, 11
capitalism, 100–102, 106–9
care, ethic of, 21
Caritas in veritate, 71, 108–9, 127n65
Carter, J. Kameron, 154
Castañeda-Liles, Socorro, 81, 96n134
Catholic Church
  and grassroots movements, 123
  and social sin, recommendations for, 49–54,
  158
  and solidarity, 118

9 781589 019300